# South Carolina Scalawags

# South & Carolina Scalawags

Hyman Rubin III

THE UNIVERSITY OF
SOUTH CAROLINA PRESS

Hardback edition published by the University of South Carolina Press, 2006
Paperback and ebook editions published in Columbia, South Carolina,
by the University of South Carolina Press, 2021

www.uscpress.com

Manufactured in the United States of America

30 29 28 27 26 25 24 23 22 21
10 9 8 7 6 5 4 3 2 1

Library of Congress Cataloging-in-Publication Data can be found at
http://catalog.loc.gov/.

ISBN: 978-1-57003-625-5 (hardcover)
ISBN: 978-1-64336-249-6 (paperback)
ISBN: 978-1-64336-250-2 (ebook)

*For my parents, without whom I could not have begun this project,*
*and for my wife, Jennifer, without whom I would never have finished it*

# CONTENTS

# ILLUSTRATIONS

# PREFACE TO THE PAPERBACK EDITION

I am grateful to the University of South Carolina Press for the publication of a paperback edition of South Carolina Scalawags. Among other reasons is the opportunity, fifteen years after the publication of the original edition, to reflect on what the book got right and wrong. The passage of time, further archival research, reading the work of other scholars, and even the events of the past fifteen years have all affected my thinking, to a greater or lesser extent, about the Reconstruction period. Overall, I believe the main arguments in *South Carolina Scalawags* hold up well, but a few particular points should probably be modified.

In the original preface, I listed the main conclusions as follows: (1) the scalawags "were few in number but disproportionately important" to the Republican Party's success; (2) there would have been more scalawags without the threats, violence, and social pressure brought to bear against them by Democrats; (3) while whites joined the party for reasons other than promoting the rights of African Americans, many of them evolved into advocates for those rights; and (4) "White supremacy was not the normal or natural political program of white South Carolinians." All of these propositions are debatable, but I remain convinced that each is basically right.

As to the numbers of white Republicans, it is hard to form a basis sturdier than speculation. There are no nineteenth-century exit polls to study, and statistical analysis promises only to extend guesses to additional decimal places. Observers at the time were in a position to formulate reasonable estimates, since voting was done openly. Unfortunately, they also had every incentive to shade the truth. Reasonable observers put the lower limit at 3,000 white Republican voters and the upper limit at two or three times that. Of course, to turn that estimate into a percentage would reduce reliability still further, since the denominator is also based on guesswork. How many white South Carolinians voted in any given election? It clearly varied a great deal; the number of white voters was largest in 1876, but that election also saw massive fraud, violence, and intimidation, not to mention a heightened degree of social pressure on white South Carolinians to vote for Democratic candidates. An 1876 estimate of white Republican voting would seriously understate the Reconstruction average.

If I am less sure than ever how many scalawags there were, I remain convinced that they had tremendous importance, both symbolically and practically. The amount of attention focused on them by Democrats—both "respectable" newspaper editors and violent vigilantes—are sufficient to prove their symbolic importance. Their practical importance is, if anything, understated in the book. In the few years after the end of slavery, the vast majority of African Americans had not built up the economic security, the literacy and numeracy, or (not least in importance) the military experience and skill necessary to challenge the Democrats. White Republicans were essential to the success of the party.

The second conclusion, that Democrats' threats, violence, and social and economic pressure decreased the number of white South Carolinians who cooperated with the Republican Party, is borne out by election returns; more Republicans voted when it was safe to do so. Of course, the important question is what that meant. Was it good news for the Republican Party that many whites would support the party once it was safe? Or was it bad news, because safety could never be guaranteed? In 2006 I wrote, "it is possible that a few more years of support from the federal government could have given the party space to win over enough whites to be able to sustain itself financially and militarily. The more time Republicans had to achieve effective government, the longer they controlled jobs in a depressed economy, and the longer blacks enjoyed equal rights without Democrats' dire predictions of a 'war of races' coming true, the better chance there was that the state would develop an effective two-party system." I still believe that is true, but "a few more years of support from the federal government" were highly unlikely to be offered.

The third conclusion, that white South Carolinians who joined the Republican Party for other reasons became advocates for the rights of African Americans, may also be too optimistic. It is accurate as long as the Republican Party held power; at least in the South the fortunes of the party were inextricably bound to the rights of African Americans. Even after Reconstruction ended, the few white Republicans who remained active in the party continued to defend the party's biracial essence. However, I now believe the overall conclusion is more accurate for white Republican leaders than it is for white Republicans in general. Leaders would have had ongoing collaboration with leading African Americans; that would not have been the case for whites who had voted for Republicans once every year or two for a decade during Reconstruction but had no deeper relationship to the party. It is certainly hard to see evidence in the Jim Crow era that a substantial number of white South Carolinians opposed segregation, discrimination, and disfranchisement.

As a result, it may be misleading to write, as I do in the book, that "white supremacy was not the normal or natural political program for white South Carolinians." White supremacy was, at the very least, not the top priority for thousands of white South Carolinians during Reconstruction. White South Carolinians, like most people everywhere, wanted peace and prosperity. They sought an alternative to the devastating war and long economic crisis their state had experienced, and thousands of them were willing to cooperate with African Americans and other Republicans—or even vote Republican themselves—in pursuit of those aims. On the other hand, of those thousands, all but a handful seem to have made their peace with white supremacy in the years after 1877 without much dissent. As a political program for white South Carolinians, white supremacy might not have come naturally, but in the decades that followed Reconstruction it did indeed become normal. As the state and its people experienced generations of poverty and backwardness, a succession of uninspired leaders provided them with little else.

Hyman Rubin III
*Columbia, South Carolina*
*March 2021*

# PREFACE TO THE FIRST EDITION

## *Reconstruction in South Carolina*

The Union victory in the Civil War reunified the nation and ended the institution of slavery in the United States, but it also raised a troublesome issue. How could Congress restore self-rule to the states of the former Confederacy without risking another attempt at secession or a reimposition of slavery? Presumably self-rule would result in the same secessionist planter-aristocrats returning to power in the southern states. Preventing secession or the oppression of former slaves would require the continued presence of the Union army in the South and the continued involvement of Congress in southern local affairs—in other words, a far cry from self-rule. Democrats in Congress tended to favor self-rule for the South, even if that meant former slaves would not enjoy full freedom. Republicans, however, proposed the radical solution of extending the right to vote to black men. Since former slaves were the southerners most loyal to the Union and most interested in protecting their own rights, giving them an influence in southern politics would guarantee the results of the war.

The enfranchisement of black southerners led to the founding of local and state Republican Party organizations all over the South. With blacks now comprising more than 50 percent of the voting population of some southern states (in South Carolina, 60 percent of voters were black), the Republican Party was triumphant in southern elections beginning in 1868. Most white southerners, however, were adamantly opposed to being governed by former slaves, and they used every means at their disposal, including violence and terrorism, to retake control of their states. One by one the southern Republican governments fell; some were voted out of office, others fell to violent coups, but by 1878 all the former Confederate states had been returned to white Democratic control. From that point on, the influence of black southerners on their states' politics faded rapidly, and the Republican Party became a nonentity in southern elections for four generations.

The period of Republican rule in the southern states is referred to as "Reconstruction," and the various state governments themselves are referred to as Reconstruction governments. In addition to the black southerners who contributed by far the largest share of Republican votes, the Reconstruction Republican organizations included two other groups, which have been known by the derisive terms applied to them by southern Democratic opponents of Reconstruction: "carpetbaggers" and "scalawags." A carpetbagger was an immigrant (of either race) who came from the North or West to the South during or after the war and entered the Republican politics of his adopted state, supposedly in order to dupe the former slaves into voting for him, fleece the southern people, and return home. A scalawag, on the other hand, was a white southerner who joined with former slaves and voted for the Republican Party, thus incurring the enmity of his Democratic and white supremacist neighbors.

These last Republicans—those of the white southern variety—are the subject of this study. Focusing on one state, South Carolina, I draw several conclusions about the scalawags: (1) they were few in number but disproportionately important to the success of the party, (2) their numbers would have been higher had it not been socially and economically disadvantageous—indeed often physically dangerous—to support the Republican Party, and (3) most joined the Republican Party in order to put forward an agenda unrelated to racial equality, but the experience of political cooperation with blacks led many of them to embrace racial equality as a core political principle.

The most important conclusion of this study is that white supremacy was not necessarily the normal or natural political program of white South Carolinians. It was central to the politics of some, and it was accepted with more or less reluctance by others. But some white southerners rejected it outright, and its imposition—by force—preempted their attempts to build a very different South Carolina from the one that would emerge in the 1880s and 1890s.

# ACKNOWLEDGMENTS

While a graduate student at Emory University, I received invaluable advice and insight from my professors and fellow students in the Department of History. The financial support provided by departmental fellowships, a Mellon Fellowship, and a National Endowment for the Humanities summer stipend allowed me to conduct research. The first draft of the first chapter of this endeavor was presented at a Mellon Fellowship seminar, where Professor Elizabeth Fox-Genovese and my fellow Fellows, Bobby Donaldson, Steven Oatis, and Larissa Smith, rightly and helpfully carved it up. For comments on subsequent drafts and suggestions for further research I am indebted to fellow graduate student William Carrigan and to Professors Dan T. Carter, Michael Bellesiles, Leonard Carlson, and, most of all, James L. Roark, my adviser and mentor. I thank him especially for his encouragement during the early, floundering stages of the project, when I otherwise might well have abandoned it.

During my research, I was generously and expertly assisted by the archival staffs at the Houghton Library at Harvard University, the Library of Congress, National Archives I in Washington, D.C., National Archives II in College Park, Maryland, the Southern Historical Collection at the University of North Carolina at Chapel Hill, and especially at the South Carolina Department of Archives and History and the South Caroliniana Library at the University of South Carolina at Columbia. At Caroliniana, archivists Henry Fulmer, Robin Copp, and Beth Bilderback deserve special mention for directing me to source materials I otherwise would not have found. Rebecca Phillips provided much appreciated research assistance at a critical stage of the project. Professor Eric Foner, whose professional courtesy and generosity set a standard to which I will always aspire, graciously shared his research files with me. Horace Harmon, curator of the Lexington County Museum, was a vital source of information on the parts of that county's history that never got into the books. I also owe a great debt of gratitude to Richard and Belinda Gergel for discussing their research with me, for frequent and enlightening discussions of Reconstruction politics, and most of all for introducing me to my wife.

My colleagues and students at Columbia College have provided me with many pleasant distractions from this project, but they have also sharpened my thinking about key aspects of the arguments presented here.

Finally, I want to express my gratitude to the anonymous reviewers commissioned by the University of South Carolina Press for saving me from embarrassing errors and otherwise helping me improve the manuscript, to Karin Kaufman for her meticulous copyediting of it, and to my editor at the press, Alex Moore, for his encouragement and for his patience in the face of my conviction that "deadline" is a relative term.

# INTRODUCTION

## *The Scalawags and the Historians*

On November 8, 1998, after the election of a new governor of South Carolina, the *State* newspaper contained a special section with a feature on the best and worst governors in the more than three-hundred-year history of the colony and state. "Without question the state's worst governor" was Franklin J. Moses Jr., a native white southerner who served as a Republican during Reconstruction; one of the five best was Wade Hampton III, who led the paramilitary overthrow of Reconstruction in 1876.[1] Clearly, thirty years of historical revisionism have done little to change traditional attitudes toward South Carolina's Reconstruction.

To be fair, Governor Moses was indeed spectacularly corrupt, and Governor Hampton was not as violently racist as his successors would be. Nevertheless, it seems clear that the thoughts of black South Carolinians were not much consulted in the formation of the "best and worst" list. While personally immoral, Moses was the champion of a more moral South Carolina, one that would treat all citizens alike before the law. Hampton, on the other hand, although personally honest, came to power only because many blacks were forcibly prevented from voting, and his administration almost completely eliminated blacks from influential offices.[2]

The newspaper article is only one example of the failure of historical revisionism to penetrate very deeply into the public mind. The southern white Democrats who overthrew the Republican Reconstruction regime immediately set out to justify their actions to both those at home, who knew what methods they had used, and those in the North, who had the political power to reverse their revolution. Their campaign was so successful that for years it was generally accepted that southern whites who practiced intimidation, fraud, and murder to seize power were in fact the "Redeemers" they claimed to be, saving the state from corrupt and incompetent blacks, carpetbaggers, and scalawags.

The terms, of course, refer to the three groups of people who supported the Republican governments. Blacks were by far the most numerous, composing 60 percent of the state's population (and probably more than 90 percent of the Republican Party) for most of the period. "Carpetbagger" was the derisive term used by Democrats for Republican immigrants from the North; they were said to have arrived in South Carolina with nothing but a carpetbag, which they presumably intended to fill with loot before returning north. The final category is the subject of this study: native white southerners who supported the Republicans.[3] They were particularly odious to southern Democrats, who searched for a term harsh enough to convey their contempt for such "traitors to their race." The term they chose was "scalawags." As Wade Hampton explained, it was "used by drovers to mean the mean, lousy, and filthy kine that are not fit for butchers or dogs."[4]

Vilification of native white Republicans was so extreme because they were, both practically and symbolically, so important. Despite South Carolina's large black majority, the success of Reconstruction there, just as in majority-white southern states, depended on the ability of the Republican Party to attract white adherents. The most recent study of the subject, Richard Zuczek's *State of Rebellion: Reconstruction in South Carolina,* points out that even though 60 percent of the state's voters were black, the whites were vastly superior in armaments, military experience, and organization. Gun ownership was practically universal among whites and very rare among blacks. Far more whites than blacks had fought in the war, and most whites had experience in the antebellum slave patrols or vigilance committees—exactly the type of experience that would prepare them for an extralegal war of resistance against the government. And a war of resistance would be all but inevitable if the Republican government failed to gain legitimacy (in the eyes of northerners as well as southern whites) by attracting some minimal percentage of native white South Carolinians.[5]

Opinion in the North was therefore crucial as well, as it was Union troops who protected the duly elected southern governments from overthrow. And it was southern whites who had the power to grant legitimacy to the Reconstruction governments in the eyes of northerners. As long as the divide was along the line of race, white northerners would eventually side with white southerners, so deep and pervasive were the prejudices of the times. Only by appealing to a sizable minority of white southerners could the Republicans build a party in the South.

Knowing the stakes, southern Democrats, often calling themselves "Conservatives" in order to appeal to southern whites who had never been Democrats, set out to eliminate southern white support for the Republican Party. Social ostracism was almost universal; white Republicans were expelled from clubs, organizations, and even churches on occasion. Old friends passed them on the street without a word. Occasionally families disowned Republican members.

Violence was also a constant threat; the state government never had the ability to protect the lives and property of its supporters. Even those Republicans who earned grudging respect for their integrity had to fear bushwhackers and Klansmen. Of course, white Republicans were no different from blacks in this regard, and because of the numbers involved, the vast majority of the Klan's victims were black. But scalawags were arguably bigger targets for violence, at least to the extent that their Democratic neighbors perceived them as leaders in the Republican Party.

Given the hostile and dangerous atmosphere in which Republicans existed, it is perhaps no wonder there were so few of them. But the question of numbers has two facets to it. While it is one of my principal arguments here that the paucity of white Republicans was a disproportionately important factor in the defeat of Reconstruction, it is also important to note that their numbers were actually much greater than southern tradition teaches (and would have been even greater without the threat of violence).

The story of the South Carolina scalawags is actually two stories, one historical and one historiographical. This study is concerned with the historical story: what motivated the white Republicans, what they did, and what happened to them. But the historiographical story—the way historians have written about the white Republicans—is fascinating as well and worth consideration. Studies about scalawags have focused on five questions: What kind of people were they? How many of them were there? Why did they become Republicans? How effective were they? And what happened to them?

Southern tradition has ready answers to the first two questions: there were very few white Republicans, and they lacked education, character, and public-spiritedness. This tradition is both oral and literary, the latter based on a long line of neo-Confederate histories going back to Reconstruction itself.[6] Easily the best of the traditional accounts is Francis Simkins and Robert Woody's *South Carolina during Reconstruction,* long the standard work on the subject and still an invaluable resource. This study has sometimes been termed "revisionist" because its condemnation of Reconstruction is not quite so thoroughgoing as some; nevertheless, Simkins and Woody remark of the state's white Republicans that "their apostasy from the white race was induced either by hopes of personal aggrandizement or by pique for some misfortune suffered at the hands of the heretofore dominant element."[7] If anything, their judgment is a rather mild one, attributing to white Republicans motives of ambition and resentment. More typically they were portrayed as having acted out of sheer greed or outright moral perversion.[8]

Perhaps even more representative of South Carolina's public memory of Reconstruction—because they have often been written by nonacademic historians—are the many local and county histories. These almost always stress a version of Reconstruction in which the state's white citizens were oppressed by corrupt Yankees and ignorant former slaves, and in which Hampton's counterrevolution in 1876 marked the "Redemption" of southern civilization. Interestingly, the one point about native white Republicans that these histories never fail to stress is their inconsequential numbers. County and local histories compete with each other to cite the fewest "scalawags." For example, according to local histories, at Spartanburg Court House, out of 339 white men, "only two cast Radical votes," while "there were no white people in Williamsburg who had been born here who were Republicans in this reconstruction period."[9]

But there is some deception in this. For example, the Spartanburg history cited above mentions Javan Bryant several times as a Conservative or as a candidate for office on the Conservative ticket, on which he won election as one of Spartanburg's representatives in the state legislature. But nowhere is it mentioned that while in the legislature he cast a vote in favor of ratifying the Fifteenth Amendment, or that he was expelled from the Conservative Party and threatened by the Ku Klux Klan for his pro-black sentiments, or that after his term of office he began a Republican newspaper in Spartanburg.[10] Nor was Bryant alone; in fact, Allen Trelease notes that white Republicans in Spartanburg amounted to "a considerable number," and a Republican leader estimated that there were 450 of them. I have identified more than twenty by name.[11]

The degree to which white Republicans have been edited out of local histories is impressive. One such volume, *A Laurens County Sketchbook,* includes a sketch of "the Joe Crews house, a sturdy building shrouded in legendary mystery." It seems that "Mr. Crews was said to have been involved in a political movement which could not be sanctioned by a majority of the leaders of the local government. As a result, he was ambushed while making his way to the state's capital and died from the attack." Of course, the mysterious political movement was the Republican Party. But the name of that infamous entity is omitted—nor are there any telltale dates to let the reader make an inference.[12] But Joe Crews's Republicanism is no mystery. He was a delegate from Laurens to the 1868 Constitutional Convention, after which he represented that county in the South Carolina House of Representatives for four consecutive terms. He voted consistently with the "Radical" faction, and he was assassinated in 1875.

What some writers leave unsaid, W. W. Sellers spells out in his 1902 history of Marion County: "I would mention the names of some of the scalawags in Marion, but out of respect to the families or descendants of some of them, the writer forbears, knowing that the present generation is not responsible for what was then done."[13] With this construction, Sellers brilliantly discredits all of Marion's white Republicans simultaneously, without having to adduce charges against any of them.

Revisionist authors have written more nuanced analyses of South Carolina's scalawags. The first such work, written well ahead of its time, was Alrutheus Ambush Taylor's 1924 dissertation *The Negro in South Carolina during the Reconstruction.* While focusing on black South Carolinians, Taylor was the first to take a more evenhanded approach to the state's scalawags.[14] Joel Williamson, whose *After Slavery* is perhaps the best revisionist work, agrees that while "some native whites became Republicans out of expediency, . . . it is also certain that many adopted the party out of principle."[15] But his focus too is on black Republicans, not whites. Generally speaking, while revisionist authors have recognized that venality is not a sufficient explanation for the actions of the scalawags, they have not offered any systematic analysis of those actions.

Revisionists have added important facets to our understanding of white Republicans. Joel Williamson notes the diversity of their backgrounds, occupations, and motivations.[16] Thomas Holt elucidates the policy conflicts and political contests between white and black Republicans.[17] Richard Zuczek and Lou Falkner Williams show the white Republicans as victims of Democratic violence.[18] But all these works have devoted comparatively little space to white Republicans, as they have focused on either white Democrats or black Republicans.[19] The impression given is that the tradition's equation of party and racial lines is in the main accurate. Thus the great majority of South Carolina's native white Republicans have remained shadowy figures at best, and the story of the party's attempts to recruit more of them has been relegated to the footnotes.

On the other hand, studies of other states and of the region have often inquired more deeply into the character and origins of white Republicanism. The most important of these is Eric Foner's *Reconstruction: America's Unfinished Revolution, 1863–1877.* Foner recognizes that scalawags were "men of prominence and rank outsiders, wartime Unionists and advocates of secession, entrepreneurs advocating a modernized New South and yeomen seeking to preserve semisubsistence agriculture."[20] Ultimately, though, he decides that most scalawags were upcountry Unionists; in particular, of those who served in state constitutional conventions, "nearly all had opposed secession."[21]

The "persistent Unionism" explanation of white Republicanism has been the dominant view. Carl Degler, in referring to the "Unionist Foundation" of the southern Republican Party, called it an illustration of "the remarkable continuity in Southern history."[22] And surely in the upper South, the great majority of white Republicans had been Unionists.[23] In addition, Unionists "made up the great majority of white Southerners who joined the Louisiana Republican party," and in Alabama and Arkansas as well they offered the largest white base upon which the party could draw.[24]

But studies of other southern states have not always confirmed this judgment. For example, David Donald, writing on Mississippi, concluded that most scalawags there were former Whigs residing in the black belt.[25] His conclusion sparked a debate with Allen Trelease, who maintained that the bulk were upcountry Unionists.[26] The debate ultimately hinged on statistical methods, and because of the limits of the data, the resolution is uncertain.[27] It is quite possible that Mississippi followed the same pattern prevalent in the upper South, whereby Whigs became Unionists and then Republicans. As James Baggett put it, white Republicans "were a Whig-unionist residue formed after the eruption of the Civil War."[28]

What is true for other southern states is frequently misleading for South Carolina; so too with the problem of scalawag origins. It may well be that South Carolina was the only state in which most postwar white Republicans had been Confederates. In upstate Greenville County, for example, I have identified twenty-eight scalawags by name; of these, twenty-four (86 percent) probably served in the Confederate army.[29] The explanation lies in the near universality of Confederate service in South Carolina; perhaps 88 percent of the state's white men of military age served.[30] If that is true, the 86 percent participation rate among later Greenville scalawags seems entirely plausible.

Of course, fighting in the Confederate army does not necessarily imply support for secession. Some Unionists were undoubtedly conscripted against their will. It is therefore possible that most scalawags could have been Confederates and also that most could have been Unionists, as James Baggett contends in his study of scalawag leaders.[31] But it is also possible that most were simply swept along by the secessionist tide and did not seriously challenge that movement until it proved a failure. While other states vigorously debated secession, in South Carolina the "fire-eaters" had the field almost to themselves.[32] The Republican Party there may well have been based on men who originally accepted the disunionists' appeal but after four years of destruction and privation determined that secession had been a "swindle" and that those leaders who presided over such a thorough disaster should not be permitted to rule again.[33] As Jeffrey Crow has shown, the devastation of the war had a powerful impact on the thinking of those who had fought it.[34]

It is doubtless true, as Degler says, that the Republican Party could never "be built on the number of Southerners who became Republicans because of the Surrender," but he discusses conversion as a matter of honor, whereby the vanquished cede moral authority to the victors.[35] Surely few southerners would have agreed that might made right in that way. But it is different, and much more persuasive, to argue that the experience of devastation and defeat made them trust their leaders less. Degler agrees, for example, that scalawags often seemed to find their primary motivation in punishing secessionists.[36]

The question of social class is also important in the study of southern Republicanism. Republican leaders called theirs the "party of the poor man."[37] Such appeals have led some historians to a class-conflict explanation of the white Republicans, first propounded by W. E. B. Du Bois and later touched on by Armstead Robinson, Michael Fitzgerald, and J. Mills Thornton III.[38] But while Republicans clearly made an appeal to poor whites, they tried at least as hard to recruit the "wise and experienced" former leaders to the party.[39] Even class-conscious Republicans had to admit that the old elite comprised "the wealth, experience and intelligence" of the South, and that the party could never succeed by excluding those elements.[40] The results were simultaneous, and contradictory, appeals by the party to the poor (join the Republicans and throw off the chains of oppression) and to the rich (join the Republicans to put the brakes on Jacobinism and "class legislation").[41] Economically as otherwise, white Republicans were a diverse lot.

Of course, this is to be expected; in joining the Republican Party, southerners were making a political decision, not necessarily an economic one. The key question in politics, as several historians have recognized, was how inclusive democracy should be. Paul Escott makes this point directly in reference to North Carolina: "Long resentful of undemocratic social and political arrangements in the state, [scalawags] took the opportunity presented by Reconstruction to ally with black voters and work for a more open, more democratic society."[42] James Baggett, for example, finds a clear difference between scalawag leaders and later "Redeemer" Democrats in antebellum office holding. In South Carolina, Democrats were almost twice as likely as scalawags to have been local officeholders before the war and almost three times as likely to have been state or federal officeholders. This difference was also tied to social class, as Baggett's data indicate: he finds South Carolina's scalawag leaders about twice as likely as Redeemer leaders to have had prewar estates worth less than ten thousand dollars and half as likely to have had estates worth more than twenty thousand dollars.[43] The Republican Party clearly offered an opportunity for political leadership to men outside the antebellum ruling class, and many white Republicans saw this widening of opportunity as a good in itself. A belief in true democracy, rather than the oligarchic version practiced in South Carolina before the war, may have motivated many of the state's white Republican voters.

The number of scalawags is an even more basic, but still unresolved, question addressed by the literature. Allen Trelease estimated the white Republican vote for the South as a whole at 20 percent of white voters, but indicated that in South Carolina it was probably much less.[44] Joel Williamson speculated that the number of Palmetto State scalawags "probably fluctuated between three and four thousand, although groups of white voters entered and left the party at various times."[45] That is a much smaller number than Republicans claimed, and even Democrats admitted that three thousand would be a conservative estimate.[46] Edmund Lee Drago guesses that five thousand was "the number of whites who had voted Republican at the peak of Reconstruction." Drago, unfortunately, does not explain the derivation of this approximation.[47]

Republican newspapers at various times speculated that there were five thousand, ten thousand, or twelve thousand white Republicans in the state. Of course, these figures were sharply disputed by the Democrats, but even the Democratic *Greenville News* reportedly acknowledged that there were three thousand as a conservative estimate.[48] At some point a Republican newspaper claimed that five thousand whites had voted for Grant in 1868.[49] If that many white southerners braved the dangerous 1868 election and voted for the national Republican Party, it stands to reason that many more might have voted for local Republican candidates in safer years. The *Columbia Daily Union* speculated in 1872 that there were ten to twelve thousand white Republicans in South Carolina, about 18 to 20 percent of whites, and while that is surely too high for any one election, it may be close to the number of whites who *ever* voted Republican during Reconstruction.[50] Exact numbers are necessarily impossible to ascertain. In any case, it seems clear that the number of scalawags varied greatly, depending on how safe it was to be a Republican in a given place at a given time.

The subject of violence brings up a related issue, the assumption that the few native whites who joined the Republicans represented the full extent of the party's *potential* voters. To make that assumption is to deny the extreme courage and determination required to join the party in the face of social ostracism, threats, and outright violence. What is surprising is that such a denial is attempted not only by traditionalist histories but by revisionist studies as well. Joel Williamson remarks casually that "very generally anti-scalawag snobbery was much more a post-Redemption myth than a Reconstruction reality."[51] (Such a position cannot be sustained; antagonism toward scalawags was as intense as tradition says it was.) Williamson, however, qualifies his assertion somewhat by stating that "scalawags, of course, always ran the risk of social ostracism." The crucial factor, he believes, was social class. Poor white Republicans might be shunned, but, "far from condemning the best class of scalawags . . . for becoming Republicans, many native whites praised them for attempting to save their state by elevating the character of the dominant party."[52]

Williamson's equivocation on the issue of ostracism is appropriate, but the determinative factor was probably not class. Instead, it seems that relations between white Republicans and Democrats varied according to time and place. For much of Reconstruction, for example, Democrats willingly served as sureties for Republican officeholders—in effect, lending them the means to take office. But during the Red Shirt campaign of 1876, Democrats made a concerted effort to prevent Republicans from qualifying as officeholders.[53] Place made a difference too. Some counties saw substantial cooperation between the leading Democrats and Republicans; in others, Democrats showed no tolerance at all for "renegades."

Studies of the South or of South Carolina have not addressed in any depth the issue of county differences. If indeed all politics is local, this would seem a significant omission. Those who have touched on the subject come to one of two conclusions: volatile counties typically had especially corrupt or bellicose Republican leaders or volatile counties typically had especially irresponsible Democratic opposition. The usual case study for the former is Laurens County, where the boss was Joe Crews, a white Republican singularly talented at infuriating the white opposition. For the latter, the case study is Edgefield, where Democratic leaders such as Matthew C. Butler and Martin W. Gary were seen even by other Democrats as undisciplined and dangerous.[54]

Laurens and Edgefield were exceptionally violent—or, in the language of the time, "disturbed." In many other places, Democrats and Republicans were capable of cooperation, as is noted in local histories such as Louise Ayer Vandiver's classic on Anderson County and John Hammond Moore's more recent work on Richland County.[55] Indeed, as Eric Foner notes, even in Edgefield, leading "Democrats temporarily put aside their white supremacist convictions to join black officials in an effort to attract a railroad."[56]

But it is also true that even the "safer" counties saw periods of political intensity. In Richland County in 1868, the University of South Carolina's Euphradian Society expelled two of its members—Thomas J. Robertson and Franklin J. Moses—declaring that in joining the Republican Party they had "proven false to their race."[57] Also in that year, it was reported that Richland Democrats would discriminate against Republicans in hiring decisions.[58] And in Anderson, John R. Cochran's Republicanism had social consequences as well. An Anderson Democrat, while denying that the county was dangerous, admitted that Cochran's "relations with his fellow citizens have become very much embittered" as a result of his politics.[59]

Another group of questions historians have asked about the scalawags has been, What were their goals in joining the Republican Party? How well did they achieve them? And what was their impact on the party? As for scalawags' ideological goals, historians seem to be in agreement on one point: the scalawags were racially more conservative than their black or northern colleagues. As Foner puts it, their "alliance with blacks remained a marriage of convenience."[60] What, then, were they doing in the "Black Republican Party"? Williamson suggests that "many native whites voted Republican not because they really approved of political collaboration with Negroes or hoped to achieve office, but because they found appealing a program that endorsed an expansion of educational, economic, and political opportunity."[61] Michael Fitzgerald and Mills Thornton echo this view. Both, however, see whites' attraction to Republicanism as being shallow and destined for failure, Fitzgerald because of racism and the impracticability of the Republican program, Thornton because of the tax burden imposed on whites by Republican spending.[62]

If the scalawags, as these accounts suggest, had less to lose by the failure of Republicanism than did carpetbaggers or blacks, we would expect to find that in states where they dominated the party, Redemption came sooner. That is exactly the finding of Peter Kolchin's study of the question: "In the top ranks of the party the appearance of [a] sizable number of scalawags was clear evidence that the Republicans were in trouble."[63] On the other hand, William C. Harris argues that a Republican Party under more moderate, native leadership would have had a better chance at forming a successful biracial party than many have assumed.[64]

South Carolina, once again, is a case unto itself. It was the only state in which blacks were represented "in the top ranks of the Reconstruction governments."[65] Even though a black man was never governor or U.S. senator, the state's representatives in Congress were usually black, and the state house of representatives had a black majority. And again, there was a strong black majority in the electorate. The role of scalawags in South Carolina was therefore different from what it could be in other southern states. For the most part, scalawag officeholders were not more conservative than carpetbaggers on racial issues. If they had been, they could not have been elected. Williamson concludes that by the end of Reconstruction, "no white Republican politician could expect long to survive who was not willing to grant Negroes access to all offices."[66]

There were conflicts, of course, between white and black Republicans. "White Republicans," Williamson notes, "were irritated and alarmed by the flooding tide of black officeholders."[67] And there were issues on which they tended to disagree, usually on the merits of "social equality," or what we would call nondiscrimination laws.[68] But for the most part, the racial positions taken by the state's scalawags were much closer to those taken by blacks than to those of Democrats. And on economic issues, "the most important of which were those expanding the credit of the state and supporting railroad construction," legislators both black and white, Republican and Democrat, were in agreement.[69] This agreement was even more apparent at the national level, where South Carolina's representatives and those from other southern states voted with their region more than with their party.[70]

Perhaps the most important measure of the scalawags' effectiveness was whether they got the offices they sought. If scalawags joined the Republican Party because they wanted to participate in government, how well did that decision pay off? White Republicans undoubtedly did better than black Republicans in winning office, especially those offices appointed by the governors. But scalawags often believed that offices that should rightfully be theirs were occupied instead by carpetbaggers, blacks, or, worst of all, Democrats. In filling the ranks of the judiciary, for example, all of South Carolina's Republican governors made competence and experience top priorities and consequently appointed a great many Democrats. White Republicans made frequent protests, but even positions requiring less expertise—like those of census taker or postmaster—often went to their political enemies or to outsiders. Anderson County Republican John Cochran wrote in frustration that such a pattern "convinces native republicans that they have been upon a 'Fools Errand' in advocating and sustaining a party that refuses to recognize any merit amongst the natives."[71]

Cochran even ranked this "freezing out" the natives as among the top reasons South Carolina's scalawags left the Republican Party, arguing that in 1876, "not a native did more in that campaign than he thought was absolutely necessary to save Hayes," the Republican presidential nominee.[72] Historians' accounts have frequently presented the conversions from Republican to Democrat as representing the weakness of South Carolina's Republican Party—but the precise nature of this weakness is the subject of dispute. Thomas Holt blames factionalism within the ranks of black Republicans.[73] J. Mills Thornton III argues that some "poorer whites did indeed support the Republicans early in Reconstruction," but he blames the end of this support on the Republicans' shift of the tax burden toward the yeomen.[74] Joel Williamson goes the farthest in this vein, blaming the defeat of Reconstruction on the Republicans for their "absence of a sense of responsibility to the whole society, white as well as black."[75] Finally, Michael Perman reaches the exact opposite conclusion, contending that the party abandoned everything it stood for, from attempts to improve the lot of sharecroppers to measures to preserve law and order, out of an "overwhelming obsession with proving itself responsible and reasonable" to white voters.[76]

But none of these analyses (including Cochran's) adequately explains the completeness or the rapidity of the collapse of white Republican voting in 1876. Just as Williamson claims, "the scalawag element very nearly evaporated."[77] The reason was fear. The campaign of 1876 marked the Democrats' determination to submit to Republican rule no longer. They used every means at their disposal to intimidate Republicans into voting with them, or "crossing Jordan," as the Democrats put it. Simkins and Woody rather coyly surmise that "no doubt many found it convenient to ally themselves with the Democrats even though at heart they were sympathetic with the Radicals."[78] But Richard Zuczek puts the matter starkly: "Republicans backed down, knowing that opposition would result only in further bloodshed, not in lasting peace."[79]

Given the seeming contradiction between Democratic violence against Republicans and cooperation with them, it is crucial to note that another variable in the equation was time. Democrats made two determined efforts to threaten, cajole, or destroy white Republicans. The first, from about 1868 to 1871, was put down by federal force. An interval of relative quiet followed. The second period of proscription and intimidation, in 1876, was successful, largely because the federal government did little to intervene. The continued support of the North, then, was crucial to the success of the state's Republican Party. The reasons this support was withdrawn have been analyzed rather thoroughly. As Richard Abbott and William Gillette point out, northern Republicans always looked first to their own political interests, and when southern Reconstruction became unpopular, the national party sacrificed it.[80] Terry Seip has shown that northern and southern Republicans had very different economic interests; it is not surprising, then, that the former should cut loose the latter for political advantage.[81]

Finally, there was the matter of northern racism.[82] Northerners' refusal to believe that blacks were capable of self-government led them to distrust white Republicans allied with blacks. This lack of trust even applied to carpetbaggers, much to their confusion and dismay. As a Louisiana carpetbagger put it, "It has always seemed strange to me that the Northern people should so readily have believed their young men the infamous wretches which the South represented them to be."[83] But believe it they did, and the results were disastrous for the southern Republican governments.

What happened to the scalawags after 1876 is a matter of substantial agreement. A few had been or would be killed for their political beliefs. Some remained loyal Republicans for years afterward. But most either joined the Democrats or retired from political life altogether. The Republican Party itself was doomed to become a hollow party, existing for whatever patronage came from Washington during Republican presidencies.[84] And South Carolina's experiment in biracial democracy was all but defeated. All that remained was the complete disfranchisement of blacks and the institution of Jim Crow segregation during the 1890s, part and parcel with the emergence of a reactionary pseudo-democracy that would leave South Carolina languishing in poverty and race hatred for generations to come.

White supremacists' use of history itself was an important element in their victory. Before South Carolina's Reconstruction government had enacted its first law, white supremacists in the state were ready to call it a failure, and they used history to support their cause. In March 1868 the *Sumter News* editorialized, "*None but white men* have ever had other than *a despotic government.*" The *Charleston Courier* later that year predicted that "negro rule" would result in "another Hayti" —a reference to the Haitian Revolution of the early nineteenth century, which many whites considered as proof that without slavery a black republic could be neither prosperous nor stable. South Carolina planter Alexander P. Wylie made the point explicit when he told a black audience that they "had done nothing in the advancement of civilization in this world except what has been forced on you through slavery to white men."[85]

After the end of Reconstruction, white supremacists' skillful use of history continued to strengthen their cause. Their evocation of the "horrors of Reconstruction" served to render almost unthinkable any discussion of black voting or, indeed, two-party politics for decades to come. The basis of this understanding of history was the assertion, made over and over in traditional accounts, that Democrats' assertion of white supremacy was natural and even inevitable. This study demonstrates the falsity of that assertion. It examines the thoughts and experiences of white South Carolinians who found white supremacy neither inevitable nor desirable.

The organization of this study is chronological. It begins with an examination of the first postwar leaders of South Carolina. Many of them had personally resisted secession, and as a group they marked a shift away from the lowcountry aristocracy who dominated the state's politics before the war and toward greater representation of the upcountry. They believed in moderation and practical politics, and they attempted to reconcile white South Carolina with the Republican-dominated national government. Their attempt failed because they did not sufficiently please either side. While they were willing to democratize the state's politics, as northerners demanded, they were unwilling to grant substantial rights to the freedmen or even fully accept the results of the war. On the other hand, they went much too far to suit the former fire-eaters and Confederates who advocated resistance to any meaningful change. The advent of black suffrage sealed the fate of the moderates; by 1868, there was an unbridgeable gap between what was demanded by the new majority-black electorate and what was even remotely acceptable to most whites.

The main subject of this study is then introduced: the native whites who, in this polarized environment, sided not with the old leaders (and the masses of their own race) but with the northern Republicans—and more directly, with black South Carolinians. While diverse in background, the new men coming to power through the Republican Party had one important similarity: they were united by their commitment to democratic ideals. (The state constitution of 1868 illustrates, in many ways, this commitment.) In practice, they were intent on displacing the old lowcountry aristocracy from its position of political dominance. Whether or not they had been Unionists before or during the war, they blamed the aristocracy for the devastation of the war, and they demanded the opportunity to run the state themselves.

The inevitable reaction of the Democrats (sometimes appropriating the name "Conservatives") from 1868 to 1871 is the next subject taken up. White Republicans, like their black comrades, were always criticized, often persecuted, and not infrequently assaulted for their political opinions. This experience led to a renewed commitment to personal freedom. The main unifying principle for all Republicans became no more or less than that they had rights: the right to participate in their government, the right to have the will of the majority enacted, and the right to disagree with their opponents without fear of reprisal. Thus the one measure of most utility to Republicans would have been one that assured the protection of life and property, and the rule of law—a measure that, despite their unanimity, they were powerless to enact. White Republicans thus learned a lesson with which black Republicans were intimately familiar: theoretical equality lost its meaning without the practical power to back it up. The number of scalawags plummeted during this period, and it was only federal intervention that kept the Republicans in power.

The deployment of federal troops in South Carolina from 1871 to 1874 created an uneasy peace. This was, in a sense, the heyday of the scalawags, at least in terms of numbers. Native whites joined the party in perhaps the greatest numbers since 1868. But the Republicans' chief weakness was still the lack of a monopoly on the use of force; this weakness was only papered over by the federal presence. This false sense of security led Republicans to take their dominance of the state for granted; seeing no real threat from the Democrats, they turned against one another in a scramble for office. Widespread and bitter factionalism within the party led Republicans to hurl at one another accusations of corruption that Democrats gleefully repeated. Northern voters turned in disgust against the southern Republican governments, and federal intervention in the South became increasingly unpopular.

The major trend of the Chamberlain administration (1874–76) was a return to moderation. Unlike the first attempt at moderation, this time the ruling group's base was Republican, and it was white moderates to whom they reached out. Still, the problem was the same: the two sides were too far apart for moderation to be practicable. Chamberlain was in an impossible position; Democrats demanded more than his party could permit. In retrospect, it is easy to blame him for misjudging the character of the opposition. He should have known that the Democrats who praised him for honesty and cooperation would depose him if they had the chance, and he should have strengthened the state government accordingly. But this misses the point: he relied on federal protection because there was no other viable option; when it was removed he was at the mercy of the enemy.

Nevertheless, Chamberlain's naiveté had consequences. When he appointed "well-known and bitter Democrats" to key positions, white Republicans in particular were not given sufficient reason to adhere to the party, and many bolted at the first sign of trouble. Faced with the near-fanaticism of South Carolina Democrats in support of Hampton, continued concerns about the honesty of the state's Republicans, and the northern public's growing weariness with Reconstruction, the national party abandoned Chamberlain and the rest of his party to their fate. The result was, for practical purposes, the end of Republicanism in South Carolina.

The epilogue deals with the white Republicans in South Carolina after Redemption. I have chosen to view Reconstruction as an episode in the continuing struggle for political democracy in South Carolina. Those who became Republicans, whether they were black or white, rich or poor, believed in democracy. In contrast to their Democratic opponents, they believed that every citizen was capable of participating in the government and had a right to do so. They believed that freedom of thought should be protected, and they believed the majority should rule. The Democrats believed none of these things. In their view, only those with a stake in society should be citizens; speech considered detrimental to society should be suppressed; and the "capital, wealth, and intelligence" of the state, not the majority, should rule. This conflict over the principles of democracy was too dichotomous, and too fundamental, for compromise. It was inevitable that it should be decided by force of arms. It was probably inevitable too that the Democrats would win.

The Democrats also won the battle over how the Civil War and Reconstruction would be remembered in South Carolina, as should be clear from the *State*'s list of best and worst governors. The victors wrote a story of a noble and chivalrous Old South, a glorious and gallant Lost Cause, a corrupt and tyrannical period of Negro rule, and finally the Redemption of southern civilization in 1876. There was, however, a competing version of these events, believed also by white southerners, albeit many fewer. According to this story, the Old South was oppressive and undemocratic, the Civil War was a disastrous blunder, Reconstruction was a new birth of freedom, and the Red Shirt campaign achieved the defeat—or at least the long postponement—of democracy in South Carolina.

# South Carolina Scalawags

# ONE

## Origins of the Scalawags, 1865–1867

South Carolina did not have white Republicans in any politically significant sense until the formation of the Republican Party in the state, which did not occur until the enfranchisement of the freedmen in 1867.[1] That monumental transformation of the state's body politic provided the voting strength that made a Republican Party possible. Nevertheless, prior to 1867, the state did have *potential* white Republicans—many more, in fact, than it ever had actual white Republicans. Upcountry farmers and Charleston artisans, country lawyers and urban shopkeepers, these men had in common a deep mistrust of the secessionist prewar elite and their political vehicle, the Democratic Party. They considered the Democrats undemocratic, and they wanted to pry open the political process for new men and new ideas. Even more, they believed that the disasters of secession and defeat were caused by the prewar leaders' political extremism. White dissenters, then, set out to replace South Carolina's characteristic extremism and reaction with moderation and progressive change. They got their chance during presidential Reconstruction, the period from 1865 to 1867 when Reconstruction policy followed the lenient approach of President Johnson, a Democrat, rather than the more demanding system later put in place by the Republican Congress.

They failed. During presidential Reconstruction they learned that their program of moderation and progressive reform was unworkable for two reasons. In the first place, politics had become too polarized to permit a moderate solution. In Michael Perman's apt phrase, they slowly became aware of "the irrelevance of the moderates."[2] In the second place, the kinds of reforms they favored—education, economic development, social welfare—were decidedly secondary to the main issue of the day: race, or, more specifically, the place the freedmen would occupy in the new society. The centrality of the race issue, and especially the enfranchisement of black men, gave moderate white southerners two options: they could give up on their reformist ideas and fight for white supremacy or they could join the Republican Party and attempt to implement their policy goals with the help of the freedmen. Most chose the first path, but a surprising number chose the second. This chapter describes their route from moderation to Republicanism.

The most prominent South Carolinian who would become a Republican was surely James L. Orr of Anderson County. Having achieved a national reputation as Speaker of the U.S. House of Representatives in the late 1850s, Orr served as governor from 1866 to 1868. He followed a careful course, trying to maneuver South Carolina past military rule and provisional government back to full membership in the Union. Accused by extremists of selling out principle for personal gain, Orr during Reconstruction was in fact true to the principle he had fought for all his life: moderation.

Orr achieved national prominence in the antebellum period through a decidedly pragmatic approach to politics. Thus he adhered to the Democratic Party (to do otherwise in South Carolina would have been political suicide) but readily supported Zachary Taylor, a Whig, for president when Taylor seemed to southerners "sounder" on the slavery question than the Democratic candidate, Lewis Cass of Michigan. Orr adopted Democratic positions on issues such as the tariff, which he abhorred, but sounded much like a Whig when advocating diversification of the southern economy, manufacturing, and internal improvements.[3]

But it was in the sectional conflict, the most heated political fight of the antebellum period, that his moderation was most notable. Orr, a slaveholder, staunchly defended the status quo in the South, but he was deeply suspicious of movements for southern independence. A nationalist at heart, but no supporter of a strong central government, he straddled the fence on the question of South Carolina's relationship to the Union. At times he used strong pro-southern rhetoric. In 1850, when outrage at the California Compromise threatened to spark secession, Orr called the compromise a bad bargain and referred to the Union as a curse to the South. During the Kansas crisis of the mid-1850s, Orr stood strongly for slavery in that state, contributing to sectional tension. And after the founding of the Republican Party on an antislavery platform, he insisted that the election of a Republican president would warrant secession: "If the South should think upon this subject as I do, no Black Republican President would ever execute any law within her borders, unless at the point of a bayonet, and over the dead bodies of her slain sons."[4]

On the other hand, as inflammatory as Orr's statements could be at times, in the context of South Carolina he was clearly a moderate. In 1850, while Orr protested the California Compromise, he stopped short of advocating secession, favoring cooperation with other southern states. Orr's position is properly contrasted not with that of unconditional Unionists (there were very few in South Carolina) but with that of "fire-eaters" such as Robert Barnwell Rhett, Maxcy Gregg, and Governor Whitemarsh Seabrook, who argued for immediate secession. And when Orr (and other southern Democrats) embarrassed northern Democrats by pressing for slavery in Kansas, his goal was to prove to South Carolinians that the Democratic Party—the *national* Democratic Party—was the best guarantor of their southern rights. It must be remembered that until 1856 South Carolina was not officially represented at the National Democratic Convention, and it was largely at Orr's urging that this aloof posture was ended.[5] (Orr's colleagues in Washington understood his position; it was the trust of northern Democrats in his "pacific Union sentiments" that led to his election as Speaker of the House in 1857.)[6] And finally, if his call to resist a "Black Republican President" seems extreme, not to say apocalyptic, it should be borne in mind that even after making this statement, he continued to oppose separate secession and to view any secession as reversible.[7]

Once war broke out, Orr, like many southern Unionists and conditional Unionists, "went with his state." He raised a regiment known as "Orr's Rifles" and was elected colonel by the approximately one thousand men who joined. After he completed the organization of this regiment, but before it saw combat, Orr resigned his commission to accept a seat in the Confederate Senate.[8] In that body, he continued his vigorous advocacy of moderation. The question of the draft, perhaps the most controversial issue faced by the Confederacy, forced a choice between state rights and individual rights, between military necessity and personal freedom. Orr, deeply committed to all of the above, proposed a halfway measure: a "conditional" draft based on requisitions on the states. It is unclear how the system would have worked, and Orr's colleagues rejected it.[9]

As the war ground on, the Confederacy was faced with the question of how far it would go to prolong the struggle. Some military and political leaders favored the use of black troops in the Confederate army. Others objected that the use of black troops would lead white troops to desert in protest or that it would be a stepping stone to emancipation.[10] Orr, predictably, tried to conciliate the two sides by arguing for the use of limited numbers of slaves in noncombatant roles but not as troops.[11]

The final controversy in the Confederate government concerned when to concede that the war was lost. True to his pragmatic nature, Orr was willing to accept defeat (or at least to seek a negotiated settlement) in March 1864, well before most Confederate statesmen. Although offended by "the humiliating terms of peace tendered us by Lincoln" at the Hampton Roads conference—the terms included abolition—he concluded that Union victory was certain and saw no benefit in fighting to the last man. "I fear now that we will not be allowed to retain slavery—if at all it will be only temporary, but even with that great loss and humiliation it is to be preferred to a hopeless and desperate prosecution of an impossible war," he declared. He bitterly condemned Confederate president Jefferson Davis for failing to work seriously for peace.[12]

Political Reconstruction in South Carolina began auspiciously with a meeting between a delegation from Charleston and President Andrew Johnson in the summer of 1865. Both sides seemed conciliatory. Johnson's intention was to return the southern states to civil government as quickly as possible, provided that southerners conceded the results of the war. To that end, he requested from the South Carolina delegation, headed by moderate Charleston judge (and future Republican) Edward Frost, a list of suitable candidates for the position of provisional governor of the state.[13] The name the president chose was that of Benjamin F. Perry, an upcountry legislator and perhaps the leading antisecessionist in the state. He had cooperated with the Confederacy once the war broke out, but otherwise his political outlook was in fact much like that of President Johnson. Both conformed to northern opinion by favoring the expansion of democracy in the southern states, but both angered many in the North by supporting a strict policy of white supremacy. Furthermore, both drastically overestimated the president's power and influence.

In 1865 the leadership of South Carolina enjoyed an excellent opportunity to take charge of the course of Reconstruction in the state. The Constitutional Convention of that year, necessary to repeal the Confederate-era state constitution and to abolish slavery, enjoyed wide latitude for reshaping the state's politics in ways that would set northern minds at ease. Orr, for one, indicated a willingness to view the North with more admiration than bitterness: "I would have [South Carolina's] acres teem with life and vigor and industry and intelligence, as do those of Massachusetts."[14]

Orr's attitudes, however, did not prevail at the convention. Instead, the delegates sent an unacceptably mixed message to Washington. They gained the approval of observers by democratizing South Carolina's politics, but they appeared petty and hostile in their unwillingness to comply with Johnson's mild terms for reunion. The president had directed that at a minimum the convention should repudiate secession, slavery, and the Confederate war debt. The delegates grudgingly accepted the first two conditions, but in such language as to advertise their spite. The convention refused to abolish the debt. The state's secession ordinance was repealed, not annulled, implying that when issued, it had been valid. The convention declined to abolish slavery itself, announcing instead that the "slaves having been freed by the action of the United States authorities, neither slavery nor involuntary servitude . . . shall ever be re-established in this State."[15] The opening clause was meant to underscore the fact that, as delegate and Confederate general Samuel McGowan put it, there were not "ten men in the Convention who would favor the abolition of slavery as an independent proposition aside from the events of the last four years." Whether this frank acknowledgment was meant to increase the likelihood of compensation, whether southern gentlemen who had lost all but honor were determined to tell the whole truth at any cost, or whether the resolution was merely a childish exercise in spite, it remains for the reader to determine.[16]

It was, however, on the issue of the freedmen's rights that southerners who considered themselves moderates made their worst misjudgment of northern opinion. After emancipation, the feeling was nearly universal among southerners that free blacks would not work, and in anticipation of such a problem, the southern states passed restrictive labor laws that applied only to the freedmen: the so-called Black Codes. Provisional Governor Perry deemed the codes essential, and the first state legislature after the 1865 convention passed a typical one. It defined as "persons of color" those who were less than seven-eighths white, and it barred them from any profession other than farmer or servant absent special permission and the payment of an enormous tax. Intermarriage was prohibited. Capital punishment was a possible penalty for blacks for a much wider range of crimes than for whites. Blacks who committed certain crimes could be rented out to employers as veritable slaves; one such crime was vagrancy, or the lack of an employment acceptable to the authorities. Runaway "servants" were to be returned to their "masters."[17]

The outraged reaction from the North was predictable, although not to the southern leadership. Most found the Black Codes eminently reasonable, and some thought the provisions made for the protection of servants were too lenient. Moderates such as Orr originally applauded the laws. In fact, when in late 1865 South Carolinians (or some few of them) voted for a successor to Provisional Governor Perry, there was little difference between the public positions of the two leading candidates, Orr and the revered Confederate general Wade Hampton III. Hampton, who would later lead the military overthrow of Reconstruction in the state, stood in 1865 and 1866 for compromise and "accepting the situation." He gave conciliatory speeches on race relations, advising fellow whites, "As a slave he was faithful to us; as a freeman let us treat him as a friend." He also advised reconciliation with the North and even suggested that the election of a high-ranking Confederate like himself might be counterproductive.[18] Orr may have won the narrow gubernatorial race only because of Hampton's requests *not* to be elected.[19]

The existence of a vocal minority opposed to compromise is not to be doubted; prominent among them was former Provisional Governor Perry. The moderates, though, seemed to have the upper hand throughout 1865. In addition to Orr and Hampton, other well-known and well-respected leaders were making the case for conciliating the North. One of these was William Henry Trescot, a statesman and diplomat from Orr's home county of Anderson and through the early years of Reconstruction a sort of ambassador from South Carolina to Washington.[20] The leading newspapers of the state also took a pragmatic approach to the situation. The *Charleston Courier,* for example, criticized the state legislature for antagonizing the North.[21] The *Anderson Intelligencer* advised acquiescence, proclaiming that it was not unmanly to be "a willow and not an oak."[22]

The strength of the moderates was an illusion. South Carolinians were willing to compromise because compromise at the time did not seem too much to bear; for example, most southerners, including the normally perceptive Orr, expected emancipation to be *compensated.*[23] Changes in northern politics would demonstrate the fragility of the South's conciliatory posture. As long as the North seemed united, and the terms of reunion seemed lenient, there was a broad consensus in South Carolina and in other southern states in favor of doing what needed to be done, no matter how distasteful.[24] There were limits, however, to what the South would be willing to accept, and these limits were far short of what northerners viewed as minimal.

These points first became apparent in the matter of the Black Codes. Moderates such as Orr, Trescot, and the *Courier*'s correspondent at first supported the laws. In fact, although Perry had appointed the committee to draw them up, it was Orr who signed South Carolina's Black Code into law. When they realized the extent of northern outrage over the codes, however, Orr and Trescot reversed themselves, and Orr secretly persuaded the military commander of South Carolina, Gen. Daniel E. Sickles, to invalidate South Carolina's Black Code.[25]

Most whites were willing to abandon the code for the sake of restoration, but the rumored enfranchisement of the freedmen was entirely a different matter. Mainstream white South Carolinians could not imagine that blacks would be allowed to vote in their state, and their resolve to oppose such an innovation was stiffened when President Johnson took their side. In late 1866 rumors were floating around the state that South Carolina would be required to adopt the Fourteenth Amendment, disenfranchising most former officeholders, in order to achieve readmission to the Union. State legislator T. C. Weatherly, a moderate who almost uniquely remained moderate throughout Reconstruction,[26] went immediately to Washington to inquire about the matter. After meeting with Republican congressmen, who indicated that adoption of the amendment would be the final condition for readmission, Weatherly went to see the president, who privately cautioned against taking the Republicans at their word and expressed the hope that the South would reject the amendment. Somehow the *Charleston Courier* came into possession of these facts and promptly published them. Johnson denied the story; Weatherly had no comment. The state legislature, however, acted immediately on it, overwhelmingly rejecting the amendment.[27] After Johnson's support for the South became clear, South Carolina's moderates rapidly lost ground.

National politics continued to squeeze moderates such as Orr. He tried to keep pace with events, but news from Washington made it difficult for him. In January 1867 Orr received word that, unless his state extended suffrage to at least some blacks, universal male suffrage would be imposed. Having long feared such an eventuality, Orr pleaded with the state legislature to enfranchise literate or property-holding blacks. He received nothing but abuse for his efforts.[28] On March 2, 1867, Republicans in Congress passed the first Reconstruction Act over President Johnson's veto. This legislation placed South Carolina (and other former Confederate states) under military rule, provided for disfranchisement of most former Confederate officials, and—most shocking of all—provided for the registration of the freedmen to vote in an election for delegates to a new state constitutional convention.

At first Orr reacted with disbelief and confusion, asking the attorney general, "What is best for us in this terrible extremity to do?"[29] Fearing future measures such as the confiscation of estates, Orr determined that his only option was to accept the act and try to gain the confidence of the freedmen. By the end of 1867, according to his biographer, Orr "was the only white conservative leader who advocated compliance with the Reconstruction Acts."[30] But his status as a conservative was in jeopardy. It is surely going too far to say that "he was from that time dead to his own people,"[31] but it is true that many southern partisans began referring to the governor as the "Buzzard in Columbia," and the Democratic press flayed him for his alleged opportunism.[32] Eventually it was reported that the ostracism and proscription had become too much for him and that he was moving to Missouri.[33] Rumors of Orr's surrender were greatly exaggerated. He had seen worse; or as he put it, "My epidermis is very thoroughly case-hardened in consequence of the continual pricking received from numerous admirers in this and other States."[34]

Orr was determined to stay and fight, but pressure against him came from the North as well. Northern Republicans insisted upon unconditional suffrage for freedmen rather than some halfway measure that would have allowed only literate freedmen to vote. Predictably, Orr supported a halfway measure. In the 1865 convention, he had opposed enfranchising blacks because "they are not prepared to receive that privilege, and by bestowing it upon them the best interests of the State must suffer."[35] As late as 1866, he was willing to trust President Johnson to defend the South from any black suffrage.[36] Less than a year later, it had become clear that Johnson was powerless to prevent at least some freedmen from voting, and Orr argued for a literacy qualification. Such a requirement, he argued, would spur the desire for education among the freedmen.[37] Of course, Orr was being disingenuous; he had no intention of requiring *white* voters to qualify themselves for the franchise. He was merely trying to find a middle position between two extremes.

For Orr and many moderates, race was not the key issue in Reconstruction but a distraction the impact of which should be minimized. More important was the replacement of the old planter elite with the more dynamic leadership that the moderates themselves could provide. An incident from 1867 illustrates an important characteristic of the moderates: their resentment of the pretensions of the lowcountry elite. In an address to the Charleston Chamber of Commerce on the rebuilding of war-damaged sections of that city, Orr took the chance to criticize the snobbishness of Charleston's old-money social elite. Claiming that their exclusivity drove off new money and new blood, which were desperately needed, he strongly urged his audience to be more accepting of self-made men. He referred to the case of his own father, "a humble country merchant" who had gone to

Charleston on buying trips and had felt the disdain of the seaboard elite. Mayor P. J. Gaillard, intentionally missing the point, averred the right of the individual to associate with any other individual, or not, as he or she saw fit. He then denied that Charleston's social mores had retarded the rebuilding effort and predicted that they would not change in the near future. The audience rewarded Gaillard's remarks with sustained applause. Orr angrily walked out of the event.[38]

Orr here was typical of the moderates of 1865 to 1868. They tended to represent the same part of the state in which Unionism had been strongest in 1860: the upcountry districts.[39] Unionism and moderation in the upcountry had been much more widespread than in the state as a whole. The animosity between upcountry and lowcountry, illustrated by the reception Orr's ideas received from the Charleston Chamber of Commerce, had a long history and involved more substantial matters than social snobbery. Since Revolutionary times, representation in the South Carolina General Assembly had been dominated by the lowcountry parishes. The Constitution of 1808 was devised to solve this conflict.[40] It provided that representation in the legislature would be apportioned on the dual bases of white population and taxation, and the tax code was set up in such a way that the tax on slaves provided the bulk of the state's revenue. The lowcountry elite, then, paid more than their share of taxes in order to be overrepresented in the legislature. This seems to have been satisfactory to upcountry farmers, who desired little from their government. Upcountry planters, on the other hand, had to pay the same disproportionate taxes but did not enjoy adequate representation. These planters, men such as Orr, continued throughout the antebellum period to have their differences with the aristocracy over the issue of representation.[41]

They also criticized the dominant lowcountry planters for their heavy-handed methods of quieting dissent. Taking seriously the proslavery argument that black slavery allowed white freedom, upcountry dissidents opposed the restrictions on whites that an air-tight slave system required. Their relatively lax attitude toward freedom of speech, for example, led to substantially more political debate than was possible in the lowcountry. Never was this more clear than in the secession crisis. The upcountry was decidedly less unified behind secession in 1860 than was the lowcountry, and in the mountain districts Unionist sentiment was considerable.[42]

The outbreak of conflict at first excited considerable enthusiasm in all sections of the state. But as the war dragged on, upcountry Unionism began to reassert itself. As worsening economic conditions began to affect their families, upcountry soldiers increasingly questioned the cause for which they risked their lives. Beginning with desertions from the Confederate armies, this disaffection soon turned to outright disloyalty. Upcountry deserters banded together to defend their home districts against the Confederate authorities. Conscription officers and tax collectors rarely met success in these areas, and they sometimes met armed opposition. The reputation of South Carolina's "dark corner" was well known to state and Confederate officials—and to northern prisoners of war who escaped South Carolina prison camps. An unknown number of such escapees received aid and comfort in the upper districts before making their way to safety in East Tennessee.[43] Although South Carolina was the only Confederate state that did not produce a company of white troops for the Union army, deserters sapped the southern war effort by diverting precious resources and manpower to the home front.[44]

Upcountry farmers had long remained loyal to the state, largely because it made so few demands on them. But with conscription, heavy wartime taxation, and impressment of property, the Confederate and state governments brought the war home to poor South Carolinians long before Sherman did. The destruction and death brought by the war would remain a reproach against the prewar leaders in many upcountry areas. Even after the cult of the Lost Cause had rendered unthinkable any criticism of the Confederacy, the decision to secede remained suspect. In 1902 the *Lexington Dispatch* recalled that "South Carolina, in a spasm of political excitement, committed the fatal blunder of secession."[45]

In the aftermath of the war, it was opposition to the political extremism that produced secession and war that held the greatest appeal for moderates. On racial issues, however, it was the North's position that seemed radical to these men. They generally believed in white supremacy as a matter of faith, and advocating full citizenship for former slaves was heresy. When, for example, Judge Frost of Charleston declared to the 1865 convention that blacks were "unquestionably destined at no very distant day to have political rights," he was immediately accused of being a "Black Republican," according to Sidney Andrews, a northern journalist who attended the convention.[46]

What distinguished those moderates who became Republicans from those who returned to the Democratic Party was their weighing of these two kinds of extremism. Which was more important: to oppose the return to power of the men who had destroyed the state through secession, or to oppose those who would enfranchise former slaves? This dilemma was one reason Orr was dissatisfied with both existing political parties, the Democrats for holding out false hopes to the South and the Republicans for preventing the necessary reconciliation. In Orr's mind, the South could better its condition only through unity—most importantly, unity between the blacks and whites. If this could be engineered, South Carolina could "go back into the Union, holding the balance of power, and then both parties will court us."[47]

The problem, of course, was how to achieve this unity. For some self-styled moderates, it was obvious that the freedmen would naturally adhere to their former masters. It was commonly noted by planters that their former slaves asked and took their advice on all matters except politics, and this baffled them. Wade Hampton asked an audience of freedmen, "Why should we not be friends? Are you not Southern men, as we are? Is this not your home as well as ours?"[48] The obvious reply was that the freedmen chose to vote for the party that freed them, but Orr replied with a history lesson that has only recently come back into fashion: it was not the Republican Party that freed the slaves but the efforts of blacks themselves.[49] Therefore black South Carolinians owed no loyalty to the party of Lincoln, but should side with their white countrymen. Orr hoped to convince blacks that the Republicans were a purely sectional party, as illustrated by their support for an exorbitant cotton tax that penalized both white and black southerners.[50]

That the freedmen overwhelmingly rejected such arguments was a source of great frustration and confusion for former masters. When Hampton asked, "Why should we not be friends?" he meant it rhetorically, but one cannot help but imagine that he would have liked some answers.[51] As Judge Frost had said in the convention, "We assumed that we knew all there was to know about the negro; and that where the world differed from us in opinion, it was wrong. Events would seem to indicate that we were wrong in at least some very important particulars."[52] Two years later most planters had still not made that realization.

One who had, however, was Orr. He quickly abandoned the idea of turning blacks against their liberators and began trying to win them over to moderation. Unfortunately for the governor, his appeal did not win the trust of the freedmen. His preference for a "white man's government" was remembered, and although he urged whites to support Republicans' call for a new constitutional convention, he made it clear that he did so with the purpose of electing "the intelligence of the State" to draft the new document. On questions of "social equality" Orr was even more conservative, opposing the integration of schools and the University of South Carolina because, he believed, students of both races would learn more separately "than in an institution where antagonism will surely prevail."[53] Finally, when the 1868 Constitutional Convention was held, it is unlikely that Orr won many Republican friends with his address to the mostly black delegates. He informed the delegates that they were "representative only of the colored population of South Carolina" and, therefore, "it cannot be denied that the intelligence, refinement and wealth of the State is not represented by your body." Calculating that even given the Democratic gains in Congress that were expected, the constitution being framed would be in effect until 1871, Orr remarked that he felt compelled to attend the meetings of the convention so that he might "accomplish something in securing from the Convention a liberal, just, and wise Constitution."[54] As it happened, the delegates produced a document that served as the organic law of the state not only throughout Reconstruction but also for eighteen years after the whites seized control of the government in 1876—and without Orr's help at that.

As his term as governor ended in 1868, Orr was without a constituency. He had gone much too far toward accepting racial equality to be acceptable to white supremacist Democrats and not far enough to please the Republicans. The latter party had much more toleration for dissent within its ranks, however, and Orr recognized that he could influence events only by joining the dominant party. Thus he rejected former governor Perry's appeals to depend on the northern Democrats for deliverance and heeded the pleas of conservative Republicans to throw his talents behind their cause. In the antebellum period, of course, Orr had been a fervent Democrat, believing the Democrats to be the party of moderation. But with the antebellum issues settled by the war, Orr judged that the Democratic Party had nothing to offer except reaction. He resolved to become a Republican, and when his political disabilities were removed and he was offered a circuit judgeship, he accepted it.[55] The consequences of Orr's affiliation with the Republicans and his relationship to the party will be examined in the next chapter. The point here is that his attempt to find a third way, a middle road between what he saw as the extremists on each side, met with complete failure. He could not hope to have influence with the freedmen unless he became a Republican, and he was spurned by fellow whites for refusing to remain a Democrat.

Orr was far from the only moderate to experience this dilemma. After the war, it was common for white South Carolinians to oppose both parties, feeling (not unjustly) that politics and partisanship had brought the war that devastated their state. But to the state's Democrats, nonpartisanship was not an acceptable option. In upcountry Union County, for example, a local Democratic club resolved to treat any white man who failed to vote as if he were a Radical.[56] In Orr's home county of Anderson, a fifty-seven-year-old farmer, R. N. Wright, though affiliating "more with the Democratic [Party] than the other," declined to join the local Democratic club when it was organized in 1867 or 1868, a decision his neighbors would not accept. "We had just got through a bloody war," Wright explained, "and I thought we had been led off by our leaders, and I determined to take no part with either party, but be a conservative man." He was threatened with ostracism, and it was rumored that he was "a Radical." In an attempt to clarify his position, he resolved "to come out in a card in the newspaper, and deny it, and state I belonged to no party, and was always a conservative man." Wright's attempt at moderation fared no better than Orr's, and both came to the same conclusion: men of their beliefs were more appreciated in the Republican Party. Wright was appointed by Republican governors to three terms as a trial justice in Anderson County.[57]

In other counties, too, those who believed in moderation were forced to abandon that position or act with the Radicals. In Spartanburg County some of the wealthiest, most politically experienced planters at first cooperated with Governor Orr's program. Among them was Gabriel Cannon, a Unionist in 1852 and 1860 who supported the Confederacy even though he opposed secession.[58] He owned a personal fortune of one hundred thousand dollars, had an above-average education, and had served in the state senate for sixteen consecutive years before the war. He declined to be a candidate for office in the Confederacy and took the oath of allegiance as soon as he could. He supported Johnson's program of Reconstruction, defending his stand by declaring that "there would be no more abandonment in principle in our people as citizens acknowledging their acceptance of the situation than there was in General Lee's surrender, holding that both were necessitated by unavoidable and overpowering circumstances."[59]

Cannon's friend James Farrow took the same ground, writing privately to Orr, "I would not like to go 'ahead of the music' or 'behind time' but with those who contemplate steps looking to the obtaining of some measures of *stable security* to the industry and labor of the south even should the term 'political rights' have been struck from our vocabulary."[60] The intention of these elite landowners was twofold: to restore peace and to steer a middle course in politics. For some, the former motive was controlling. J. H. Carlisle, for example, cooperated because "he could stand tyranny and despotism, but he couldn't stand anarchy."[61] (In fact, it had been fear of anarchy that had made many of these wealthy slaveholders opposed to secession in the first place.)[62] Just as important to some was the desire to prevent radical Democrats from regaining control *and* prevent Radical Republicans from building up a party in the state.[63] These planters wanted events in their own hands largely because they distrusted extremists on both sides.

Men such as Cannon and Farrow were frustrated in their attempt to impose a moderate course on their section because passions made extremists of most of their constituents. The local paper, the *Carolina Spartan,* accused them of "forgetting the glorious days of '62 and '63 and . . . begging favor of those . . . who would spit on us as we bow."[64] Even though Spartanburg had a large white majority, the Republicans won the first biracial elections in large part because men such as Farrow could not convince whites to vote. "Many of them will have nothing to do with it," he reported to Orr.[65] The elite planters were not used to having their advice spurned by yeomen farmers, and it is likely that cooperation lost much of its appeal for them when they saw its unpopularity.

It was probably even more galling to them that the freedmen, even their own former slaves, would not trust them in politics.[66] As it became clear to these moderates that they would have little influence in the Republican Party, they abandoned their flirtation with it and returned to the Democratic fold.[67] Alexander P. Wylie, for example, a physician and cotton planter of Chester County, was a strong Unionist from a strong Unionist family and was in 1865 one of only three convention delegates to advocate full civil rights for blacks.[68] For his opposition to secession and support of racial justice, "some extreme men have cursed me, and called me an abolitionist," although he retained the confidence of many of the "respectable part of the people" of Chester. He was also respected by blacks. When he told his laborers to take precautions lest his cotton be burned, he was told, "No danger of burning your cotton. You treat the colored people with justice."[69] Wylie tried to be a moderating influence in his town and county, and in 1868 he would vote for the occasional Republican. He did not, however, join the

Republican Party because of his perception of local Republicans as corrupt and extreme.[70]

On the other hand, Wylie probably would not have had much of a Republican constituency in any case. Whatever he had of personal integrity and goodwill, he nevertheless had fully absorbed the prejudices of his society. At a political meeting attended almost exclusively by blacks, he announced to the crowd, "You should be satisfied with your condition. You have done nothing in the advancement of civilization in this world except what has been forced on you through slavery to white men. . . . I do not think you are as smart as we are, but you have an opportunity in this country to save yourselves . . . though you never before did it."[71] However highly Chester County blacks thought of the doctor, they could hardly be blamed for voting for Republicans who voiced more enlightened views. Wylie quoted their philosophy as "our race, right or wrong"; that seems to be all the sense he could make of their choosing measures over men.[72]

Neither Wylie of Chester nor the moderate planters of Spartanburg could fathom why the freedmen would vote for inferior men who happened to agree with the freedmen's politics. But Cannon went further than Wylie. When moral suasion did not achieve the purpose of winning freedmen's votes, he and other large planters were not above reminding the freedmen who paid their wages. Cannon gave a speech to the freedmen in which he reminded them that nine-tenths or more of them worked on land owned by Democrats and told them that if they had to depend on Republican leaders for employment, they would go the way of "the Indians, whose bones are now whitening the western hills."[73]

He also condoned, if he did not participate in, the process by which the threats were carried out: the Democrats appointed men to attend the election and write down names of blacks who voted Republican, so that they could be denied employment. Those freedmen who voted the Democratic ticket were given certificates, which they could present to prospective employers.[74] When questioned whether he believed it was right to discriminate against Republicans in hiring workers, Cannon responded that he "had no objection to it" as "we all generally employ our friends, you know."[75] Of course, in taking this position, and in blackballing Republican workers, Cannon and other Democrats were doing exactly what they accused the freedmen of doing—placing party politics above the personal qualities of individuals.

Not all of Spartanburg's moderates chose the Democratic Party, however. John Winsmith, a physician and one of the wealthiest planters in the district and a prominent politician for years, remained a Republican throughout Reconstruction and even after Redemption, as will be described in a later chapter. At first glance, Winsmith's adoption of Republicanism seems anomalous. He fit the profile of a moderate such as Cannon or Farrow, and he was a slaveholder and a lifelong states' rights Democrat who opposed both the Black Code and black suffrage as extreme.[76] Although Cannon and Farrow ultimately decided that the Republican

Party was more extreme, Winsmith came to the opposite conclusion—and for a very good reason: armed Democrats invaded his house and riddled him with bullets.

The attack was made by Spartanburg Klansmen who had heard that Winsmith was a Radical and had guns in his home that he intended to distribute to the freedmen. They came at night to demand a meeting with him, but he determined that they were trespassing on his property and constituted a threat to his safety. He located his pistols and walked out into the night, guns blazing. The Democrats returned fire, wounding Winsmith in seven places but somehow failing to kill him. The gunmen then fled.[77]

The effect of the attack was to convert Winsmith from moderation and conservatism to enthusiastic support of the Republican Party. Unlike other moderate planters who became Republicans, he never wavered in his support of the party, although he proudly announced in 1874 that he had "worked hard to redeem the character of the Republican Party in Spartanburg" and anticipated "the upward and forward movement of Republicanism in our County."[78] Of course, the more common result of Democratic persecution was exactly the opposite. Most moderates who flirted with Republicanism and then were "visited" by the Klan retired from politics or joined the Democrats in order to avoid whippings, beatings, or worse. What these more numerous cases have in common with Winsmith's singular case is that all show the unworkability of maintaining a moderate course, given the inflamed passions of the time.

Another moderate whose passions were inflamed by Democratic violence was Lemuel Boozer of Lexington County. Even though a slaveholder, he was a lifelong Unionist. Back in 1851 Boozer had used his influence to oppose the calling of a convention to discuss secession.[79] In 1860, when the southern delegates walked out of the National Democratic Convention, only two delegates from South Carolina remained: upstate Unionist B. F. Perry and Boozer.[80] Boozer personally campaigned against secession, holding meetings at which he condemned that course. His son, Baylis Earle Boozer, who shared his father's politics, was shot and killed by a secessionist.[81] A friend who visited Lemuel Boozer that night described the "spectacle of woe" he presented at that moment: he was "paralytic, both in body and brain. His very reason tottered on its throne. Unutterable anguish was depicted on his features. When he had recovered the power of speech, a wild cry for vengeance burst from his lips, and could he have commanded, at the instant, a flaming electric bolt, he would have dashed it at the head of the slayer of his son."[82]

Boozer would likely have opposed secession in any case, but his visceral hatred of the rebellion, resulting from his son's murder, rendered him a more devout Unionist than most. During the war, he gave aid and comfort to Union forces in the area, both by giving them information of the terrain and the location of Rebel forces and by sending supplies to the Union troops through his slaves.[83] At the conclusion of the war, when Union forces occupied Lexington, they made their headquarters in Boozer's house.[84] Boozer could and did take the "iron-clad oath," stating that he had not participated in any way in the rebellion.[85]

Although he participated in the 1865 convention as a delegate from Lexington, Boozer appears not to have uttered a word throughout the proceedings.[86] He illustrated his commitment to Republicanism by actions. When the state government was reorganized along the lines of congressional Reconstruction, Boozer became South Carolina's first Republican lieutenant governor, and he supported the party up to his death in 1870. In his will, he provided for land to be given for a black school in the town of Lexington.[87] At the proceedings on Boozer's death, a Democratic friend of his, who apparently came to bury Boozer, not to praise him, eulogized him thus:[88]

> He and I were antipodes in politics, but I regarded his identification with the Republican party of this State as an act of signal moral heroism, which his political opponents were compelled to respect for its perfect sincerity and purity of motive. To be dissevered from the friends of his youth, of his manhood and advanced years; to drop the hands of his own Carolinians and grasp those of strangers; to aid in seizing the government of the dear old State from the possession of her own children to be confided to the guardianship of aliens, was indeed almost to tear his body and soul asunder. But still he did it. . . . In his life I forgave him, because I knew he was honest.

This remarkable eulogy may provide some indication of the possibilities for conciliation or moderation during the period in question.

The moderate or conservative white South Carolinians of the early period of Reconstruction differ in important ways from the more liberal group who joined the Republican Party when congressional Reconstruction began. They were, as a general rule, wealthier. Before the war, they had been planters and slaveholders, and almost exclusively, they had been Unionists. Not many were as passionately or scrupulously Unionist as Lemuel Boozer, but none had been known as a secessionist in 1860 or earlier. These men—men such as Boozer, Winsmith, and Orr—had been dissenters in the prewar years. Their differences with the ruling aristocracy did not extend to an attack on slavery; they were themselves financially and morally committed to the institution as well. But there were other cleavages in antebellum society. Orr and the others were ideologically much less aristocratic than the men who had dominated the state in the antebellum period, and they had been much less willing to sacrifice white liberty to protect black slavery. When the Confederacy collapsed, they saw an opportunity to seize control of the state and reform it in their image. Later, of course, Radical white Republicans would attempt the same thing, and their vision of what South Carolina should be would differ even further from that of the lowcountry aristocracy. But the vision of the moderates was enough of a challenge to the Old South elite that it took civil war and abolition for them to get the chance to implement it.

After the war, the upcountry moderates who came to power seized the chance to democratize the state's politics, leading to open conflict with the lowcountry. This struggle was played out in the 1865 convention, and the debates were recorded for posterity by Sidney Andrews, a reporter from the North. As Andrews describes it, the long-anticipated showdown soon became a rout.[89] The upcountry members' campaign began with the abolition of the parish system, whereby the lowcountry counties had been divided into tiny parishes, each one having the same representation in the state senate as an entire upcountry county. They continued by refusing to apportion representation on the basis of total population, basing it instead on white population alone. (No one in the convention had any intention of allowing blacks to vote. Lowcountry delegates supported their representation only to increase their region's voting strength.) Finally, a resolution passed that after 1869 no county would have more than twelve representatives in the state legislature. This was obviously directed at Charleston, which had twenty.[90]

The antebellum system was not, however, thoroughly repudiated, nor was democracy embraced, even for whites. As a concession to the lowcountry, representation in the state house of representatives continued to be determined on the dual bases of white population and property. It would remain for the Republican-dominated Constitutional Convention of 1868 to abolish this last remnant of elitism in South Carolina's organic law. Furthermore, the oligarchy still controlled the state supreme court, and they used it against the measure of most importance to the yeomen: debt relief. With poverty rampant in the upcountry, and farmers often banding together to resist, sometimes violently, the forced sale of their property, two stay laws were struck down by the court, and debt relief was secured only when Governor Orr appealed to the district federal military commander to impose it by fiat.[91]

Although Orr and many other upcountry moderates became Republicans, it is important to bear in mind that most whites in the upcountry never did. White Republicans were more numerous in the upper counties than elsewhere, but it is likely that they amounted to no more than 20 percent of whites in any county at any time even there.[92] The point, rather, is that the minority of upcountry politicians who did become Republicans used the party to put forward a program they had long had in mind, and one geared to their constituents. Orr, for example, later defended his decision to be a Republican by pointing out all the party had done "to ameliorate the condition of the white people of the State—ameliorations which the Legislature of the State in 1865 and 1866 refused to grant."[93] Ironically, the Republican Party was only an effective vehicle for the upcountry agenda after the enfranchisement of the freedmen—but their votes once again shifted the weight of the state's population back to the lowcountry. Upcountry white Republicans would continue to complain about lowcountry bias in patronage appointments throughout Reconstruction.

Upcountry leaders lost out to slaveholders, then to former slaves. The irony must have frustrated them. But this aspect of the conflict too had antebellum antecedents. Many of the upcountry moderates described, such as Boozer, had favored stricter enforcement of the slave laws, a position that set them in opposition to the large planters. Their motives were usually to limit slave competition with white artisans or craftsmen, thus supporting nonslaveholders over both slave and master. Although Boozer himself was a slaveholder, he lived in the town of Lexington, and his constituency was composed largely of nonslaveholders. Others who became Radicals during Reconstruction, such as Franklin Israel Moses and Thomas J. Coghlan of Sumter and Alexander Stuart Wallace of York, had taken up the same causes in the prewar era.[94]

What changed when blacks began to exercise the franchise was that their interests had to considered and their votes solicited, which was, after all, the point. The Reconstruction Act resulted largely from Republicans' realization that the southern governments would not be responsive to the concerns of blacks unless they depended upon them for votes. Once this change occurred, politics also changed. Moderates who would and could work with the freedmen often became leaders in the Republican Party, especially if they were well educated and well off. But those who refused to appeal to blacks relinquished their leadership positions, which passed to Radicals more willing to embrace equality.

# TWO

## The Republican Alternative

While moderates were trying to discover Congress's minimum demands for readmission and convince their fellow citizens to compromise, a few South Carolinians had already decided that changes had not gone far enough. In particular, the retention in office of former Rebels was a sore point with white Unionists. On February 6, 1866, Simeon Corley, a Lexington tailor who had been forced into the Confederate army at bayonet point, wrote Thaddeus Stevens, the Radical Republican leader from Pennsylvania, an extraordinary letter in which he asserted that the old leaders were "still the enemies of the Government." He warned that their "great desire to get back into the Union" was merely a desire "to take hold of the reins of Government." The obvious problem was the lack of sufficient numbers of Unionists to carry elections or possibly even to fill all the necessary local offices. The problem led Corley to a solution well beyond what the moderates had found acceptable: "I have slowly but deliberately come to the conclusion that negro suffrage is our only hope for peace and security in the future."[1]

Corley was a lifelong dissenter from southern orthodoxy. He had opposed his state's secession in 1850 and 1860, even to the point of advocating the abolition of slavery. He had served in the Confederate army only when forced to do so and had taken the oath of loyalty as soon as he was offered the chance. After the war, he had advocated the congressional plan of Reconstruction, opposing Andrew Johnson's more lenient plan.[2] When the former won out, Corley served first as a representative of Lexington County in the 1868 Constitutional Convention, then as congressman for South Carolina's Third District. The following excerpt from his campaign broadside illustrates his political principles:[3]

> The Democrats declare that white men must rule America, and that the white man who did all he could to destroy the Constitution and the Government, is entitled to all his former rights and privileges under it; while the colored man, who periled his life to defend it, has no political right whatever beyond implicit obedience to the will of his enemies and the

> embittered enemies of the nation. What nonsense! Are South Carolinians such fools as to swallow a dose so disgustingly filthy and nauseating? . . . The only constitutional provision these un-repentant leaders are clearly entitled to, is the gibbet.

Corley was a devout democrat, advocating voting rights for all without regard to race, wealth, education, literacy, or even gender.[4] The only people he would disenfranchise were the former leaders of the state, whom he saw as tyrants and traitors. As a Christian, he professed not to hate them. "I forgive them, for they know not what they do," he said. (Indeed, a former Confederate, fifty-seven years after the war, recalled meeting Corley in a prisoner-of-war camp in Maryland and remained ever after impressed by the "kind words and offered deeds of Comrade Corley," who had "offered substantial aid to us in the hour of dire need.")[5] As an American, however, he was determined that "they shall not rule again, only to ruin us."[6]

He arraigned the former oligarchs not only for the "impetuous madness" of secession but also for the way they had ruled before the war. He deplored their "selfish disregard for the rights of humanity" and their "branding as 'fanatical' the desire to improve and elevate the masses." They had, "like another Cain . . . embraced the theory, asked *politically,* 'Am I my brother's keeper.'" He rejoiced for South Carolina that the "musty dogmas of her chivalry are buried with their conceited authors," and now he vowed, "I am not so tired of freedom as to basely surrender it to those who will pervert it to our mutual ruin."[7]

As for the former slave, Corley proclaimed that he "is to-day worth a thousand times more as the State's voter and defender, than he could ever have been as its chattel and slave," and he declared that "the hue of a man's skin shall never divest him of the claims of a virtuous heart and an active brain." White laborers should rejoice in emancipation, he argued: "The blow which struck those chains from the hands of the slave, severed them also from mine." He pleaded with his white audience to recognize that "the safety of the nation . . . depends upon the political union of the races" and to "save your State and country from further bloodshed, evidently sought by" the Democrats. As a politician he claimed to have "the entire confidence of the colored people," who knew of his prewar abolitionism.[8]

Corley had no qualms about incurring the wrath of the Democrats, as he had a long history of dissent and resultant persecution. When he came out for abolition, he was "preached at, sneered at, hated and despised." He later recalled finding his "signboard and door besmeared with something as black, but more tangible than rebel hate." In 1850 he had been threatened and warned to leave the state, but he ignored the threats and continued to write Unionist articles for Benjamin F. Perry's Greenville newspaper, the *Southern Patriot.* Corley seems not to have been molested by his neighbors during this period, but the crucible of war strained their indulgence. By 1863, they could no longer tolerate a dissident in their midst, and they offered Corley the choice of enlistment in the Confederate army or immediate martyrdom. Deciding that a "live dog was better than a dead lion," he entered Lee's army and served for two years. He later called this service "the most humiliating position . . . he ever occupied." When captured by the Union army, he "gladly" took the oath of allegiance and returned home, only to find that his home, having lain in General Sherman's path, was "almost a desolation."[9]

Having withstood these threats, insults and injuries, Corley was in no mood to back down now that "loyal men of both races" dominated the government. It was critical to him that the aristocracy not recapture the government because, having learned nothing and forgotten nothing, they would "drive the machine a *second* time to destruction." He would stand firm, "without fear," in support of "the welfare of the whole people."[10]

Perhaps what is most remarkable about Simeon Corley is that he won. First he won election to the Constitutional Convention of 1868 from Lexington County, which had nearly twice as many white as black voters, and then he won a seat in Congress by a large majority over his Democratic opponent (who, coincidentally, had been Corley's commanding general in the Confederate service). Corley concluded that his address to the voters, quoted above, "doubtless brought many white men to his support."[11]

Simeon Corley was, to put it mildly, not typical. Active in the southeastern Lutheran synod, he was an opponent of drugs and tobacco. He favored the abolition of the death penalty.[12] He was also a teetotaler. And a vegetarian.[13] It is difficult to imagine a more anomalous figure in South Carolina, where a table without pork is a table that has not been set. Personal eccentricities aside, however, Corley illustrates very well the tremendous difference made by the extension of the vote to freedmen.

The question of why he supported the measure is also crucial to understanding the character of white Republicanism. Corley explained to Thaddeus Stevens that he "had never thought of refusing [anyone] the ballot *because he was a negro,* but [only] on account of the general ignorance of the race." This position, perhaps supporting a literacy or educational qualification for voting, would have appealed to many of the moderates. But for Corley, such distinctions were no longer tenable: "Still such objections might be urged; yet, when we look at the ignorance of the whites, and their mad disloyalty, it becomes a matter of necessity" for blacks to have the vote. He added an impassioned plea for the rightness of the action as well, nothing that "it is but *just* too that men who periled all in defense of their country . . . should, at least, after saving that country, be entitled to all its privileges and benefits." He further warned of the consequences of failing to extend equal suffrage: "Any nation fostering such injustice and ingratitude . . . *would,* and I think, *should* perish!"[14]

Despite such rhetoric, and despite the undoubted sincerity of Corley's personal commitment to equal rights, it is important to acknowledge that his chief purpose was the removal from office of ex-Rebels and that enfranchisement of blacks was a necessary means to that end. Indeed, even his moral argument for black voting was not based on universal rights. Blacks should vote, according to Corley, because they had *earned* equality by supporting the Union; the logic could not be applied to the Indians, Chinese, or other racial groups.[15] And even in the case of blacks, race remained a meaningful distinction for Corley. For example, when accused by a rival of favoring interracial marriages, Corley responded, "*Every man* and *woman* has a right to marry any one they may want, and *can get;* but I trust that no one, white or colored, male or female, is so lost to the instincts of their nature as to seek a partner of the opposite race."[16]

Thus, although white Radicals such as Simeon Corley supported political and social rights for blacks, they were in no sense color blind. Indeed, Corley surpassed most Republicans in his lifelong commitment to justice for southern blacks. Many had been, in the prewar period, indifferent or hostile to African Americans. A case in point was Thomas J. Coghlan. An Irish immigrant mechanic, Coghlan had been in the antebellum years a populist politician who opposed both the large planters and free blacks and had objected to blacks practicing the mechanical professions.[17] When it became clear that the prewar elite would be displaced only with black votes, however, Coghlan became an ardent supporter of racial equality. He was active in registering black voters for the 1867 election, and in the convention he proposed South Carolina's first hate-speech law, which would have banned the use of "the epithets 'negro,' 'nigger,' and 'Yankee,' as used in the opprobrious sense."[18]

Another convert to antiracism was Alexander Stuart Wallace, Republican congressman from the Fourth District, the whitest congressional district in the state.[19] Wallace, like Coghlan, had been a popular politician before the war, winning election to the South Carolina House of Representatives several times in the 1850s from his native York County. He too seems to have won yeoman support in the antebellum period through opposition to both planters and free blacks.[20] He had also been a slaveholder, and if his enemies are to be believed, not a particularly kind one.[21]

On the other hand, Wallace had always been a Union man, running for the legislature as a Unionist in 1851 and 1860. He does not seem to have aided the Confederate cause, and he took the "iron-clad oath" in 1865—although his son Robert fought in the Confederate army. After serving briefly in the 1866 state legislature, where he opposed the Black Code, Wallace resigned his seat to accept an appointment as collector of federal revenue. At the onset of congressional Reconstruction in 1868, he joined the Republican Party and ran for Congress on that ticket.[22]

His defection led to charges of opportunism from Democrats, who noted that he had been a slaveholder "as long as he could be one" and therefore he had no standing to criticize the Democrats as the "slaveholder's party."[23] Historian Lacy K. Ford Jr. has taken this position as well, arguing that "Wallace's shift to the Republican party was extraordinary," and that the "most plausible explanation" of his actions was "sheer political opportunism."[24] Ford suggests that his conversion may have resulted from a deal with Republicans for the revenue-collector position, or perhaps for an acquittal by the military court investigating Wallace's killing of a freedman in 1865.[25]

In fact, however, it is difficult to see how "the Republicans" could have arranged either of these things, as President Johnson was still in control of Reconstruction. Wallace more likely received the appointment because he was the rare man in his district who was both a prominent, popular politician and a Unionist who was cooperative with the federal government. (His acquittal, too, was probably on the merits; the *Yorkville Enquirer* presented the case as one of "plain duty in the defense of private rights.")[26] In any case, Wallace's conversion to Republicanism, though rare, was not extraordinary. He had always opposed the leading planters of his district and the state and had always supported the Union. His position on race relations changed, but the key here seems to have been the war itself. Just as the war changed attitudes in the North about blacks (however shallow or temporary the change might be), it changed the attitudes of southern Unionists as well. (The fact that blacks fought for the Union was clearly important in this regard.) Early in the Reconstruction period, before he was a Republican, Wallace voted against the Black Code, and after changing parties he adopted the Republican position on the freedmen with consistency.

Even as he began appealing to black voters, Wallace continued to be popular with a large minority of whites in his district. Many upcountry whites who refused to vote for Republicans at the state level or the local level supported Wallace for Congress.[27] Like all Republicans, he depended heavily on the votes of freedmen to remain in office; nevertheless, he was the rare Republican who could be elected in a majority-white district. As such, he was one of the most controversial white Republicans in the state, the subject of all-out attacks by Democrats and of spirited defenses by Republicans.

Race, of course, played the largest role in the debate over Wallace's character. As was typical, Democrats attacked from both sides. They accused him of loving blacks too much and of loving them not at all but using them to win office for himself. The former allegation took on two forms. More respectable opponents accused Wallace and other Republicans of favoring not only "political equality" but also the more radical "social equality," something they felt sure was unacceptable to Wallace's white constituents. Social equality—equal access to public accommodations, integrated schools, and the like—was considered more extreme, probably because it threatened everyday relations between the races and thus diminished the privileged status of whites in southern society in a way that universal suffrage did not. Of course, most white South Carolinians did not favor that change either, but for most, it was not as viscerally disturbing as the idea that blacks would cease to show deference to whites in public.

Another tactic for portraying Republicans as too favorable to blacks, one utilized by less respectable Democrats, was to imply that the man in question was sexually attracted to black women. An example of this tactic as applied to Wallace by the *Yorkville Enquirer* described his speech at a York County Republican gathering: "The speaker basked in the smiles of his charming countrywomen who favored him with their presence, and drew fresh inspiration when he spoke especially to the ladies. It is proper to add that the only 'ladies' present were colored."[28]

The allegations that white Republicans desired black women were obviously first and foremost an insult to black women; thus we see that these remarks were never made by blacks but always by whites about one another. The background against which whites battled on this issue assumed that it was shameful for a white man to be attracted to a black woman. As was mentioned, such "allegations" were made against Simeon Corley as well, and it is likely that every white Republican at some time was accused of desiring black women. An extreme case was that of William Champion, who was taken from his Spartanburg home late at night by disguised men and whipped for being a Republican. According to his testimony, he was then forced to perform sex acts on a black woman. His accusers then "asked how I liked that for nigger equality."[29]

The almost universal retort made by white Republicans was that it was not them but the former slaveholders who desired sex with black women. The intimation that planters commonly had sexual relations with female slaves was seen by northerners and white opponents of the planters as a devastating reply to planters' insults. For example, William De Forest, a Union officer with the Freedmen's Bureau, recounts the following exchange on a southern train:[30]

> On my way from Charleston to my station I was amused at a conversation which went on behind me between a rough, corpulent, jolly old planter of the middle class and a meek-looking young Northerner, apparently a "drummer" from New York. The old fellow talked incessantly, sending his healthy, ringing voice clean through the whole car and denouncing with a delightful fervor the whole "breed, seed, and generation of niggers." . . . The six or eight Southerners in the car seemed mightily taken with the old man and laughed heartily over his phillipic.
>
> . . . "I tell you the nigger is a no-account creetur," went on the old planter. "All the men are thieves, and all the women are prostitutes. It's their natur' to be that way, and they never'll be no other way. They ain't worth the land they cover. They ought to be improved off the face of the earth."
>
> Here the New Yorker spoke for the first time in an hour.
>
> "You are improving 'em off pretty fast," he said meekly. "Got some of 'em 'most white already."

> So unfair is the human mind that nobody but myself laughed at this retort. The planter turned the conversation on crops, and the audience looked out of the windows.

Southern white Republicans also found this riposte irresistible. When the Democratic *Charleston Mercury* termed the 1868 Constitutional Convention the "ring-streaked-and-striped" convention because it was integrated, a white member (apparently unaware that his remarks might be objectionable to black or mulatto delegates) responded: "I asked who made this convention ring-streaked-and-striped. . . . I know as much about the men who call us ring-streaked-and-striped as any body, and if I choose to tell, I could astonish you with a revelation of secrets that would account for some of those streaks."[31]

Some, such as Corley, drew the obvious distinction between the forced prostitution that sometimes accompanied slavery and any consensual interracial relationships that followed emancipation. Corley, for example, opposed outlawing interracial marriage, but he can hardly be seen as condoning it, as was discussed above. In this respect, he was typical of white liberals in the North. As George Fredrickson has pointed out, while championing black rights, they retained beliefs in important differences between the races and the undesirability of intermarriage, often for presumed health reasons. For example, the New England Freedmen's Aid Society published the view that "mixture of blood diminishes vitality and force, and shortens life."[32]

As distasteful as some of the comments made by South Carolina's white Republicans were, then, they must be understood in context; if these men were not color blind, neither were their northern counterparts. It is their liberalism on questions of race, not their prejudice, which is remarkable. Although the debate over civil rights seems to indicate that there was a rift between white Republicans and blacks, the issue is easily overstated. Blacks knew that white Republicans, however disappointing they might be at times, were much to be preferred over the alternative. For their part, white Republicans objected to social equality less in principle than for practical reasons—such measures, they knew, would seem radical to their fellow white southerners, thus endangering the rest of their goals. At the outset of Reconstruction, their primary goal was the removal from office of former Confederates.

The white Republicans' aversion to the antebellum leaders of the state was complete enough to include even moderates such as James L. Orr, at least until he formally joined their party. A Greenville County Unionist named Samuel Tinsley wrote to Thaddeus Stevens urging him not to pardon Orr, "for he is one of the worst men we have." He warned that if former Rebels retained power they would "baptize the Nation in blood agin [*sic*]." Tinsley had been a hard-core Unionist. When he encountered some Union troops, "chast by dogs and all most starved to deth," he led them safely back to Union lines. One of the officers, a Lieutenant

Welsh, took Tinsley to his home in Pennsylvania for the rest of the war. Now that it was over, Tinsley found many former Confederates "in a wors state of rebellion now than at aney time" and felt that they "hate me as if I was the devel" because of his Unionism. He concluded by again urging, "Don't parden rebells nor change the oath of offis," as there were plenty of loyal Americans in the South to take the places of the disloyal.[33] White Republicans, no less than black Republicans, continued to argue that Democrats did not truly recognize their defeat in the war. Edgefield County Democrats certainly lent credence to this belief when, as late as 1868, they discussed whether "they should on the day of Election march to the polls with the Confederate flag at their head."[34]

Racial issues were far from paramount for Unionists such as Tinsley. Whereas Simeon Corley's loyalty to the federal government was rooted in his abolitionism, Tinsley had opposed secession primarily because he foresaw the destruction it would bring to the South. Once he was proved right, Tinsley strongly opposed retaining former Confederates in power. Perhaps even more typical were those who had supported secession in 1860 but after four years of war had come to the conclusion that it was a grievous error. As Tinsley wrote, "I tol the people what Secession woud do for the country and all proved to bee[.] So a large portion of the people are goin with me in national afars."[35]

Whenever they became supporters of the Union—before, during, or after the war—whites who sided with the national government found life in postwar South Carolina difficult. In addition to the economic pressures faced by all classes in the state, they often suffered added distress as a result of politics. Unforgiving of what they regarded as treason to the state, pro-Confederate southerners sometimes refused to cooperate economically with Unionists. The most vulnerable Unionists were those who did not own land, such as A. G. Hayes of Lexington County. Hayes complained that because of his politics, his neighbors "refuse to grind my corn [or] to give me any employment." As a result, he hoped to raise enough money to leave the state.[36] But even men of means suffered economically for their support of Congress. William M. Thomas, the proprietor of the Enoree Cotton Factory in Greenville, wrote in 1868 that his plant had turned a profit the previous year, but "this year party spirit runs so high, that I must stay at home for the protection of my family and to counteract the assaults of my enemies."[37]

Persecution by their pro-Confederate opponents made Unionists such as Wallace, Tinsley, Hayes, and Thomas into strong supporters of Thaddeus Stevens and other Radical Republicans in Congress. When the Radicals advocated disfranchising former Rebels, southern white Republicans cheered, even if such measures might disfranchise them personally.[38] They viewed Andrew Johnson's retention of Rebels in office as a betrayal, and they considered the removal of these men the first priority of Reconstruction. A particular sore point was the retention of Rebel postmasters. During the antebellum years, they had routinely tampered with the southern mails, censoring any material deemed likely to promote insurrection.

Corley complained that "it was at one time debated here, whether copies of the N.Y. Tribune, [which] I had paid for[,] should be delivered to me. I doubt not, in many instances, such matter was destroyed." He had nominated a loyal man for the post, but the former Confederate was retained in office.[39]

The passage of the Reconstruction Act of 1867, over Johnson's veto, gave great encouragement to South Carolina's white Republicans. Military commanders in the southern states were to register voters—of both races—for the election of a constitutional convention to revise the fundamental law of the state. Many former Unionists and current supporters of Congress offered their services in registering voters. T. B. Milford and John A. Hunter of Abbeville, James M. Allen of Greenville, and Thomas J. Coghlan of Sumter were registrars in 1867 who were or would become Republicans.[40]

Although Congress did not remove disunionist officials from their posts, it was clear that the upcoming convention would control the creation of a new state government. With the registration of black voters, the majority of delegates would be black. Democrats railed that the convention was illegitimate; meeting in Columbia for an informal convention, the leading Democrats declared that "the Negro is utterly unfitted to exercise the highest function of a citizen," that "an ignorant and depraved race is placed in power and influence," and that whites "would never acquiesce in Negro equality or supremacy." Outraged but hopeless of carrying the election, Democrats determined to boycott it in order to underscore their position. As a result, Republicans were elected from every county in the state, even in the whitest areas.[41]

The Constitutional Convention of 1868 was radical before it ever convened. Of 124 delegates, 73 were black.[42] This number corresponds almost precisely to the percentage of blacks in the electorate; the state's new government was framed by a convention truly representative of the state's people. We may understand how radical this was by looking at the issue through the eyes of William Henry Trescot, a member of the former ruling elite and in many respects a moderate and broad-minded statesman. In 1865 and after, he played the role of peacemaker, attempting to effect some reconciliation between South Carolina and the federal government. Although he claimed to accept the results of the war, he understood these to be only the defeat of secession and the abolition of slavery. The principle of majority rule he did not acknowledge as established by the outcome of the war. He was thus able to claim that the Republicans of the state were not, "in property, ability or character, representatives of the people of South Carolina." His fear was that a government not representative of the wealthy would enact "agrarian domestic legislation" that would cripple the state's economy.[43]

Here Trescot was exhibiting "the autonomic fear typical of the low country gentry for anything that smacked of democracy, or which threatened to divide the state."[44] When he thought of the state, he thought not of the mass of its citizens but of "the spirit of independence which settled it, the courage which won its liberty and has maintained its existence, the brain which devised its constitution, the enterprise which expanded its territory, the capital which freights its ships, ploughs its fields, digs its mines and builds its railroads." He gave the credit for these achievements not to the people who did the work but to the few who financed and directed it. (Can there be any wonder why Simeon Corley would accuse Trescot's class of having "ignored the dignity of labor"?) It was the old aristocracy's deeply held conviction that they were the state. Thus what was good for them was beneficial to the society at large, and what was bad for them was at best divisive and at worst—literally—the destruction of civilization.[45]

No wonder, then, that Democratic newspapers were scathing in their condemnation of the 1868 Constitutional Convention, as well as its members. Although the genteel *Charleston Daily News* showed a willingness to give some of the devils their due, the fire-eating *Charleston Mercury* seemingly could not bear to admit that any of the delegates possessed a shred of humanity. The president of the convention, Albert Gallatin Mackey, was a successful Charleston physician, a nationally respected author on masonic subjects, and a strong Unionist. The *News* credited him with "judgment and prudence" and attributed to his influence "much of the reputation [the convention] appears to have acquired in the North, for dispatch, moderation, and consistency."[46] To the *Mercury,* he was a drunk and a fraud, a Republican for profit who had become rich through politics. "We now behold him receiving a salary yet uncertain in its greatness for performing the duties of chairman of the great negro convention," the paper sneered, even though Mackey had announced almost a month earlier that he would accept no payment for his service "as President or delegate."[47]

The *Mercury* often denied the Unionist credentials of white delegates, thus implying that they had become Republicans for selfish motives. Lemuel Boozer, the antebellum planter and politician mentioned previously as a lifelong and determined Unionist, one who sent supplies and information to the Union army, was slandered by the *Mercury* as a hypocrite because he was once "a tolerably sound States Rights man."[48] James M. Rutland of Fairfield was conceded by most, including the *News,* to have been "a Union man throughout the war."[49] The *Mercury,* however, insinuated that he was not, alleging that "before he adopted his present miscegenative notions the only political occasion on which [his] name was brought prominently before the public" was to raise money to buy a cane for South Carolina congressman Preston Brooks to honor his 1856 assault against Senator Charles Sumner. Another favorite tactic of the paper was to question the designation of the white delegates as white. Thus William S. Collins was "a white man, so-called"; he was white in complexion and blood, "but in his associations and character he is a negro." John K. Terry was "said to be a white man, [but] could easily be mistaken at a short distance for a cross between a grizzly and a hyena."[50]

The scathing, often libelous criticism of white Republicans by the most rabid southern Democrats should come as no surprise. It was clearly in their interest to portray their opponents in as unfavorable a light as they could. Nor is it surprising that northern Democratic papers eagerly passed along the most unflattering characterizations of the Reconstruction governments. What does require explanation is the substantial concurrence of many northern Republicans in these withering indictments of their southern allies. Part of the explanation is political. Republican moderates were involved in a fierce struggle against northern Radicals—men such as Thaddeus Stevens, Benjamin Butler, and Benjamin Wade—seeing them as demagogues with "agrarian sympathies." They saw southern white Republicans as counterparts to these men. They sensed the possibility of southern demagogues using black votes the way northern demagogues used immigrant votes.[51]

Another part of the northern prejudice against southern white Republicans was based on class. When scalawags excoriated the South's upper class, upper-class northern Republicans were distinctly uncomfortable.[52] Moderate publications, such as the *Nation, Chicago Tribune, Boston Advertiser,* and *New York Times,* were much more comfortable with South Carolina moderates such as Governor Orr than with native white Radicals.[53] This class bias shows itself, for example, in a reference to "poor whites" as being "without character, education or position."[54]

Unfortunately for the northern moderates, aristocratic Republicans were not many in South Carolina. Faced with the choice between unreconstructed southern Democrats and southern Radicals, northern moderates seemed willing to choose the latter, but not gladly. The *Times,* for example, could see fit to compliment only two white Republicans in the 1868 convention, both of them men of conservative economic principles.[55] These northerners were more willing to see merit in some of the black delegates (as were southern Democrats, curiously enough), but these were always referred to as "exceptions," and they were usually praised as a way of further diminishing the white delegates: they "far outshone in intellect any of the white members," for example. Mostly, though, northern moderates chose to believe the worst about all southerners, black and white, Democrat and Republican, and for the future they could foresee nothing but bloodshed or, in the language of the day, "a war of races."[56]

As a result, before the South Carolina Constitutional Convention ever met, its black and white delegates were already in the uncomfortable position that the state's Republicans would occupy throughout Reconstruction: white Democrats had declared war on them, and their northern allies had evinced strong reservations about whether they were worth fighting for. In combination with the critical need for measures of relief for all South Carolinians, and the demands of the freedmen for recognition of their equality, the delegates who met in Columbia for two months in early 1868 faced a formidable challenge.

Almost immediately the delegates were placed in the position of either ignoring the needs of their desperate constituents or providing ammunition for northern Democrats to use against the national Republican Party.[57] Richard H. Cain, a black minister and editor from Ohio, proposed a resolution that would request that Congress appropriate a million-dollar loan to South Carolina to provide land to the homeless poor.[58] Charles P. Leslie, a white carpetbagger from New York, responded that although he was sympathetic to the intended beneficiaries of the proposal, it was impossible that it would succeed—"I would be willing to go to Hades, provided he gets the million dollars"—and he was prevented from supporting the measure by his concern for "what the Northern people would say about it."[59] After much pointless debate about whether the Treasury did or did not have money in it, a Massachusetts carpetbagger named Niles G. Parker cut to the heart of the matter: "I am of the opinion that if Congress should pass the appropriation called for at just this particular time, that every State from Maine to California would roll up such a Democratic vote in the coming election that was never heard of, or dreamt of, by the most ardent Democrat in this country. . . . Where would be our reconstruction if Andrew Johnson and the Democratic party had the handling of us?"[60] Eventually, and after acrimonious debate, the body passed a compromise measure whereby Congress would be asked what money it could send to South Carolina.[61]

The debate over the rather insubstantial issue of the loan petition illustrates the extreme concern on the part of some of the delegates for northern opinion. They recognized that the South Carolina party depended on northern support and judged that asking too much help from the North would be counterproductive. Most of the delegates, however, seem to have agreed with the proposal's sponsor that the need for relief should be uppermost in their minds.

Other relief measures sparked controversy as well, although for different reasons. One especially divisive plan would have nullified all debts contracted in the purchase of slaves. The argument of the plan's sponsors was straightforward: an exchange had occurred between buyer and seller. The buyer no longer had the slave because of emancipation. The seller should also lose any debt he had not yet collected; otherwise, the one was punished twice for the sin of slavery, the other not at all. To this was added the sentiment that for the state to enforce contracts for payment for slaves would be to condone the traffic in human flesh. Much better, they argued, to decree that slavery had never been legal and that contracts involving it were unenforceable.[62]

Opponents argued that the plan seemed to be motivated by a "spirit of revenge" upon slave traders, that the matter was for the courts to decide, and that slaves had indeed been property under the law, however immoral the law was.[63] Simeon Corley, who had perhaps the best antislavery credentials of any white delegate, argued for enforcing the debts in language that betrayed its own spirit of revenge against the planter:[64]

> I can see no good reason for denying the seller's right to collect the purchase money from him, whose pious clamor now denounces the contract as an outrage upon justice and right. If the pious purchaser were not an

> idiot, incapable of entering into a contract—if he got, in his own estimation, at that time, value received for his obligation to pay, it is not the right nor the legitimate business of this Convention to decide whether or not he was a fool in accepting as property that which, I trust, we all hold could not be rightfully claimed as such.

At issue was more than the moral question of whether slaves had ever really been property and more than the legal question of whether cancellation of the debts was allowed by the federal Constitution. The real issue was the practical political question of what the convention could or should do to mollify the planters, who would of course be the main beneficiaries of the cancellation. Although some delegates thought such gestures advisable, Corley did not mind going on record as opposed to any and all measures to conciliate planter opinion.

The most important question affecting the planters was whether former Confederates would or would not be disfranchised and disqualified from holding office under the new constitution. Corley, who sponsored many resolutions in the convention, spoke for the first time on this issue. Predictably, he advocated the "speedy removal" of all the "present disloyal officers of the Provisional Government."[65] No wonder the *Charleston Mercury* said of Corley that, after his actions in the convention, he could "hardly again pretend to be the friend of the white people of South Carolina."[66] Corley was not alone; other white Republicans advocated similar measures. Solomon George Washington Dill, who claimed that he was "always known to be on the side of the poor," wanted to see to it that after the convention adjourned "every civil office in the State be declared vacant of its present incumbent."[67]

White Unionists were not unanimously in favor of disfranchising former Confederates, though. The president of the convention, Albert Gallatin Mackey, presented a different conception of the issue. Government, he asserted, was only legitimate if it came with the consent of the governed, and if the previous rulers of the state had ignored that principle, that was no excuse for the Reconstruction government to ignore it. He argued for as little disfranchisement as possible and made an impassioned plea for the result of the convention to be submitted to a vote of the people for the first time in the state's history. To him, as well as to Corley, the Old South elite had tyrannized whites as well as blacks. "It was but consistent that those who deemed one-half of their fellow-citizens to be chattels, should forget, or overlook the political rights of the other half," he noted. But in order for the new government to do better, it had to recognize the rights of the old leaders.[68]

The right of suffrage was thus extended to all adult men, with no disqualifications for participation in the rebellion—but also with no requirements as to education, property, or literacy. There was some debate on all these points. Governor Orr had greeted the convention with a speech in which he "urgently" implored the delegates to ratify a qualified suffrage.[69] He suggested a literacy requirement, to be imposed without regard to race. A few of the delegates argued for such a qualification on the ground that a republican form of government required an informed citizenry. At times the discussion became heated. Solomon G. W. Dill bitterly condemned the proposal, doubting that "any person who has a Christian heart in his body, or who expects to see the light of Heaven, would introduce such a bill." Dill was called to order and not allowed to proceed with his remarks. In the final analysis though, the literacy requirement seems not to have been seriously considered by the assembly. Given the extent of illiteracy, the measure would have belied their claim to represent all the people of the state. Most of the delegates who favored an educational requirement of voters did so only to encourage education, and when attendance at school was made compulsory, support for the qualification on suffrage vanished. The final vote on the issue was 107 to 2.[70]

No property qualification was even debated, but there was some support for a requirement that voters pay a poll tax of one dollar a year or be deprived of the suffrage. R. J. Donaldson, a Chesterfield shopkeeper who may have been English, stated bluntly that "men not able to pay one dollar a year for educational purposes should not be entitled to vote, and they are no honor, nor of any use in any community." More commonly, however, the delegates raised the concern that if the poll tax were to support the state's schools, its payment would have to be compelled. J. M. Runion, a white Republican preacher from Greenville, supported the measure on that basis, as did a handful of black delegates. Most members of the convention, though, decided that punishing a man for not having a dollar would not provide him with a dollar. The poll tax requirement failed by a vote of 81 to 21.[71]

Although various reasons were adduced to support qualifications on the suffrage, in the end none of them was as strong as the appeal of universal manhood suffrage. This radical democratic urge was also uppermost as property qualifications for offices were eliminated. In the antebellum period, these had been substantial, and the 1865 constitution, the work of the Democrats, had removed them only for members of the state legislature. The 1868 convention extended the provision to include all state officials, including the governor and United States senators. Another democratizing provision of the 1865 document, the direct election of the governor and presidential electors by the voters instead of the legislature, was extended to include other state officers.[72]

The native white delegates showed in a variety of ways their commitment to popular sovereignty. They could generally be counted upon to favor shorter terms of office, fewer appointive and more elective offices, and the like.[73] In this regard, an important break from the past was the convention's reform of local government. The old districts were designated as counties and given more autonomy. County officials, including the sheriff, clerk of court, and coroner, would be directly elected rather than appointed by the legislature. (In theory, justices of the peace, now called trial justices, were also to be elected, but that reform never became reality—the Reconstruction governors appointed all trial justices.) Newly created local officials were the judge of probate, whose duties included the maintenance of records and the care of wards, formerly performed by the commissioner of ordinary and the court of equity; the county commissioners, who supervised county taxation and disbursements and maintained public highways; and the school commissioner, who administered the newly created public schools.[74]

These reforms of local government are important for two reasons. First, it was local officials "with whom the people at large would have the most direct contact day by day," so it was at this level that democracy was likely to be most important in the long term—that is, after the crisis period in which the state's new politics, economy, and society were taking shape. Second, these reforms may indicate the convention's willingness to promote democracy even in opposition to the interests of the Republican Party. The party was strongest at the statewide level, where the state's large black majority aided the Republican electoral effort. Congressional districts were consciously gerrymandered to take advantage of high concentrations of black voters. Here, though, the Republican-dominated convention took power away from the state legislature and circuit courts (appointed by the legislature) and gave it to the voters in the local counties, many of which had white (Democratic) majorities. Local autonomy, then, is one bit of evidence that the Republicans' commitment to democracy sometimes went beyond their desire to win and maintain offices.[75]

The convention again appealed to democratic sentiments in its plans for a system of universal free education, the first such system in the state's history. The antebellum elite had banned education for the slaves, and they considered it a waste of money for most citizens who could not afford to pay for it. Their 1865 convention paid lip service to the need for schools, but lack of funds prevented the issue from being addressed.[76] The Republican convention, however, began the task in earnest. They budgeted for the construction and staffing of 1800 public schools, as well as schools for the disabled and a teachers' college.

Imprisonment for debt, "that disgraceful remnant of legal barbarism," was eliminated by the new constitution's Bill of Rights. The convention also demanded that the legislature pass a homestead exemption of five hundred dollars' worth of property that could not be confiscated for nonpayment of taxes.[77] These measures were thought to be of greatest benefit to the working class and were cited frequently in Republican appeals for the votes of poorer whites.[78]

Nevertheless, the opposition to the homestead measure was led by two native white delegates, Thomas James Robertson and James M. Rutland. Robertson was the wealthiest member of the convention and, at least since the war, one of the wealthiest men in the state. He and Rutland opposed the homestead measure because of its retroactive quality: it made certain debts, enforceable at the time they were contracted, now unenforceable. For example, Robertson had lent money to a man knowing the man had five hundred dollars' worth of property that could be seized as a last resort. Now the five hundred dollars was untouchable, effectively removing the reason Robertson had seen fit to lend to the man in the first place. As Robertson saw it, this was unconstitutional and impolitic—unconstitutional because it impaired the obligation of contracts and impolitic because it stood to benefit "the very class who inaugurated the war," that is, the planters rather than the freedmen. He also warned that capitalists would not invest their money in a state known to cancel debts. Rutland, a lawyer, then chronicled a series of precedents finding retrospective homestead laws to be unconstitutional.[79]

As cogent as this argument was, the desperate need of the people to be relieved from debt and the determination that the poor should not be evicted from their houses in the end decided the matter for a majority of the delegates. Corley, for one, felt the need for a homestead law so greatly that he railed, "If the Constitution is now claimed to demand such a foul wrong upon the poor [as to evict them], who were generally as loyal as they were permitted to be, I beg leave to say that the *loyal* nation has completely outgrown it."[80] Although few were willing to go that far, the convention passed the homestead law intact by a vote of 103 to 4. In fact, even Robertson and Rutland voted for it. Both had favored a homestead law as long as it was not retroactive, and in the end they determined to secure the act and take their chances with the courts.[81]

A final category of democratic legislation that could have no ulterior political motive was the enlargement of the rights of women. The convention granted the right of a woman to own and control property even when married and determined that a woman's property could not be confiscated to pay her husband's debts. White Republican James M. Allen noted that the only women likely to own property were white women who supported the cause of secession; still, even though "these women may be sneering at us to-day . . . I wish to see the law laid down which will protect them in the enjoyment of every dollar of property which they own."[82] Furthermore, judges were given the authority to grant divorces, where once it had taken a special act of the state legislature to end a marriage.[83]

Indeed, given the strongly democratic flavor of the convention, it is striking how little support women's suffrage received in the convention. The issue was never seriously contemplated; the delegates seemed to believe that it was a passing fad. White Republican James M. Allen, after defending the right of women to own property, was asked whether he was in favor of women's suffrage. "I am not," he replied, "nor do I believe in that class of persons who carry poodle dogs, and follow in the trail of mere fashion."[84] One delegate, however, William J. Whipper, a black Detroit native who came south with the Union army, did speak on behalf of complete democracy: "The systems of legislation have been laid upon insecure foundations, and they will never be permanent until women are recognized as the equal of men."[85]

Although measures for political equality enjoyed broad support at the convention, those to provide social equality were more divisive. The first such proposal, made on the fifth day of the convention, was sponsored by George Lee, a black lawyer from Massachusetts. It provided that "no Company, Municipality, Parish or Corporation, shall make any rules or regulations creating any distinction between persons on account of race, color, or previous condition." It was postponed without debate. Benjamin Franklin Randolph, a mulatto army chaplain and graduate of Oberlin College in Ohio, next proposed specifically barring racial discrimination; the chief argument against his proposal was the unwillingness to have the words "race or color" appear in the constitution at all. It was argued that the constitution as it stood barred any discrimination. One delegate, Charles P. Leslie, did at least question the notion of racial equality. When Randolph closed his argument by saying that "God created all nations to dwell upon the earth," Leslie asked Randolph "if it would not have been a little better for his theory if the Scriptures had added 'without distinction of race or color.'"[86]

The real debate came on the question of whether the newly created public schools would be segregated by race. It was the one measure on which the white and black delegates stood most divided, with the former expressing grave reservations about the future of the school system if segregation were not required. Benjamin Odell Duncan, the son of a Newberry planter, argued that forcing integration before educating the people was backward. "If we begin by educating the masses, we end by overcoming their prejudices," he said. "But if we begin by attempting to overcome their prejudices by force, and educating them afterwards, I am convinced that the whole plan will result in failure."[87] Jonathan Jasper Wright, a black lawyer from Pennsylvania, replied that "the colored people do not want to force what is called social equality," and that in his opinion, blacks and whites would naturally choose separate schools where possible but the issue here was the necessity that "all children will have the benefit of all schools for which the public pay."[88]

Francis L. Cardozo, born in Charleston a "free person of color," made two points in favor of nondiscrimination in education. The first was the mirror image of Duncan's argument: "The most natural method to [remove these prejudices] would be to allow children; when five or six years of age, to mingle in schools together, and associate generally. Under such training, prejudice must eventually die out." His second concern was more practical: in populated areas the races would choose not to mix, "but for ten or fifteen white children to demand such a separation, would be absurd."[89]

The result of the debate was an overwhelming margin in favor of integrated schools; it passed ninety-eight to four. Native white delegates were much more divided, however. All four votes against were cast by scalawags, as were twelve of nineteen abstainers. Although it is certainly possible that those abstaining did so for other reasons than to avoid the vote, the fact of the matter is that nineteen scalawags voted for the school bill without a discriminatory provision and sixteen did not.[90] Antidiscrimination legislation continued throughout Reconstruction to be the most racially divisive issue among Republicans.

With the benefit of hindsight, a final issue should be addressed. The great failure of the Reconstruction government was its inability to secure a monopoly on the use of force. It was thus unable to defend the lives and property of its adherents, and it ultimately fell victim to an armed rebellion. It is therefore of interest to inquire how far the convention's members were mindful of such a possibility and what steps they took to prevent it. Unfortunately, the delegates seem not to have taken any concrete steps to ensure the viability of their government. Perhaps the presence of the Union army was reassurance enough for them. Or perhaps they were naive about the lengths to which Democrats would go to ensure white supremacy. In any case, the only substantive measure the delegates took was the formation of a state militia without distinction of race.[91] Simeon Corley and Jonathan J. Wright alone seem to have looked to the possibility of a renewed insurrection. They criticized the provision of the militia article that excluded from service those citizens who were or would be disfranchised, noting that this played into the hands of the former Rebels. As Wright noted, if there were an insurrection, and the disfranchised whites were not required to help put it down, "they would support our enemies." Corley argued that the "safest place would be to put them into the military, where they would be under restraint." Their efforts failed, however, and the militia article passed as proposed.[92]

It is difficult to tell whether such a provision would have been effective, as the Democrats would surely have objected strongly to serving in an integrated militia, and in fact the militia did in practice become almost all black (whites formed extralegal "rifle clubs"). To the extent that the Corley-Wright amendment would have forced the issue while federal power over the South was at its strongest, however, it might have made some difference.

Overall the convention must nonetheless be termed a success. The delegates framed a constitution with several radically democratic features. In addition to provisions for political democracy such as universal manhood suffrage, increased local autonomy, and increased responsiveness of officials to voters, the delegates also democratized South Carolina's social relations with measures such as universal education, private ownership of property by married women, and judicial divorces. Provisions for economic democracy included the enactment of a homestead exemption, the abolition of imprisonment for debt, and the call for a state land commission.

But at the same time, the delegates had not resorted to any measures likely to lose support for the Republican Party in the North. Confiscation was never seriously considered, nor was disfranchisement of former Rebels. Where the convention courted northern disapproval, they did so only in the face of manifest and urgent needs of their constituents, notably in the cases of the stay law, which prevented immediate collection of debts, and the retroactive homestead law, which prevented the seizure of a certain amount of a debtor's property (his "homestead") to pay his debts, even if those debts had been contracted before the passage of the law. Both these laws were seen by many fiscal conservatives (and creditors) as unconstitutional.

Spirits were high as the South Carolina Constitutional Convention of 1868 adjourned—only to reform immediately as the South Carolina Republican Party Convention in order to nominate candidates for the 1868 elections. The constitution would be submitted to the people for ratification, something that had not happened previously in the state. Many of the delegates submitted themselves to the people as candidates as well. Their pride in their accomplishment was no doubt justified; northern opinion seemed impressed with the document, and even the Democratic *Charleston Daily News* found kind words for some of its provisions.[93] Still, the state's Republicans had hardly prepared themselves for the coming onslaught.

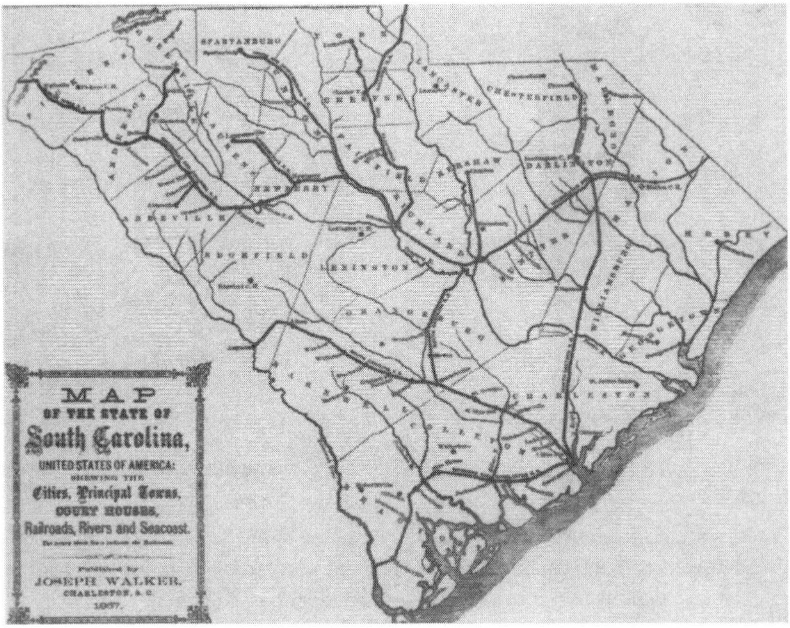


South Carolina counties in 1867. Other counties referred to in the text are Oconee and Aiken. With its county seat at Walhalla, Oconee was formed in 1868 from the western part of Pickens. The town of Aiken was the center around which Aiken County was created in 1871 from parts of Orangeburg, Lexington, Edgefield, and Barnwell. Courtesy of South Caroliniana Library, University of South Carolina, Columbia

"Secret Meeting of Southern Unionists." From *Harper's Weekly,* August 4, 1866. Courtesy of South Caroliniana Library, University of South Carolina, Columbia

ABOVE LEFT: James L. Orr. Courtesy of South Caroliniana Library, University of South Carolina, Columbia

ABOVE RIGHT: Simeon Corley. He described himself as follows for the congressional directory: "Of German descent, tough and wiry, and is forty five years of age, but looks younger." From a copy, courtesy of South Caroliniana Library, University of South Carolina, Columbia

Solomon L. Hoge. An officer of the U.S. Army during the war, Hoge settled in South Carolina after the surrender. He served as a justice of the state supreme court, then was elected to the Fortieth Congress for one term. In 1872, he ran for state comptroller general on the bolters' ticket, telling their convention he "admired those men who were natives, and had the moral courage to stand up for Republican principles." From a copy, courtesy of South Caroliniana Library, University of South Carolina, Columbia

Radical members of the South Carolina legislature. Scalawags in italics. TOP ROW: *George Dusenberry,* W. J. McKinlay, *Elias E. Dickson,* C. M. Wilder, *W. R. Hoyt,* B. F. Randolph, David Harris; SECOND ROW: J. P. Mays, J. K. Jillson, Hutson Lomax, B. F. Jackson, H. W. Webb, B. A. Boseman, Reuben Tomlinson, J. J. Wright; THIRD ROW: *Francis DeMars,* W. J. Brodie, Eben Hayes, Lawrence Cain, H. J. Maxwell, *James Martin,* Wilson Cooke, *Franklin F. Miller;* FOURTH ROW: P. R. Rivers, H. W. Duncan, *Lemuel Boozer,* unknown, Powell Smythe, J. B. Wright, *Franklin J. Moses,* Sancho Sanders, Samuel Nuckles; FIFTH ROW: *T. B. Milford,* J. H. White, Barney Burton, J. Boston, H. L. Shrewsbury, E. C. Mickey, J. A. Henderson, *G. Holliman,* H. E. Hayne, J. S. Mobley, James Hutson, W. B. Nash, unknown; SIXTH ROW: A. W. Smith, C. H. Pettingill, *J. B. Hyde,* S. J. Lee, W. M. Simons, J. A. Chestnut, Harry McDaniels, *John Wooley* (?), John Gardner; BOTTOM ROW: S. A. Swails, Wade Perrin, Burrell James, W. E. Johnson, L. W. Wimbush, *E. S. J. Hayes,* Simeon Farr, J. W. Meade, B. A. Thompson, J. H. Rainey. Courtesy of South Caroliniana Library, University of South Carolina, Columbia

Frederick A. Sawyer. A native New Englander, Sawyer came to South Carolina in 1859 to establish a normal school for women. He tried to remain neutral during the war but had to flee north to avoid conscription. He returned in 1865, becoming collector of customs and, in 1868–72, U.S. senator. He supported the bolters against the regular Republicans and was not renominated for his Senate seat. Courtesy of South Caroliniana Library, University of South Carolina, Columbia

ABOVE LEFT: Franklin Israel Moses. Chief Justice of the South Carolina Supreme Court from the onset of Reconstruction until his death in 1877. He was also the father of Governor Franklin J. Moses and was often (mis)identified as Franklin J. Moses Sr. Courtesy of South Caroliniana Library, University of South Carolina, Columbia

ABOVE RIGHT: John Robert Cochran. Courtesy of South Caroliniana Library, University of South Carolina, Columbia

ABOVE LEFT: Jonathan Jasper Wright. Associate Justice of the South Carolina Supreme Court throughout Reconstruction. Courtesy of South Caroliniana Library, University of South Carolina, Columbia

ABOVE RIGHT: John T. Green. Courtesy of South Caroliniana Library, University of South Carolina, Columbia

Francis L. Cardozo. Son of a Jewish economist and a free black mother, Cardozo was born free and attended schools in Charleston. He became the first African American to win statewide office when he was elected secretary of state in 1868. Serving as state treasurer from 1872 to 1877, he fought against corruption, but when Democrats regained power they prosecuted him for corruption. Despite his probable innocence, he was found guilty. After a pardon by then-governor W. D. Simpson, Cardozo and his family moved to Washington, D.C. Courtesy of South Caroliniana Library, University of South Carolina, Columbia

Joseph Crews. State representative and Republican boss, Crews persistently warned Republican governors that "Democrats are murdering and threatening People on account of Political Opinions." He was assassinated in 1875. Courtesy of South Caroliniana Library, University of South Carolina, Columbia

Robert Brown Elliott. As a two-term U.S. congressman, Elliott won a national reputation in an 1874 debate over the civil rights bill. In defending the bill, Elliott was considered by many to have gotten the better of Alexander Stephens, who had spoken against it. Courtesy of South Caroliniana Library, University of South Carolina, Columbia

William J. Whipper. Courtesy of South Caroliniana Library, University of South Carolina, Columbia

ABOVE: "The Commandments in South Carolina." The caption reads, "We've pretty well smashed that; but I suppose, Massa Moses, you can get another one." This Thomas Nast cartoon from *Harper's Weekly,* September 26, 1874, shows that in the North, even partisan Republicans regarded the Moses administration as corrupt—and that they often held grossly prejudiced attitudes about southern blacks. A black man, drawn in stereotypical fashion and wearing prison stripes, has a pardon from Governor Moses in his pocket. Courtesy of South Caroliniana Library, University of South Carolina, Columbia

Daniel H. Chamberlain. In other photographs and in cartoons, Chamberlain is bald; here he may be wearing a toupee. Courtesy of South Caroliniana Library, University of South Carolina, Columbia

State representative Thomas Hamilton of Beaufort. Drawing by Harry Ogden published in *Frank Leslie's Illustrated Newspaper,* December 23, 1876. According to the caption, Hamilton is "weeping over the corruption of his party." During the "dual legislature" controversy in November 1876, the Republican House of Representatives had declared elected five Republican candidates from Barnwell County who had lost on the face of the returns. Hamilton made several speeches in protest, calling the committee's action "an infamous outrage." On December 4, he presented his certificate of election to the Speaker of the Democratic House; his actions and those of a few other defectors deprived the Republican House of a quorum and added to the Democrats' momentum. Courtesy of South Caroliniana Library, University of South Carolina, Columbia

Wade Hampton III. Courtesy of South Caroliniana Library, University of South Carolina, Columbia

# THREE

## The Democratic Counterattack

White opponents of Reconstruction, still calling themselves Democrats, met in convention in Columbia on April 2, 1868, to denounce the new constitution, choose delegates to the National Democratic Convention, and nominate candidates for state offices. Apparently still hopeful of winning black support, the convention resolved that whites, "when we have the power," would grant qualified suffrage to blacks. Predictably, this proposal pleased no one. Black voters would hardly choose to place qualifications on their franchise, and even limited black suffrage was too much for the hard-line whites—most prominently W. D. Porter, the convention's nominee for governor. Porter refused to run unless the plank were retracted, which it promptly was.[1] The dispute was not the last between Democrats who favored adopting conciliatory tactics and those who insisted on an all-out defense of white supremacy. Such arguments recurred throughout Reconstruction. Hard-liners triumphed in 1868, and for the next three years Democrats mounted a campaign of terrorism against Republicans, killing scores of them. The violence provoked a response by the federal government, however, and by 1872 Democrats were no closer to retaking control of the state.

The 1868 South Carolina Constitution was then and remains today the only one the state has ever submitted to the electorate for ratification. Although that distinction was certainly a point of pride for Republicans, the vote provided an opportunity for their enemies. Foreseeing the violence to which Democrats would resort to prevent the ratification of the new constitution, Maj. Gen. Edward R. S. Canby, who replaced Gen. Daniel E. Sickles as military commander of South Carolina, deployed troops to each county to protect the freedmen's right to vote. As a result, the election went off without major incident. The Democrats, still largely unorganized, were crippled by white apathy. The new constitution was ratified, and in the interim elections for offices, the Republicans scored almost a clean sweep. They won all statewide offices and all seats in Congress, and even in local contests Democrats were successful only in counties where they vastly outnumbered their opponents.

Democrat planters still did not fully grasp the reality of Reconstruction; they clung to the hope that Congress would reconsider, realize the enormity of its errors, and refuse to accept the new South Carolina Constitution. To that end, Democrats in mid-1868 lodged a protest in the form of a document presented to the U.S. Senate.[2] In their attempt to appeal to both parties in the North, the signers scrupulously avoided the label "Democratic." They claimed to represent the "conservative people of South Carolina" and signed themselves the "State Central Executive Committee," neglecting to specify that they were, in fact, the State Central Executive Committee of the Democratic Party. The bulk of this document consisted of a systematic survey of the amount of taxes paid by each and every member of the convention and state government. It was the Democrats' contention not that the members had committed any form of impropriety or had evaded any taxes, but simply that, as evidenced by their low tax bills, these men were poor:

> It will be seen that they represent not the wealth of the State, neither its commercial, nor its agricultural, nor its mechanical interests. That they do not represent its intelligence, its tone and its sentiments, may be regarded as a self-evident proposition, to establish which requires no argument.

The constitution produced by such men was of necessity "a political abortion, the offspring of incapacity and prejudice and hate."[3]

The underlying assumptions were those of a body of thought sometimes referred to, confusingly in this context, as "traditional republicanism." The assumptions of this body of thought were (1) in a republic the people rule through their representatives, not directly; (2) there is such a thing as the "public good," and representatives who are virtuous will pursue it, even at the risk of their own benefit or that of their constituents; and (3) virtue is only possible for those citizens who maintain "independence," that is, those wealthy enough not to depend for sustenance on others. There are two reasons for the necessity of independence. First, because the richer the man, the greater his "stake in society," and second, because poorer men have greater temptations—to be dishonest in office, to do the bidding of wealthier men on whom they depend for financial support, or to support measures that benefit their particular economic interests rather than the "public good."[4]

This political theory was on the wane in most of the nation, even most of the South, before the Civil War. In South Carolina though, representation in the state legislature was still apportioned on a dual basis—white population and property —until the constitution of 1868 took effect. In protest against this change, the Democrats revived a slogan from the colonial era: "Taxation without representation." In their minds, their payment of taxes actually entitled them to govern, even to the extent that any government of which they were not a part was unrepresentative and illegitimate.[5] Historians have stressed Democrats' accusations of Republican wastefulness, but what is most clear in documents such as the Democratic appeal to the U.S. Senate is the blatantly class-conscious nature of their attacks. They opposed the expenditures called for in the new constitution, but their principal accusation was that the delegates were poor and therefore unfit for the public trust. The U.S. Congress, unimpressed with this logic, accepted the new South Carolina Constitution on May 22, 1868.

Having failed at the ballot box, and having failed to win the federal government's intercession on their behalf, the Democrats adopted a strategy aimed at carrying the fall election by any means necessary. This election featured the presidential contest, and they hoped that a Democratic victory in the presidential race would put an end to Reconstruction. The Republican ticket was headed by the triumphant Union general Ulysses S. Grant, while the Democrats headed theirs with Horatio Seymour, a bitter opponent of Reconstruction.[6] Democrats used several means to prevent Republicans from participating in the campaign. By far the most prevalent was the economic pressure available to Democrats who employed Republican sharecroppers or farm laborers. Several local Democratic clubs passed resolutions stating that they would not hire workers who voted Republican, and many Republicans reported that they did not vote for fear they would be fired, evicted, or both.[7]

Usually these workers were black, but in places where large numbers of whites worked for wages, white Republicans suffered the same pressure. For example, James McLesky, a lifelong resident of Centreville in Anderson County, told investigators of "a dozen white Republicans, and many colored, in my neighborhood, who did not go to vote" because of such economic pressure. Alexander Campbell, an election manager in Anderson, affirmed that "many colored persons did not vote for fear of insulting their employers by so doing, and I know poor white men who did not vote for the same reason."[8] John H. McDevitt, a white Republican and the sheriff of Edgefield County, reported that the superintendent of the Graniteville Mill, which employed only whites, "told me he wouldn't allow any one to remain on his place that voted the Republican ticket" and that he followed up on his threat by firing "one or two for affiliating with the Republican Party."[9] In October a Charleston doctor reported that "merchants on Hayne Street & the Bay have determined to give employment to none but Democrats. . . . Hundreds are now out of employment as a sequence following this fact."[10]

White Republicans who practiced trades were also vulnerable to Democratic retaliation. Jesse Pickrell, a watchmaker in Greenville, had to leave his native Williamston because of his Republican affiliation. He "was going round repairing clocks, as I could get no work in Williamston, and had to go away where I was not known politically."[11] P. J. O'Connell, a white Republican of York County, told federal investigators that in that county, Republicans were "tabooed," which meant that "the democrats would not transact any business with them that they could avoid—nor would they permit others to do so."[12]

Refusal to associate economically with Republicans was also widespread, and to many Democrats, scalawags were especially deserving of it. In July 1868 the *Charleston Courier* reprinted an announcement by a grocer from Augusta, Georgia: "No native 'scallawags' or their money are wanted in my store from this date. Negroes and Eastern men are excusable, even if they are in some cases in opposition to the people of the South; but a native that turns traitor to this country ought not to be tolerated by law-abiding people."[13]

Economic sanctions, however, were not the answer for the Democrats. Many leading Republicans of both races were financially independent and thus nearly immune from Democratic threats. Some even had the means to provide for fellow Republicans. When Chesterfield Democrats threatened to lay off farm workers who voted, county Republican boss R. J. Donaldson "had posters printed offering homes & long leases of land to 200 families without distinction of color."[14] Such was not the case for the vast majority of Republican voters; nevertheless, despite the seemingly tremendous power of economic coercion against the freedmen, Democrats faced several difficulties in implementing the policy. In the first place, employment resolutions sometimes failed because of a general shortage of farm labor that required the use of all available hands, regardless of politics. When resolutions did pass they were not universally adhered to by employers. For example, Democrat T. M. Christian recalled two fellow Democrats' statement that "they had colored Republicans hired, and that they were going to keep them, (as they liked them better than other hands,) although it was contrary to the rules of the Democratic Club."[15] A black farmer named Squire Wideman could take an active role in the Republican Party at least partly because his employer "showed me no hard feeling or prejudice" for doing so.[16]

Nevertheless, the most important reason for the failure of economic pressure was the determination of the freedmen not to submit to such threats. Sampson Duncan, for example, lived fifteen miles from the nearest poll and was warned by his employers that any black who voted would lose his job; furthermore, "they said if any of the blacks came [to vote] they should not stay on their places. Notwithstanding this, I came." He soon found work on another farm.[17] Charles Morris of Anderson also voted despite warnings from his employer, and he paid the same price. Less fortunate than Duncan, Morris could not find a new employer. Instead, he "had to go into an old field and build a house, and I am living there yet." Isaac Walker's employer told him "if I voted I would have to leave the place. I answered him, I would vote if I would have to leave." He too was soon homeless.[18]

Given the determination of the Republicans, it is unlikely that such intimidation would have been at all effective without the reality of Democratic violence, and there can be no doubt that such violence was rampant. Sheriff McDevitt stated that every day in the period before the election, "colored men would come in and report the death, also whipping and abusing of persons; I have heard of fully twenty such cases, and have seen the wounds on the parties." W. P. Harris, a white Republican from Newberry, counted four political murders in town and over forty in the county.[19] Truman Root, a white Republican merchant from Edgefield, knew of twenty murdered or shot in his county.[20]

The most famous practitioners of such violence were the Ku Klux Klan. Much has been written about the Klan, or the Ku-Klux as it was known at the time. Usually depicted wearing white sheets, these "night riders" became legendary following D. W. Griffith's 1915 film, *The Birth of a Nation,* which depicted Klansmen as valiant heroes rescuing the South from tyrannical "negro rule." Although mass audiences found the film thrilling, elite white southerners were more nostalgic for Wade Hampton and his Red Shirts than for the Klan, which they remembered as a dangerous, lawless organization composed of and instigated by the poor whites.[21] Traditionalist southern historians also sought to demonstrate "how truly . . . unimportant the South Carolina Klan was" in comparison to the Red Shirts.[22] The distinction is easily overstated. Important studies have shown that the Klan was no more independent of "respectable" Democratic control than were the Red Shirts.[23]

Historians have also debated the purposes of the Klan. Did it exist primarily for the economic purposes of disciplining farm laborers and keeping black South Carolinians in their place?[24] Or did it exist for the purely political purpose of carrying elections? The judgments of modern historians have been nearly unanimous: the Klan was "the terrorist arm of the Democratic party."[25] It almost always targeted Republicans, both white and black, or Unionists—all of whom were seen as traitors to the South.[26] Furthermore, Klansmen almost always indicated a political purpose for their "visit," usually asking victims how they had voted in the election or forcing a promise from them to vote Democratic next time. Attacks were meant to coerce victims into supporting (or at least not opposing) the Democratic Party or, in the case of the obstinate, to kill them and make examples of them. The philosophy of the outlaws was best summed up by one of their number, William K. Talbert, who announced the purpose of violence to be to "kill out the leaders of the republican party and drive them out of the state."[27] The organization was primarily political in nature, and it was brutally effective—at least until 1871, when federal enforcement of voting rights was strengthened.

It was also relentless. In counties where the Klan or other terrorist organizations existed, scarcely a single leader in the Republican Party was fortunate enough to escape a visit. The attack on Pickens Stewart, an Edgefield freedman, was fairly typical. He was whipped by three disguised men whom he nonetheless recognized. He quoted his assailants as saying that "they whipped me because I was too smart, as I was running to town too often to speeches, and bringing back the news, and reading papers too much, and carrying political pamphlets about." The more important and defiant a Republican was seen to be, the more severe the consequences when the Klan came. Joshua Wardlaw had attempted to vote Republican at the spring election, but on being told that "if a Radical ticket was voted it would be over a dead body," he replied, "If I could not vote the way I wanted, I would not vote at all. . . . I told them, before leaving, that I was a Radical, and did not care who knew it; and I did prevent a great many from voting the Democratic ticket, and I will still do so." The Democrats' reprisal was brutal; he and all the male members of his household were stripped and given hundreds of lashes:

> Mr. Richardson afterwards told me he was very sorry I had escaped from them. My brother-in-law died from the beating he got that same night; and my nephew, Harry Durgan, got severely beat that night, by the same party; and Harry Martin received about seven hundred lashes also. My cousin, Ben Pinckney, was so severely beaten that he was unable to do any work for a month or so after. I have never been back to the settlement since that time, being afraid they would kill me.

This same group whipped a man named Mack Martin senseless then "put the dog on him, and the dog attacked him, (naked as he was,) and tore large pieces from his side and limbs."[28]

Nor did Klansmen always limit their victims to men. Just before the fall election, Harriett Freeman and her niece were stripped, beaten, and whipped "nearly one hundred lashes." Her attackers, she claimed, "told us if we didn't leave before Sunday night they would kill us . . . that they would have no d——d Radical men or women about there." Klansmen raiding Stewart Moore's house assaulted his wife and aunt and threw one of his children into the fire. Investigators later confirmed that "the scars from the burns were plainly visible, disfiguring the child's forehead, nose, and lips."[29]

Such accounts could lead to the impression that Klan raids were motivated by nothing more than hatred and brutality. In other cases, Klansmen demanded money or guns.[30] But most raids had an explicit political purpose. One important Klan activity, for example, was the preelection practice of breaking into the homes of Republican leaders and demanding their ballots. There were separate ballots, or tickets as they were called, for each party. The tickets were printed in Columbia and distributed to the various county leaders, who in turn took them to the polls. Voters could then ask for either ticket (thus announcing which party they intended to vote for). But if the Republican tickets had been stolen, they would not be available at the polling place.

In Abbeville, Sherrard Butler took more than 360 tickets from the courthouse to his home in Cokesbury the day before the election. At 2:00 A.M., Ku Klux from Laurens, wearing sheets and hats, came to his door and demanded the tickets. He had guns, but because his family was present he decided to hand the tickets over.

At the election the next day, more than two hundred blacks did not vote in Cokesbury because they were without tickets. Some voted with other tickets, but Butler thought they might not have been real. The same problem faced Republican voters at the county's other boxes as well. Outside the courthouse town, the only Republicans able to cast ballots were those who had brought them from home. In Newberry only three of eleven boxes polled any Republican votes at all; at the others, "Republican tickets were not allowed to be carried there."[31]

Finally, even Republicans who survived the election campaign and possessed tickets often did not vote because armed bands of Democrats frequently guarded rural polls. At one box in Abbeville, Democrats opened fire on Republicans to drive them from the polls; four were wounded and one killed.[32] Sometimes threats sufficed, if blacks became convinced they had to vote the Democratic ticket or nothing.[33] Some black voters got around this intimidation, however. In Union County armed whites prevented blacks from voting until the blacks started a rumor that U.S. troops were on their way. At that point the whites drifted away, and the blacks voted.[34] Usually, however, black voters had to make the trek to the county seat, often a distance of ten to twenty miles, in order to vote. Hampton Edmunds of Abbeville walked twenty-six miles to vote—and that after being raided by Klansmen.[35]

For courage, though, it would be hard to match Dennis Jackson's story. Jackson, a black Abbeville resident, went to vote at Calhoun Mills. The poll was located at the top of a narrow staircase, and white men, possibly drunk, were sitting at the top of the stairs and firing their pistols at any blacks who tried to vote. Jackson, who had brought a ballot from home, attempted to get up the stairs, but before he got far, he was shot in the left shoulder. The whites continued shooting most of the day; when they had left, Jackson returned, along with over a hundred other blacks who had been waiting all day, and cast his ballot.[36]

Stories such as Jackson's notwithstanding, the combined impact of Democratic boycotts, ostracism, and violence on the fledgling Republican Party were important. Although this pressure seems to have had little influence on blacks' determination to be Republicans, it severely decreased the number of white South Carolinians willing to join the party. This assertion is based on two considerations. First, we know that the intimidation was strong enough to prevent even known and committed white Republicans from voting.[37] Other whites, not known as Republicans and not strongly committed to the party, would have had even more reason to keep quiet about their principles. According to T. P. Slider, treasurer of Newberry County, "white men who voted the Grant ticket were spotted here"; that is, their names were taken down by Democrats and published in the *Newberry Herald.* This was easily accomplished in the absence of secret ballots.[38] Sometimes "spotting" Republican voters was even easier. When white Republican William Ashley voted in Abbeville County, only Democratic ballots were available: "those who voted otherwise had to write" the tickets themselves.[39] Given such circumstances, it was perhaps understandable for many closet Republicans to choose discretion over valor.

Second, there is abundant evidence of a sizable proportion of whites who, though not Republicans, flatly rejected planters' calls to join the Democratic Party. For example, when David Wyatt Aiken took the stump at a whites-only political barbecue and railed that any white man who did not join a Democratic club was a Radical and a traitor, the meeting "broke up in a row."[40] Many whites refused, as long as they could, to choose sides. John Wilson, a pillar of the Anderson white community, decried the divisiveness of Reconstruction politics and "never attached myself to either political party." He "regarded the ultra wing or faction of either alike inimical to a good government."[41] Thomas Wadlington, a Newberry merchant for forty-eight years, was similarly opposed to extremism. Although long a member of the Democratic club, he stopped attending its meetings when it passed a resolution barring the employment of blacks who voted Republican: "I didn't think it a good policy; I don't believe in ultraism."[42]

Nor was such moderation limited to a few individuals. Some Democrats in Aiken even joined with Republicans to request the deployment of more U.S. troops to their town to keep the peace.[43] In Newberry the first county officers elected under the new constitution were nominated as "a kind of general consent ticket" put together by leaders of both parties. The compromise, it seems, met the approval of most Newberry citizens. Predictably, some hard-line Democrats "got up what they called a 'white man's ticket,'" but "it didn't make much impression, as they got but a few votes." The effects of the combined ticket were interesting. Those nominated tended, with few exceptions, to become Republicans. William Summer, a well-known horticulturist who owned a nursery in Pomaria, had considered himself a Democrat but after being nominated tried to stay "above the fray" of the election. On election day, feeling "some gratitude" that Republicans had agreed to his nomination, he tried to fulfill his duty as a rural election manager. When some whites at the poll threatened blacks with eviction if they voted, Summer assured them that they could vote. When the Republican ballots did not arrive, having been stolen the night before, Summer sent a man to the county seat to get more.[44]

For hard-line Democrats, distinctions between Radicals and moderates were not worth making. Any white man who would cooperate with Republicans was considered a Republican. All were subject to insult and ostracism, and all lived in fear of violence. Nathan McAllister, sixty years old and one of the founding citizens of Anderson, was attacked in the road and accused of Radicalism.[45] T. B. Milford, recognized even by the *Charleston Mercury* as a "respected and influential man in his neighborhood," returned from Columbia only to find "a general disposition, on the part of my old friends, to treat me with contempt."[46] Benjamin Odell Duncan of Newberry, a conservative man from a wealthy family, was openly cursed in his own neighborhood for being a Republican.[47] John Robert Cochran, later praised for saving Anderson County from the worst parts of Reconstruction, found at the time that "men who were previously my friends would not speak to me on the streets."[48]

White Republicans also lived in fear of violence. Mary Cochran, John's wife, wrote to Governor Scott in October that she could "never lie to sleep with that sense of safety which I could feel . . . if my husband's principles were Democratic."[49] Elliott Hayes of Lexington spent nights away from home during October and November 1868. Truman Root of Edgefield had his house fired into while his family was at home; he sold his possessions and moved away. Alexander Bryce Jr. of Oconee County told of several white Republicans in that mountainous region who were afraid to sleep at home. White Republicans were more numerous there than elsewhere, but white Democrats outnumbered them considerably. Moreover, the lack of a federal garrison anywhere in the county gave it something of a Wild West flavor. Bryce himself was commissioned to establish a police force. On one occasion, when he attempted to stop Democrats from harassing Republicans,[50]

> six men drew their pistols on me, and I drew mine and had it cocked first. They said "God damn you, you have been born and raised in this country; you have gone against your country; you have showed yourself this day." I replied to them, "You are several more in number than I am, put up your pistols, I will get one of you certainly, if you attempt to shoot." They cursed and abused me for everything they could think of.

The vast majority of the Klan's victims were black, and attacks on white Republicans were usually not as deadly. Nevertheless, white Republicans insisted that in some places at least, Democrats harbored more malice against them than against the blacks.[51] Furthermore, the statements of many Democrats lend credence to such a position. The situation in Laurens was typical. Democrats believed that if they could kill the white leaders, "they could carry the election."[52] The faults of such an analysis were no barrier to its widespread acceptance by Klansmen. At his trial for complicity in Klan violence, for example, Kirkland Gunn quoted his understanding of the purpose of the organization: "killing off the white Radicals" and merely "whipping and intimidating the negroes."[53]

But if it was more important to punish white Republicans than black Republicans, why did the latter bear the brunt of Klan violence? The seeming contradiction is resolved by several facts. First, white Republicans tended to be leaders in the party and were thus able to post armed guards of Republicans at their houses. John R. Cochran of Anderson was one example. "I considered it necessary to fortify my house," he told investigators, "and for that purpose I purchased a lot of sheet iron, greased it, and placed it around my house; bought ammunition and armed a guard of colored men for my protection at night." This safeguard was adopted by black leaders, too, when they could do so. Hutson Lomax of Newberry recalled telling a Democrat who threatened him with death that he had guards at his home every night, along with "about seventy-five muskets over there, and all loaded with buck shot; and if any of them came over there they would be killed."[54]

A second factor was that white Republicans were more likely to live in town. Towns provided not only the safety of numbers but also the protection of any federal troops remaining in the county. In Abbeville, Democrats and Republicans all acknowledged that a "Republican was safe in town, but in the country, probably not." After being attacked, Winnie Moore moved to Anderson Court House "because I am afraid to live in the country."[55] Finally, many white Republicans escaped reprisal because they enjoyed the safety of Columbia or Washington. Because a higher percentage of them achieved high office, fewer of them were within striking distance of the Klan.

But even in towns Republicans were vulnerable, guards were no guarantee of safety, and representatives eventually had to return home. White Republicans in all these categories would fall victim to assassination. Indeed, the first man assassinated in the 1868 reign of terror was newly elected state senator Solomon George Washington Dill, a white man native to Kershaw, South Carolina, who had served in the constitutional convention. Although Democrats sometimes claimed that only corrupt Republican officials were attacked by the Klan, in this instance that is obviously not the case, as Dill had not yet taken office. It seems clear that the crime for which he was executed was that of heading the local Union League, a secret Republican society that instructed the freedmen as to their political rights. Dill knew that his Republicanism could result in retaliation from Democrats and always had bodyguards and dogs stationed at his house overnight. These were of no avail on the night of June 1, 1868, though, as he and one of his guards fell dead under a volley of musket balls.[56]

Dill's murder was the first of many. The Klan targeted prominent Republicans, either officeholders or local organizers.[57] Although Democrats claimed that only "bad men" were targeted, the evidence shows that any Republican would do. For example, in Newberry County a black politician named Sam Dogan had angered local whites with his enthusiastic endorsement of Republican principles—or, as the Democrats put it, Dogan was "particularly obnoxious to the white people" because of his "meddling with matters that didn't concern him." When rowdy Democrats tried to disrupt a Republican meeting, Dogan "told the crowd to be quiet, that we don't make any disturbance at your meetings." When a Democratic mob called Solomon L. Hoge, a white Republican candidate for Congress, a "damned liar" and threateningly followed him to the train station, Dogan and other Newberry blacks interposed themselves between the speaker and the mob with "the intention, if they got on him, we would assist him as much as we could." Newberry Democrats referred to their opposition as the Dogan Radicals. They attributed so much influence to him that the Democratic sheriff was heard to remark, "If Sam Dogan was put out of the way we could influence the rest to vote the Democratic ticket."[58]

The conflict between Dogan and the Newberry Democrats escalated on the day Hoge gave his speech, possibly September 20, 1868. The Democrats, angered by the speech and unable to attack Hoge, seem to have gone looking for a more vulnerable target. They found Johnson Stuart, "a leading Radical in his neighborhood," and killed him. Stuart had apparently angered the Democrats during the spring election, when as a poll manager he made whites wait their turn to vote, just as blacks waited. At the time Tom Wadlington, a Confederate veteran, told Stuart's brother that Stuart was a marked man because of that. When the brother responded that Stuart had "treated all alike," Wadlington replied, "Well, he should not have done that way; he ought to have let the white people in."

Stuart's killers were never identified, but a young white man named Dan Ward was suspected by many of involvement. At some point, a desperado named Murtishaw, while riding on the town's main street, met Dogan and made as if to run over him with his horse. Dogan drew a pistol and forced Murtishaw to ride around him. A witness later reported hearing Murtishaw say, "I cannot go home to my wife and tell her that a damned nigger presented a pistol to my breast and I [did] not resent it." The town marshal heard the comment and took Murtishaw (and his associate, Fitzgerald) into custody. Soon thereafter, Ward was shot (although not fatally) by parties unknown. Most Democrats assumed Sam Dogan was involved, but he denied it and was never indicted. He was, however, jailed—for his own protection, according to the head of the local Democratic club. Unable to get to Dogan, Murtishaw and Fitzgerald killed Lee Nance, a leader in the Republican Party but otherwise "a quiet, peaceable citizen" whose character was "the very best that anyone could have," according to a white man who had known Nance since the time he was a slave. It was widely rumored that Dogan "would have atoned instead of Lee Nance" had he not been in jail.[59]

The murders continued in October (after the end of the legislative session), when James Martin, a white Republican from Abbeville, was killed. He was a former school teacher who had lived in Abbeville at least twenty years when he was elected to the legislature as a Republican in 1868. As a memorial to him, his seat stood vacant until the 1870 session.[60] The next victim was Benjamin Franklin Randolph, the free mulatto from Ohio who had served as a chaplain in the Union army. After working for the Freedmen's Bureau as an educator, he entered politics. He helped organize South Carolina's Union League, served in the 1868 Constitutional Convention, and won election to the state senate from Orangeburg. He was boarding a train in Abbeville County when he was shot by several men in broad daylight.[61]

The killings of Martin and Randolph provide test cases for two claims about Klan violence frequently made by leading Democrats. The first is that the Klan, and other groups claiming to represent white society, enforced what they saw as moral order. The second is that violence was committed by "a few outlaws" rather than a hierarchical, paramilitary force under elite control. For example, James Chesnut, a prominent Camden planter and husband of diarist Mary Chesnut, claimed that he could "see no reason to believe that these organized bodies have any political coloring whatever." He also asserted his belief that the violence resulted from offenses committed by the victims of Klan violence and that, in the main, the Klan murders "have been the killing of obnoxious white men."[62] The violence was a natural reaction to "an absolute despotism," Chesnut judged, and the true cause of the murders "arises from the government of the State of South Carolina." In the same breath, however, he was careful to say that "nowhere are they countenanced by thinking or good men."[63] In other words, the killings were caused by the absence from government of the best men of the state, but those men had nothing to do with them. It was, rather, poor whites who were attempting to reinstate their betters.

In the first place, leading Democrats insisted, only "incendiary" speakers and militant leaders were targeted by bushwhackers. Abbeville resident B. A. Davis did not "believe that any would have been touched had they not used incendiary language."[64] In the face of overwhelming contrary evidence, the Democrats tried to assert that there had never been "an instance of a human being who was punished for being a republican," that only "bad men" were visited by terrorists. In fact, though, it was not for any "supposed wrong and corruption" that white Republicans were ostracized and persecuted, unless the very espousal of Republican doctrine was evidence of bad character. Chesnut indicated that in fact this was the case: "We do not recognize that any of them have gone over [to the Republicans] from pure and simple philanthropy."[65]

It is much clearer that such an explanation suited the purposes of elite Democrats than that it was in any way accurate, as the assassination of James Martin illustrates. Martin's death, according to most accounts, followed a dispute about a barrel of whisky he had purchased in Columbia and brought to Abbeville Courthouse, where he lived. Democrats apparently thought a barrel too much whisky for one man, and a rumor circulated that Martin had gotten it "to buy negro votes with." Martin's fellow members of the Abbeville delegation to Columbia, T. B. Milford and George Dusenberry, both white Republicans, vouched for their colleague's integrity. They stated that the whisky was to be divided among the three of them for private use.[66]

The general opinion of the community seemed to be that Martin was "a sober, industrious man," "a quiet, unobtrusive citizen," and "a hard-working, persevering man." Such, at least, was the judgment of moderate Democrats, those who were not active club members and those who consented to be elected to office with black votes.[67] Hard-line Democrats, however, had taken to calling him "Sneak" Martin, and some of them regretted his death "no more than they would a dog's." One Abbeville Democrat wrote sarcastically that as Martin was taking the whisky barrel home, "it exploded & killed poor Sneak, another Grant & Colfax vote lost." The writer showed his knowledge of the truth by adding, "Will send you the paper containing full account of the murder."[68]

According to Republican testimony, the morning of the day Martin was killed, a Democrat named Joe Davis pointed him out and said, "There is that God damn Sneak Martin; he will not live to get home." Davis, William K. Talbert, and others were later seen following Martin on the road to Martin's house. One witness said of Martin on that occasion, "I never saw him in such a hurry before." Apparently the men caught up to him outside of town and ordered him to dismount. They then gunned him down, taking the whisky and some money from his pockets. Although Sheriff Cason did not believe the killing was politically motivated because Martin "was liked by men of all politics here," the majority opinion was that, at a minimum, "his position in the party attracted attention to him." Any mystery is resolved if the testimony of Adaline Brooks is believed. Brooks, a black domestic servant for the Shoemaker family, reported overhearing Henry Shoemaker tell his father, Oliver, that he had good news: "We have put old Sneak up." She claimed that Oliver replied, "Now, if you will go on and get Milford, Dusenberry, and Lemuel Guffin, the country will be at some peace." Those men, along with Martin and Lemuel's brother Pembroke Guffin, were the leading white Republicans in the county. Brooks's testimony, though uncorroborated, conforms to information available elsewhere.[69]

The other Democratic claim was that outrages were committed by a few outlaws, acting on their own. In fact, Richard Zuczek's recent study of South Carolina opponents of Reconstruction reveals a very hierarchical Klan, each branch exercising autonomy, but all under the command of the local elite Democrats.[70] And even on the state level, the violence stopped—as if by magic—when Wade Hampton gave the command. After a meeting with Governor Scott at which Scott mentioned the possibility of a stronger military presence in the state, Hampton, along with the rest of his "State executive committee" (which "represents nearly every white citizen of South Carolina"), issued a statement opposing political murders as bad strategy. Hampton lamented that "a few lawless and reckless men have brought discredit on the character of our people, though provocation in these cases may have been given." He made a point of opposing assassination "not only from its moral atrocity, but from its political tendency."[71] The fact that his belated denunciation of terrorism put an immediate end to the violence is at least suggestive that the Democratic elite had previously allowed it to exist.[72]

Hampton gave a further clue that the leading Democrats were largely to blame for the violence when he called on the Republicans "to unite with us to check and discountenance all incendiary language."[73] Hampton, two months earlier, had spoken in this way on the subject of white Republicans:[74]

> These scallawags and traitors should be branded with infamy and eternally stigmatized. . . . The word scallawag is used by drovers to mean the mean, lousy, and filthy kine that are not fit for butchers or dogs. . . . They have dishonored their State, and heaped everlasting shame on their families.

> . . . There are no words in the English language to express the utter contempt entertained by me for these renegades and traitors.

And two months later, two more of them were dead and the rest fearful for their lives.

Nor was Hampton alone in employing such irresponsible rhetoric. David Wyatt Aiken, perhaps the richest man in Abbeville County, became as well known for his fiery diatribes against Republicans as he was for his writings on scientific agriculture.[75] Several black residents of Abbeville recalled a speech he gave there after riding on the train with Hutson Lomax, a black man who was a county officeholder and a candidate for the South Carolina General Assembly: "He said that he had come up from Columbia with Hutson Lomax, and it provoked him so he didn't know what to do, and said he was beneath a dog's notice." Settling into his rant, Aiken continued that "Hutson Lomax was elected School Commissioner, and Henry Nash [also black] a County Commissioner, and before the white man should be ruled by the nigger, they would kill the last one of them. They wanted the nigger to understand it was a white man's government, and that they intended to kill every leading Radical, and would not leave one on the face of the earth." In the same or another speech, Aiken was quoted as accusing carpetbaggers of "trying to make the colored men gentlemen, and the white people hewers of wood, and drawers of water, and before they (the white people) would suffer that to be done they would grind the colored people into powder." Even some Democrats, such as John C. Whitefield of Anderson, thought Aiken had "made a foolish speech." Whitefield was "shocked to think a man would make use of such language in a public speech."[76]

Another outburst of Aiken's may have led to the assassination of state senator and Republican Party chairman Benjamin Franklin Randolph, a black minister from Ohio, while he was campaigning in Abbeville. Randolph was killed by William K. Talbert, John Wesley Talbert, and Joshua Logan. When they arrived at the depot, they sent "two little boys . . . down to the cars; they came into the cars, looked about, and went back again to the crowd of men." Informed of which car Randolph was riding in, they waited until he came into view and at that point began shooting. When Randolph fell dead, they rode off, all in full view of a fairly large crowd of whites and a few blacks. One of the black witnesses recalled Fletcher Hodges, a local Democrat, asking him who the shooters were. When the witness replied that they were known to everyone there, Hodges replied, "Well, you had better mind how you talk; you don't know whether they are known or not." Hodges then walked over to the body, and said, "Yesterday you boasted that negro blood ran in your veins, and you was proud of it; now, God damn you, it is running in the ground."[77]

The word around town—at least around the Republican community—was that Logan and the Talberts had acted at the urging of Hodges, Langdon Conner, and James Cochran. One witness testified that as the shooters rode past Cochran's store, Cochran called out, "Did you get him?"[78] Unfortunately, as in the killing of Martin, certainty is elusive. A magistrate in the town of Greenwood, J. A. Leland, wrote to the governor claiming that Logan and John W. Talbert had come to him to turn state's evidence against William K. Talbert, with whom they had killed Randolph—and James Martin. According to Leland, they insisted they and "Bill" Talbert were the only people involved, thus casting doubt on the involvement of prominent citizens in Randolph's murder, as well as on the involvement of Joe Davis and the Shoemakers in the Martin murder.[79]

But for Republicans, at least, responsibility lay with Aiken. Among those suspecting Aiken ordered the killing were state party chairman A. J. Ransier and Governor Scott.[80] According to several witnesses, when Aiken was forced to share a train with Randolph, he "said: 'You damn black son of a bitch, you have no business here.' He also said, if all the white men were like him, Randolph should not put his foot again in that car. . . . Mr. Randolph told him he was going in that car, and going to Abbeville to speak. Aiken told him if he went there and spoke he should never see Columbia again."[81] In fact, Randolph did not see Columbia again. He was assassinated at Hodges Depot on his way out of Abbeville. The circumstantial evidence seemed compelling to Sheriff Lemuel Guffin, a white Republican who arrested Aiken as an accessory before the fact. After two days in prison in Columbia, Aiken was bailed by Wade Hampton and Col. L. C. Childs, another prominent Democrat. His case was never brought to trial.[82] The most that can be said with certainty is that if prominent Democrats ordered these killings, they did an effective job of creating reasonable doubt.

Aiken not only claimed his own innocence but also offered his house as a refuge for other fugitives trying to escape "arrest on KKK difficulties." Aiken's wife wrote in her diary of one such fugitive who lodged with them. She felt "so sorry for him & for all others thus situated." She concluded that "we poor Southern people have more than we can bear." On another night, a Colonel Watts stayed with the Aikens; he had left his home "on account of the arrests the Yanks or radicals are making." She assumed it was "all for political effect" and that none of the parties was actually guilty.[83]

Leading Democrats claimed not to be involved in the violence, instead implicating "the lower class of white people," who, they claimed, had "a great prejudice against the negro, because he is a competitor for common labor."[84] Nevertheless, it was widely assumed at the time that these "mean whites" were but "the dupes and tools of men of higher social position in life."[85] Republicans certainly thought so. George Dusenberry thought that "there were some men appointed from every Club to assassinate Republicans." He believed that the actual assassins were "reckless men here, who would kill a man for five dollars and a little whisky," but he also felt sure that they operated under the orders of more prominent men. At a minimum, Republicans agreed with Anderson County white Republican John R.

Cochran: "In justice to the majority of the citizens of Anderson County, I would state that they condemned these outrages; it was a minority, and young men who owned but little, if any property in the County; but while the old citizens would come to me and speak of these outrages and condemn them, they never took any steps against the offenders."[86] Given the moral authority possessed by these men, their refusal to cooperate in the enforcement of the law was tantamount to complicity in the reign of terror.

The crux of the matter is that Democrats were unwilling to recognize the political legitimacy of any government they did not control. Because their interest was synonymous with that of the state, anyone who opposed their interest was selfish. The case could just as easily be made that those South Carolinians who joined the Republicans solely to win office were *all* motivated by ideology rather than selfishness in the sense that it was very radical and democratic of them to believe that they deserved office. The argument, though, merely matches one absurdity with its mirror image. Of course there were both public-minded and selfish Republicans, just as there were principled and unprincipled Democrats. The point here is that within white society the Democrats denied, and the Republicans defended, the principle of democratic pluralism.

Freedom of thought thus became a crucial principle of democracy for Republicans. It was the principle Simeon Corley defended when he admonished Congress to see that "southern Republicans shall be protected in the freedom of opinion and speech." If the nation were to "maintain its integrity," he reminded his northern colleagues, "it must protect its loyal defenders." If the former Confederates could continue to "threaten, overawe, and assassinate loyal men for no crime but their loyalty, then the war for the Union is a failure."[87] Although many whites were forced by Klansmen and other Democratic terrorists to renounce publicly their Republicanism, most Republicans held firm. Samuel Poinier of Spartanburg, for example, switched to the Republicans in 1868 and stuck with them, despite threats so continuous (and so plausible) that he rarely slept at home. (Poinier told a congressional committee that many Spartanburg Republicans had been forced to renounce publicly their Republican principles by gangs who whipped them and threatened to kill them if they did not do so.)[88] Another white Republican, W. O. B. Hiott of Oconee County, wrote to Governor Scott that he had refused the refuge of the Democratic Party, and would "rather die and fill a Republican grave than go with the Enemies of my Mother Government."[89]

The only officers to be elected in the fall of 1868 were the state's presidential electors and congressmen, and although the Republicans eventually won them all, it was clear that Democratic violence had taken a toll. Grant won South Carolina's electoral votes with 62,916 votes to Seymour's 45,237—a considerable margin but well short of a full vote. (Later Republican candidates would roll up 80,000 to 90,000 votes.) Even worse, Republicans actually lost two of the four seats in Congress on the face of the returns. The losing candidates, Solomon L.

Hoge and Alexander Stuart Wallace, contested the election in December 1868. The resulting investigations, both state and federal, elicited voluminous proof of foul play on the Democratic side, and Congress later seated both Hoge and Wallace.[90]

After the elections, Democrats in many counties resolved to follow through on threats made during the campaign. In the counties of Fairfield and Union, there were wholesale evictions of Republican tenant farmers.[91] Most of them were freedmen; in Spartanburg, white Republicans such as Green Pearson and John Payne lost their lands as well.[92] In Lancaster masked men broke into the homes of J. F. G. Mittag and John B. Cousart, prominent white Republicans, and abused and threatened them. Mittag was so shaken that he fled across the border to Charlotte, North Carolina, vowing not to return "until I shall have been informed that the Military is in the Village of Lancaster."[93] In Abbeville, rumor had it that as soon as U.S. troops were removed, "all those who had any connection with the Election on the Republican side, by distributing tickets &c are to be killed off." Many freedmen left their homes, "and all live in fear and trembling," according to a Freedmen's Bureau clerk.[94]

Although the U.S. Army was the most powerful guarantee of peace in a county, the troops were too few to guarantee peace throughout the state; moreover, it was no secret that the federal government wanted to reduce troop levels in the South even further. In November Governor Scott had commissioned a state constabulary force with mixed results. In the lowcountry parish of St. James Santee, the constabulary, composed entirely of blacks, was praised by white landowners: "We have security for our property. It is working like a charm."[95] Even in upcountry York County, a Republican leader thanked the governor for sending him a constable, reporting that since his arrival "people treat me with the greatest respect & are now condemning the recent outrage."[96] But as previous evidence indicates, the constables enjoyed only sporadic success in enforcing peace.

At the start of the 1869 session, Scott and the legislature began to look for solutions. The search led to the most controversial Republican policy of Reconstruction, that of arming a black militia. This was a move many white Republicans and almost all blacks welcomed. In July 1868, just weeks after Governor Scott took office, he called for the creation of a state militia. Once it was armed, he believed, the U.S. troops then in South Carolina could "with propriety be dispensed with." Although a military man himself, Scott adhered to the old republican tradition that "the continued presence of the military is a reproach" to a democratic government; he foresaw his administration relying "upon that willing support that the citizen should give to the institutions that protect him."[97]

Blacks had been agitating for some time for a chance to defend themselves. A black veteran of the U.S. Army immediately asked Scott to commission two companies of militia he had raised in Darlington; Scott's response is not known.[98] In fact, armed blacks had been drilling in several counties at least since that date, and Scott was rumored to approve of such organizations.[99] Whether he quietly encouraged blacks to defend themselves is unclear, but he did disband an unofficial black militia group in Union County, where a riot had taken place.[100] In October, Scott sent a representative, Thomas J. Mackey, to negotiate with the Meigs arms company of Lowell, Massachusetts, to purchase thousands of state-of-the-art rifles.[101]

Still, Scott chose his course of action only as a last resort, knowing that nothing would be considered more inflammatory by Democrats, and even by moderate whites. One such "fence man," as he called himself, was Sebastian Kraft of Union. Kraft deplored the lawless condition in his county, but to him the only remedy was the army. "One thing is certain," he warned Scott. "Arming the Freedmen, will only hasten our destruction, they are unreliable. Liquor, tobaco [*sic*] & promises will buy them over."[102] But if Kraft would only trust the army, not a militia, some black Republicans would only trust a militia, not the army. Richard H. Cain claimed to speak for black Charlestonians when he told the governor, "We have no confidence in the troops stationed here."[103]

By early 1869, Scott was more convinced than ever of the need for a state militia. Perhaps the murder of Randolph had driven him to this conclusion. He informed the national party of that event by announcing that "last Friday about fifty of the citizens of Abbyvill county collected at Cokesbury for the express purpose of seeing one of their number murdered." Praising Randolph, Scott vowed that "his death should be revenged on these scoundrels."[104] Perhaps it was the fact that violence against Republicans continued well after the election, with no end in sight. Whatever the proximate cause, in early 1869 Scott was quoted as saying of Democrats that "the only law for these people was the Winchester rifle."[105]

On February 13, 1869, Governor Scott ordered native white Republican Franklin J. Moses Jr., as adjutant and inspector general of South Carolina, to raise a state military force.[106] Moses and Scott then commissioned Republican bosses in each county to act as enrollment officers for the militia and as commanders in case the militia should be called up. Although there can be no doubt that Scott was motivated by outrage against Democratic violence, it is also clear that the creation of the militia created a new set of employment opportunities for county Republican bosses, many of whom had long sought government employment. Lem Guffin, an Abbeville constable, was one such beneficiary. Guffin immediately began enrolling men, and the results he found most gratifying. As a constable he had been "looked down on" by the local whites, but now he reported to Scott, "You have given them a good *scare*"—so much so, that the officers of the local Democratic Party promised to take responsibility for law and order themselves if Guffin would hold off on forming the militia. Guffin convinced Scott to accept the bargain, then presented the Democrats with warrants for the arrest of several outlaws![107]

Guffin was not alone in urging the governor to hold off actually arming the militia in order to see what the threat of one would do. Guffin's Abbeville colleague

Hutson Lomax agreed, as did James W. Hayward of Edgefield.[108] Even Adjutant General Moses himself seemed to agree, although he strongly urged the purchase of two thousand rifles "for use in an emergency."[109] White Democrats and even moderates strenuously pleaded with Scott to wait, at least until after the crops had been brought in. George Williams of Charleston, who claimed not to have "taken any part in politics since the defeat of Clay in 1844," warned that mobilizing the militia before harvest would "have the most disastrous effects upon the agricultural labor (both black & white)" because whites would certainly organize, drill, and challenge armed blacks. Guffin, too, was concerned that immediate enrollment would "have a ruinous effect on the farms."[110]

Republicans soon had much more serious concerns. Beginning with attacks in Edgefield County, vigilante groups continued their reign of terror.[111] Once again they frustrated all attempts by local officials to bring them to justice. From Edgefield, Sheriff John McDevitt reported that "every day colored men would come in and report the death, also whipping and abusing of persons," but that he was powerless to stop it. All of white Edgefield seemed to be in sympathy with the terrorists.[112] In Abbeville, Lem Guffin wrote to Governor Scott that he had been warned by prominent local whites not to issue warrants against any who had committed outrages against Republicans. He feared that if he did so "it would inaugurate *civil war* here at once."[113] From the town of Sumter, John Feriter, a merchant and Republican county commissioner, wrote to Scott that men in disguise were burning the stores and businesses of those who were thought too friendly with blacks. He assured Scott that "the parties committing these outrages were comprised at least in part by some of our first families."[114]

The months before the election of 1870, however, were a period of relative peace, as opponents of Reconstruction tried their strength at the ballot box and, perhaps more important, federal troops returned to most counties to prevent election-related violence.[115] Nevertheless, there were disturbing signs of what lay ahead for Republicans once the voting was over. White militants were flocking to Laurens County, purportedly "to fight the militia there."[116] A constable sent to inspect the situation reported to his superior that what he found was "no mere disturbance of the peace that can be controlled by a police force, but that it is a complete military organization."[117] Based on this and other reports, the state's chief constable, John B. Hubbard, reported to the governor that "a complete organization exists from the Savannah river to Chester, a distance of nearly two hundred miles in length, and . . . that its object is to intimidate Republican voters on Election day, and if necessary murder leading republicans." The members of this organization were well armed, and more weapons were being delivered daily. Men from other counties were well provisioned by white citizens of Laurens.[118] Nevertheless, there was no outbreak until after the election.

The election itself was the occasion for one of three serious splits in the Republican Party during Reconstruction. In each case, some disaffected Republicans aligned themselves with Democrats and challenged the regular nominees. The character of the campaign and the escalation of Republican factionalism are subjects for the next chapter. Here it is sufficient to note that the campaign itself was a brief respite from violence.

The Democrats put on an elaborate show of bipartisanship. They made a serious effort to win black support by claiming friendship, starting rumors that if their ticket won wages would go up, and finally paying blacks to participate in their meetings. At the elaborately choreographed "Union Reform" convention, Democrats offered the lieutenant governorship to several blacks, who declined, before the blacks in turn offered it to Confederate hero Matthew C. Butler, who accepted. Few were fooled by such tactics, and the regular Republicans won convincingly. Scott, for example, defeated Republican defector Richard B. Carpenter with over 60 percent of the votes to win reelection as governor.[119]

Immediately after the Reform ticket failed at the polls, Democrats reverted to violent means of achieving power. The first outbreak was at Laurens the day after the election. A detachment of the (black) state militia had been threatened by armed white militants. In the tense atmosphere, what began as a scuffle escalated quickly. When the shooting stopped, three members of the militia and nine Laurens Republicans were dead and the town was in the hands of the vigilantes. Democrats argued that the sole cause of the incident was the conduct of the black militia, and that if Scott would disband it, there would be no further violence.[120] In at least one county, black leaders seem to have believed that assertion: from Newberry, Joseph Boston, Harry Scott, and J. P. Hutsin wrote, "The election is now over, and if by taking away thes arms will restore peace for God sake let it be done And a nothir thing we are not drilled well annough if any trouble comes to defend ourselves against these desperadoes."[121] Governor Scott determined that the state militia was no match for the vigilante organization and would probably be the target of more attacks. He thus called in guns the state had issued to militia units, once again leaving Republicans without any protection.[122]

The Klan soon resumed its depredations. This round of violence was more sustained, more widespread, and more deadly than the last. In November and December, several black Republicans in York County were murdered; one of them, Tom Black, "was Shot in 17 or 18 places & his throat cut from ear to ear."[123] In Spartanburg, Anthony Johnson was killed and many others attacked.[124] Near Aiken in Barnwell County, a black Sunday school teacher and his family "escaped almost by a miracle from about ten armed ruffians" and made his way to the house of Warren Diver, a northern-born white Republican. Diver had been insulted for his politics for years, but now Democrats warned him, believably he thought, that he would be killed if he remained in the neighborhood. Asking Scott for protection, Diver wrote that he knew "one man is not a match for 20 or 30 armed Ruffians[, but] if I had 4 or 5 men of nerve here with good arms I should feel much more like faceing them."[125]

Union County was particularly lawless. On New Year's Day, a white Republican trial justice in Union, A. B. Owens, was "murdered by about 40 K.K. in masks." None was ever identified. Three days later, black Republican James Perler was killed. Numerous other Republicans of both races were brutally beaten and whipped by "masked mounted men." It was enough to convince at least one observer that the decommissioning of the militia might have been a mistake. After reporting on violence in Union County, a U.S. infantry captain mused, "Though not disposed to recommend Colored Militia it is remarkable that no Ku Kluxing is done in the county in the vicinity of the Armed Militia."[126]

By the middle of 1871, Republicanism was at low ebb in several upcountry counties. Klan violence "was quite effective at forcing Republican resignations," and Governor Scott had difficulty finding Republicans willing to take office in Union, Spartanburg, and York Counties.[127] State officials were affected as well. Many Republican lawmakers, perhaps mindful of the fate of Dill, Martin, and Randolph, remained in Columbia even after the legislative session ended. Although Republicans in 1868 had distinguished themselves by their courage, in 1870–71, discretion was the better part of valor. With no state force remotely capable of standing up to the Klan, Republicans were easy targets. Public repudiations of Republicanism became common. Those who remained in the party were generally those who had the means to be elsewhere—Congressman Alexander Stuart Wallace, for example. Wallace, a York County native, was "a man of good courage" who had worked as a federal revenuer in the upcountry and thus was used to dangerous work, but after being told by his family that "they did not think it safe for him to return home at present," he judged it best to remain in Washington after the end of the session.[128]

Between December 1870 and mid-1871, Governor Scott pleaded with President Grant to fulfill his duty under the Constitution to suppress domestic violence and take care that the laws be faithfully executed. After months of inaction, during which time dozens of Republicans were killed or wounded, Grant finally intervened, first in March 1871 by sending additional troops to South Carolina and finally in October of that year by suspending the writ of habeas corpus so that hundreds of suspected Klansmen could be arrested and tried.[129] During this period, Congress was also active, conducting an exhaustive investigation of Klan activities and passing the Ku Klux Act, which made conspiracy to deprive citizens of the right to vote into a federal crime.

Numerous problems faced the prosecutors, including lack of men, resources, and even jail space to deal with the thousands of guilty parties. One particularly important problem was that most Klan offenses were committed before the Ku Klux Act went into operation. Because of such difficulties, and because leading Democrats bankrolled the best legal defense money could buy for the defendants, convictions of Klansmen were, relative to the number of perpetrators, few. Even worse, few high-level leaders were convicted. Many were, however, exposed. In

October a Spartanburg Republican boss wrote the governor: "A few days ago I wrote you a note recommending Dr. B. F. Bates to your consideration as a true Republican; since that time it has been developed that Dr Bates is the Chief of a den of K.K.K.; and I therefore withdraw whatever I have said in Dr. Bates's favor."[130] In York a moderate Democrat also found, to his "utter astonishment," that "a large majority of my neighbors & supposed friends were Ku Klux and consequently my enemies."[131] Many former militants fled to avoid capture. In Union a white Republican leader, noting that "Union County is almost depopulated" after the flight of three hundred men, complained that "some U.S. officers are not doing their duty or perhaps they had rather run the men away than to arrest them."[132]

"After a wave of political terrorism unprecedented in the history of the United States," concludes historian Richard Zuczek, "a handful of low-ranking Ku Klux Klan members had been sentenced to a few years in jail."[133] On the other hand, the federal scrutiny brought to South Carolina by the Klan investigation caused Democrats to scale back their terrorist campaign, and election returns indicate that Republicanism, including white Republicanism, began to increase in 1872. In March, Warren D. Wilkes of Anderson reported that "peace, good feeling, and prosperity" had returned, as the citizens turned their attention to crops. "Then too, the cause of Republicanism is brightening," he added, as "many of our prominent and influential men, . . . convinced by the inevitable logic of facts, have openly pronounced in favor of the Republican party."[134] Another white Republican claimed that among poor whites as well, Republicanism was gaining ground: "The steady sober minded farmers are at length discovering that it is high time for them to learn to think for themselves." He also reported progress in the Republicans' positive agenda, noting that "Colored Schools have arisen rapidly, since the scotching of the K.K. dragon."[135] In many ways, the years from 1872 to 1876 were the golden age of the Republican Party in South Carolina; during that period, the party added new members, some of them prominent whites, and took important steps toward reforming abuses in the state government. Nevertheless, Republicans in those years severely wounded themselves through factionalism, and they never developed the ability to keep order without federal help.

# FOUR

## The Perils of Faction

Reconstruction in South Carolina was overthrown by armed force. Democrats never for a moment reconciled themselves to the Republican regime, and when they saw their chance to seize the government, they did not hesitate. Nevertheless, it is not the case that Republicans were merely innocent victims, nor that they played no part in their party's downfall. In important ways, Republicans, through their factionalism, assisted the Democrats in subverting Reconstruction. Several types of factionalism existed within the Republican Party. There were racial divisions, splits between northern- and southern-born Republicans, and conflicts between conservative and radical positions. Most common of all were personal rivalries; the other types of factionalism were often merely the weapons with which personal rivals did electoral combat. By far the most destructive intraparty battles, however, were those fought over the issue of corruption.

According to the traditional view of Reconstruction, the Republican governments in the South were uniformly and completely corrupt, and nothing short of the overthrow of these governments by the old ruling class could end the plunder. In South Carolina this view is given added credence by the voluminous *Report of the Joint Investigating Committee on Public Frauds* compiled by the Democrats in 1878 after they had regained power.[1] This "Fraud Report," based on documentary evidence and the confessions of many Republican officeholders, establishes conclusively that corruption was rampant among government officials during much of Reconstruction. The report, however, only filled the gaps in an account of corrupt practices largely unearthed by Republicans themselves. Joel Williamson has gone so far as to claim that "reform was largely achieved . . . under the banner of Republicanism well before Redemption occurred."[2]

Even more devastating to Republican rule than corruption itself was its relation to Republican factionalism. Electoral fights between different Republican factions were often vicious, and for an office seeker to accuse his rival of corruption was the rule rather than the exception.[3] From personal rivalries in the various counties to large statewide factions, Republicans accused other Republicans of all manner of crimes, and the accused usually defended himself by similarly impugning his accuser. The result was the nearly inescapable conclusion, on the part of moderate whites in the state and nation, that the South Carolina Republican Party was a pack of thieves. This perception, based on truth but so exaggerated as to become a prejudice, severely inhibited the ability of the party to attract more native whites within the state and gave the national party all the excuse it needed to abandon the state party to its fate.

Although the prevalence of corruption in the early part of Reconstruction merits careful attention, so does its counterpoint—the ability of the Republican Party to produce reform efforts and to repair much of the damage done to the state by early excesses. A more damaging tendency of the Republicans was that of factionalism. Analysis of Republican failure therefore requires an investigation of the uses and abuses of corruption rhetoric by factions within the party as well as the ways this factionalism weakened the party and played into the hands of Democrats.

South Carolina's Republican Party suffered from factional splits both at the top levels of the party hierarchy and in nearly every county organization in the state. A crucial question for understanding the state's white Republicans is whether or to what extent these divisions were racial in nature; that is, did white Republicans and black Republicans see each other as rivals or even harbor racial prejudices against each other? The existence of friction along racial lines has often been noted by scholars of the period. Two causes of such friction are preeminent: the debate over civil rights (or "social equality") and the scramble for offices.

Conflict between white and black Republicans over antidiscrimination laws began as early as the Constitutional Convention of 1868. When a proposal to create a school system was put forward without any mention of segregation, scalawags in particular were almost as likely to abstain as to vote for it. Later that year, many white Republicans in the state legislature similarly tried to avoid taking a stand on a public accommodations bill. One of the bill's champions, black House member William J. Whipper, expressed his "regret . . . that there should be so many of our white Republican members absent during the consideration of this question." Had he not known that the speaker's stand was draped in mourning for the death of Thaddeus Stevens, Whipper sarcastically remarked, he would have thought it was in memory of the white Republicans: "I should have thought that the Ku Klux Klan had killed them off, and we were now mourning their departure."[4]

When the measure came to a vote on September 15, 1868, white Republicans ducked it again. Of the thirty-four white Republicans in the state house of representatives, twenty abstained. Nine more opposed it and only five supported the civil rights bill. If carpetbaggers are excluded, the vote was sixteen abstaining, seven opposed, and three white Republicans in favor.[5] In the state senate, a civil rights enforcement measure led to similar divisions among white Republicans. On September 8, 1868, for example, the S.C. Senate voted to table a civil rights bill proposed by Jonathan Jasper Wright. Of sixteen white Republican senators, four were absent, seven voted to table the bill, and only five voted to take it up. If only scalawags are considered, one was absent, four senators voted to table the bill, and four voted to take it up—but only one of these was born in South Carolina (Charles W. Montgomery of Newberry).[6] All the Democrats present, of course, voted to table the bill.

However much the possibility of social equality with their former slaves disturbed Democrats, they took barely disguised glee in watching Republicans divide among themselves over the issue. Most black Republicans and a few whites supported civil rights bills to prevent racial discrimination in public accommodations. Many white Republican, both natives and carpetbaggers, voted against such bills or even spoke out against them—carpetbaggers Charles P. Leslie and David T. Corbin, for example, were the most vocal opponents of civil rights legislation in the Senate.[7] Democrats praised these conservative Republicans even as they wondered aloud why blacks would vote for such men. Generally speaking, most white Republicans were far more interested in economic and political issues than in civil rights, which they often wished black and Radical white Republicans would drop in the interests of party unity and recruitment of new white support.

It has been asserted that white and black Republicans were at odds over patronage and elective offices as well. Thomas Holt dedicates one chapter of his study of black leaders in Reconstruction South Carolina to the question of "Black Domination or White Control." In it, he describes the willingness of blacks in the early years of Reconstruction to stand by and allow white Republicans to hold most offices but also the assertiveness of blacks in later years, when they demanded a greater share of offices for men of their race.[8] The push for more black officeholders occurred mostly between 1870 and 1872 and resulted in success, especially at the statewide level. For example, before 1870 no blacks served in South Carolina's delegation in Congress, but after the election of that year, three of four congressmen were black.

Some white Republicans opposed this trend. According to historian Joel Williamson, "White Republicans were irritated and alarmed by the flooding tide of black officeholders."[9] The generalization is too sweeping, but some white Republicans did respond to blacks' push for office with frankly racial arguments. Thomas N. Tolbert of Abbeville called for a stronger effort at recruiting native whites into the party, as "there is not enough virtue and intelligence among the Blacks to conduct the government in such a way as will promote peace and prosperity."[10] In 1874, when four blacks were nominated as Republican candidates for Richland County's legislative delegation, the Republican *Daily Union-Herald* of Columbia flatly announced, "It is time to have at least one white man in the Legislature from this county."[11] J. F. G. Mittag, an illustrious native white who was an early convert to Republicanism but failed to win office, wrote the governor in disgust, "having sustained losses and labored sufficiently—yea to my hearts content, for an ungrateful class of people."[12]

To some extent, though, these cases are exceptional. Just as often, white Republicans recognized the claims of blacks to offices. One such case was John Wooley of Edgefield. Wooley had joined the Republican Party as soon as it was formed and had remained active in it even after the Klan threatened to murder him.[13] Nevertheless, in 1872 Wooley found his Republicanism questioned by political rivals, and he was removed as county treasurer by Governor Scott. Edgefield voters retained their confidence in Wooley; a mass meeting in May 1872 said of him, "We shall always feel grateful to him for the interest manifested by him in the education of our children." Buoyed by this support, Wooley announced his intention to run for Edgefield's seat in the state senate.[14]

Edgefield's black politicians, however, were in the midst of a campaign to win more important offices for themselves. Wooley reluctantly but willingly removed his name from consideration and had the following announcement (or "card") published in the Republican newspaper of record: "The question of color having been raised by the leading colored men from Edgefield county, I respectfully withdraw from the canvass, as a candidate for State Senator. I wish it, however, to be understood that I go for Grant and Wilson, and the Republican party of South Carolina."[15]

The situation in Edgefield was unusual. White Republican Thomas J. Mackey would complain two years later that Edgefield's government was "wholly composed of negroes elected on the race issue, asserted even against white Republicans."[16] In most counties, factions did not occur along racial lines but, rather, overlapped with them. The best-known county factions were those in Charleston; Thomas Holt gives several pages of his account of white-black divisions to the disputes in that county between white congressman C. C. Bowen and black leader Robert De Large. The conflict between these two men is not best understood in racial terms, however. The crucial fact in the Charleston situation was that Bowen, through his early control of the patronage of the customs house, had built up a political machine that allowed him to challenge the regular party. De Large was merely one of the regulars who came into conflict with Bowen because of this permanent factional split.[17] It was also not necessarily the case that Bowen represented the more conservative Republicans. Democrats in the local elections of 1875 sided with the regular Republican *against* Bowen's faction.[18]

In most other counties, too, the main factional splits were personal rivalries among leaders rather than racial disputes. The evidence for this statement is largely negative: the absence of any mention of race in most of the propaganda with which county factions attacked each other. Instead, rival Republicans cast aspersions on each other's character, often to the point of absurdity. In Lexington County competing factions were headed by Elliott Hayes and Simeon Corley.

Perhaps responding to a Corley charge, the Hayes faction in December 1870 put together a petition and sworn statements asserting that Hayes's brother Bolivar did not, on November 29, engage in an inappropriate assignation.[19] Switching from defense to offense, a Hayes broadsheet attacked Corley with the accusation that one of the men on Corley's ticket had "entered a photographic gallery in Lexington village, and, after having stripped himself of every vestige of clothing, and thereby placed himself below the level of a brute, sat and had his naked person photographed in the most beastly attitude! Does 'Mr. Corley' deny this?"[20]

More typical than charges of lewd conduct, however, were charges of corruption. Accusations of fraud were as common in intraparty conflict as they were in the Democrats' campaign against all Republicans, and they aided Democrats greatly in making their case. Before examining the role that corruption rhetoric played, however, it is necessary to define the role of corruption itself in Reconstruction South Carolina. In particular, it is important to evaluate the kinds and degrees of corruption practiced in the state and to assess the response of the Republican Party to corruption.

The Republican regime in South Carolina suffered accusations of fraud in several areas, the most damaging of which undoubtedly concerned the massive increases in the state debt during Reconstruction. Democrats accused Republicans of brazen theft; Republicans countered that they did the best they could with the impossible situation Democrats left them. The truth was more complicated than either party's rhetoric would indicate, at least during Governor Scott's first term.

In 1868, when the Republican government came to power in South Carolina, the state was indeed considerably in debt already. This existing debt dated partly from the antebellum period and partly from the years of provisional Reconstruction. (The Confederate debt had been repudiated by the Fourteenth Amendment.)[21] With interest coming due and bonds maturing imminently, and with the collection of taxes still some months in the future, the incoming state government found itself in a difficult financial situation not of its own making.

The solution legislators settled upon was to issue state bonds to raise the necessary funds. The legislature thus passed on August 26, 1868, several acts that created the Financial Board, gave it the power to appoint a financial agent in New York, and authorized him to borrow $1 million on state bonds. The Financial Board was composed of Governor Robert K. Scott, Attorney General Daniel H. Chamberlain, and Treasurer Niles G. Parker. The financial agent they chose was Hiram H. Kimpton, a New York banker.[22]

The task of the Financial Board was immediately complicated by the actions of the South Carolina Democrats. When it was made public that the legislature would issue bonds, Democrats protested in strong terms and announced that any such bonds would be repudiated as soon as the Democrats recaptured the state government. An editorial of the *Charleston Daily News* of July 17, 1868, after less than two weeks of Republican rule, proclaimed that "no 'bayonet' bond, for whatever reason issued, will ever be recognized by the white people of the State." The question was squarely put: "Would New York or Boston touch these bonds, issued by authority of a horde of negroes, and in the face of the protest of the white people of the State?"[23]

The answer was no. Kimpton found it impossible to sell the bonds. As the governor was later to admit, "At that time, it was regarded as a wild speculation to loan money on South Carolina bonds."[24] It is unclear how to apportion blame for this want of confidence in the bonds among three factors: the Democrats' threats of repudiation, general northern mistrust of the Radical southern governments, and particular skepticism about the 1868 South Carolina bond issues. All involved later admitted it had been a bad idea to print on the bonds "Loan to pay interest on the public debt." Such an admission was not likely to allay the concerns of capitalists.[25] In any case, Kimpton, unable to sell the bonds, used them as collateral and borrowed money to pay the state's debts. Thus began his practice of "hypothecating" bonds—using them as security for loans. This practice would cost the state greatly, as the interest on such short-term loans was of course much higher than that on bonds would have been.[26]

After the 1868 elections, however, South Carolina's financial standing improved greatly. With the victory of General Grant in the presidential contest, the national commitment to Reconstruction seemed firm. Further, with South Carolina continuing to show a large Republican majority, the Democrats' threats of repudiation should they gain control seemed at worst a long-term worry. As early as November 1868, certain securities of the state called "bills receivable" were selling at 85 percent of par value.[27]

Unfortunately for the state's finances, however, state officials soon commenced a series of financial irregularities that would eventually send South Carolina's credit plummeting. The first instance involved the million dollars in bonds "to pay interest on the public debt." Because such a description weakened the confidence of investors, it was proposed to replace the bonds with another set imprinted "Issued under Act approved August 26, 1868." The new bonds were printed and sent to the agent, who began to sell and hypothecate them—while the old issue remained outstanding. Thus two sets of one-thousand-dollar bonds, each set numbered from 1 to 1,000, were in use simultaneously.

It has been alleged that this sleight of hand was committed for the purpose of the private enrichment of the Financial Board.[28] But this does not seem to have been the case, at least not at that time. Instead, it appears that these officials resorted to such irregular measures with the intent of solving the state's financial problems. To acquit them on the charge of peculation in regard to the 1868 bonds should not, however, obscure two facts: (1) their actions were in fact fraudulent, and that for the selfish motive of preserving their political careers, and (2) many of these same officials, particularly Scott and Parker, and probably also Chamberlain, were involved in other affairs that reflect even less well on their personal integrity.

Whatever the motives of the Financial Board, they injured the credit of the state in sending the second issue of bonds to Kimpton while the first was still in circulation. As might well have been predicted, a certain investor eventually came into possession of a bond of each issue having the same number. This bit of bad luck spurred Kimpton to begin taking the first issue out of circulation, and a little over half of the million dollars in bonds was eventually cancelled or destroyed. The board, however, refused to acknowledge that their actions had been intended to mislead. They affirmed their right to issue the second set of bonds by pointing out that the actual language of the act—"the Governor . . . is hereby, authorized to borrow . . . on coupon bonds . . . a sum not exceeding one million dollars"—permitted the issuance of as many bonds as was necessary to realize $1 million in cash, and with bonds selling far below par, the second issue was lawful.[29] Attorney General Chamberlain later admitted that the second issue was numbered the same as the first, rather than from 1,001 to 2,000, "because, if the numbers on the bonds issued showed a larger amount than $1,000,000, it would injure their credit in the market"—presumably because it would amount to an admission that each bond was worth only half its face value at most; otherwise, it would be an unlawful over-issue.[30]

Such financial wizardry as Kimpton and the Financial Board engaged in was made possible by a fact that was crucial to the entire financial situation: no one was keeping records of the financial agent's transactions. This was made clear in 1874 by testimony before the Dunn committee, a legislative investigating committee charged with determining what bonds were outstanding at that time. The board itself kept no records, according to all its members, and Kimpton did not report to the board as such. Governor Scott stated that Kimpton reported only to Comptroller General Neagle. Neagle stated that Kimpton did not do so and that he knew of Kimpton's transactions only from the treasurer's reports. Treasurer Parker stated that Kimpton reported to him only in general terms, and Kimpton insisted he was required to do no more than that. The others confirmed there was no law requiring reports from Kimpton.[31]

The disorganized condition of the state's finances would eventually provide a temptation the agent and the board were unable to resist. The lack of record keeping allowed the agent to sell bonds at one price, claim to have sold them at a lower price, and pocket the proceeds.[32] This was in fact done as early as 1870, according to Treasurer Parker's testimony in the Fraud Report.[33] The fraud in question was that by which members of the board and other well-placed Republicans acquired the Greenville and Columbia Railroad for far less than its market value, many of them using money Kimpton stole in the above fashion and then advanced to them.

In addition to the "bond ring" or "railroad ring," composed of white, northern-born statewide officials—Scott, Parker, and Chamberlain were all carpetbaggers, and Kimpton never left the North—there was also a "legislative ring" composed of the mainly southern-born legislators, of both races, accused of accepting bribes and voting themselves excessive pay and benefits. Again, though, there is very little to suggest that such peculation occurred before 1870. The authors of the Fraud Report admit that legislators' requests "at first . . . were moderate, and included only stationery and postage stamps," and that the members "requested the Clerks to deduct the amount from their pay." Eventually though, the legislators put in orders of food, alcohol, cigars, and even furniture far in excess of their pay, and the Committee on Contingent Accounts began issuing pay certificates to cover the cost of such "expenses."[34] Such practices immediately became a touchstone for those interested in demonstrating the evils of Reconstruction. As Joel Williamson pointed out in 1965, "Few historians have since failed to use eight-dollar spittoons, one-dollar cigars, and a bar in the Capitol to lighten their prose and delight their students."[35] But the state was not bankrupted on wine and cigars. Most of the enormous expenditures for "legislative expenses" went for the more serious matter of out-and-out bribery.

The origins of bribery in the legislature are obscure. Although Simkins and Woody claim that "from the very first session in July, 1868, money was used freely and soon openly to purchase the votes of the legislators," they give no source for this claim, nor do they name any specific bill that was secured by bribery before 1870.[36] The first documented case of vote buying is from the phosphate monopoly bill of that year. On the other hand, remarks by one of the legislators involved indicate that bribery was not entirely new at that time. Prince Rivers, a member of the state house of representatives from 1868 to 1874, told Democratic investigators that he and other upcountry members "didn't find out for some time that the down country members were using us, and getting paid themselves for their own and our votes, and when we found it out we combined against it so as to secure our share of pay as well as the others."[37] Whether he meant that the low-country members were first to receive payment for the phosphate bill or that they had been bribed on previous occasions is unclear.[38] In general, the origins of corruption in the legislature have never been adequately explained.

If in fact corruption was minimal before 1870, it becomes a matter of some interest how and why it began. The commencement of stealing in earnest in that year is probably, however, attributable mainly to two rather prosaic factors. In the first place, the desperate condition of the state's finances left no money in the treasury for anyone to steal for the first couple of years of Republican rule. And in the second place, it seems to have taken some time for would-be thieves to create schemes to prevent detection. In the legislature, for example, it became standard practice to pass a bill authorizing pay certificates for several legitimate recipients, but with the inclusion "and others" at the end. The extra money, above what was owed legitimate claimants, would then be given to a member of the legislature or a Republican county officer who needed funds.[39]

By the time the 1870 election campaign was underway, enough evidence of wrongdoing had become public that the Democrats saw an opportunity. Their plan was to use the issue of fraud as a wedge, split off disaffected Republicans, and lure them into the fusionist Reform Party. In this new party, the Democrats, who supplied the organization and much of the voting strength, would presumably dominate. The strategy necessarily required that the Reformers win black votes, so they had to play down the obvious fact that it was a movement orchestrated by Democrats. They placed at the head of the ticket Richard B. Carpenter, a carpetbagger from Kentucky who had been a judge under the Republican regime and who claimed that in national politics he was a Republican yet. Twenty to 30 blacks served as delegates to the Reform Party Convention (out of 150 delegates). Democrats involved in the party also belatedly announced their acceptance of the Fifteenth Amendment and all the Reconstruction laws. Most of the Democratic press followed suit. Although a few papers protested the Reformers' concessions to "Negro equality," a majority were determined to be silent on racial issues, making the contest one of "honesty vs theft—virtue vs vice—intellect vs ignorance."[40]

The 1870 campaign marked two changes in Democratic strategy. One was the attempt to fuse with part of the Republican electorate; this would be repeated in the elections of 1872 and 1874. The other was the transition in their indictment of the government from a purely race- and class-based attack to one centered on policy. Instead of predicting that such a group as the Republicans must surely ruin the state, it was claimed that they had done so. They had raised taxes far too high, sold too many state bonds, and squandered the proceeds. When they had been dishonest, that was so much the worse.

The Republicans, of course, had to defend themselves from these charges. In an effort to do so, they published several pamphlets that put the financial situation of the state in context, so that the voters might "fairly consider the actual conditions of the problem which was given us to solve." The first point they made was that the state treasury was empty when they took office. Furthermore, they had been assigned the task of offering services to a much greater population than before the war (the freedmen were now counted as citizens for purposes of disbursements) on the basis of a much smaller tax base than before the war (of the two primary forms of taxable wealth, slaves and land, the former no longer existed and the latter was greatly diminished in value). Finally, as a result of the destruction caused by the war, the state had already incurred obligations of debt before the Republicans took office.[41]

As to the bond issues, the Republicans blamed Democrats for the necessity of so many bonds, because one reason they had to be sold so far below par was the uncertainty about whether they would be paid off—and this was caused by the Democrats' own threats that "the property-holders of South Carolina would pay no debts contracted in support of a government forced on them by negro votes and federal bayonets."[42] Democrats in mid-1868 went even further, threatening to withhold their taxes from the state government. They believed they could get away with it because the penalty for tax evasion was to have one's property seized and sold at auction. Democrats conjectured that if all in the neighborhood agreed not to bid, the tax evader could retain his property.[43] Such an extreme measure was not adopted, but uncertainty must have further weakened investors' confidence in state bonds because the interest on the bonds was to be paid from tax receipts.

In any case, Republicans argued, they had faced a choice of bond issues or even higher taxes, as the government lacked money even to pay past-due interest on pre-Republican debts.[44] Scott would later conclude that the second choice—even higher taxes—was to be preferred, because the interest on loans was so high and because paying for the government through taxation alone would have forced the legislature to practice economy or face the wrath of the Democrats.[45] This postmortem was disingenuous, though. If the collection of such an amount of taxes had been possible, it was indefensible to issue bonds, much less borrow on them. The budgetary shortfalls could not have been remedied through taxation. As it was, the property owners were shocked at what they owed. Although the tax rates themselves were not high compared to those in nonsouthern states, they were a great deal more than South Carolina property owners were used to paying.[46]

It is unlikely, though, that such questions had much to do with the actual voting in 1870. The Democrats had been implacable opponents of Reconstruction since its inception. If it made any difference, the adoption of the Reform name and the inclusion of prominent Republicans probably *reduced* the anti-Republican vote, as some Democrats found too little difference between the two sides to bother voting. For their part, South Carolina's Republicans may be forgiven if they were not yet ready to trust the opposition. It had been but five years since the war had ended, and armed assaults on Republicans had been more or less continuous since that time.[47]

Republican speakers pounded home the themes of slavery, Black Codes, and political violence at every public gathering—greatly angering the Reformers. Carpenter, the Reform candidate for governor, later pinned the blame for his defeat on such speakers. According to him, "the speeches that were addressed to the colored people were of a kind intended to arouse their passions, to make them dislike and hate the white people, by setting them at variance with the white people." As an example of such rhetoric, he cited the generic refrain, "'You used to be lashed, you used to be sold, and your wives and daughters outraged,' and all that sort of thing." When pressed whether such observations were not in fact true, Carpenter hedged, "I do not think it was the rule to mistreat or to beat slaves."[48] Once they saw the preponderance of Democrats in the Reform Party, it was inconceivable that many black voters would side with them against the Republicans.

The regular Republican ticket defeated the Reformers by a decisive margin and retained control of the government. The victory came, however, amid charges of widespread electoral fraud, which added another grievance to the Democratic litany. Although Democrats admitted they would have lost a fair fight at the statewide level, fraud may well have deprived them of a congressman and a handful of state and county officers.[49]

The specific charges (stuffing of ballot boxes and the like) were rendered more than plausible by the inadequacies of the state's laws governing elections. In the first place, all commissioners of elections in all the counties were appointed by the governor, and he refused the Reformers' requests to appoint one of their party in each county to ensure fairness. Second, ballot boxes were to be delivered sealed to the commissioners, and they had ten days to count the votes; in many cases, this was done in their own homes. Third, the commissioners did not have to produce the ballots after counting; they could, and often did, destroy the ballots and simply report numbers. Obviously this rendered objective verification extremely difficult. Finally, because state laws provided no penalties for violations, all cases of electoral fraud had to be tried in federal court.[50]

These laws were exploited by Republicans in at least a few cases. Laurens County Republican boss Joseph Crews was frequently accused of "counting in" Republican candidates.[51] And the seating of two Republican legislators from Chesterfield, a white-majority county, earned the criticism even of Republican newspapers.[52] But Republicans did not always get away with electoral fraud. Commissioners in Beaufort County were convicted in federal court for manipulating the election when forty-one men came forward and testified they had voted for a certain party—the commissioners had claimed only six in their precinct had voted for that party.[53]

After the election, the conduct of both parties grew much worse. On the Democratic side, the activities of the Ku Klux Klan, which had subsided somewhat before the election, resumed with a vengeance. On the Republican side, the variety and scale of frauds practiced by state officials increased dramatically. The largest of these frauds was the use of the Republican Printing Company, which had the contract for all state printing, as a sort of slush fund for payments to legislators. As soon as this company, directed by the clerks of the state senate and house of representatives, acquired the contract, the yearly outlays for printing rose astronomically. From $21,000 in the 1868–69 session and $45,000 in the 1869–70 session, the spending for printing was $152,000 in 1870–71 and rose to a high of $450,000 in 1872–73. The testimony of Josephus Woodruff, clerk of the Senate, and A. O. Jones, clerk of the House, establishes that the excess was pocketed, part being kept by Woodruff and Jones and the rest divided among several legislators they called "the friends."[54]

Other frauds, begun before the election, continued unchecked. Falling into this category was the purchase, by several Republican politicians, of the Greenville and Columbia Railroad. A "sinking fund" commission had previously been created to dispose of the unproductive properties of the state and use the proceeds to buy back state bonds at deflated prices, thus saving the state years of interest payments.[55] Apparently, the real purpose of the commission was to acquire the

Greenville and Columbia Railroad, not an unproductive road but a valuable one. The members of the commission—Scott, Neagle, Chamberlain, Senate Finance Committee chairman Charles P. Leslie, and House Ways and Means chairman Joseph Crews—put the road on the market without advertisement and bought it themselves—for much less than its market value. In many cases, members of the ring bought in using money embezzled by Kimpton and advanced to them. The ring, headed by railroad magnate John J. Patterson, then bribed Franklin J. Moses, Speaker of the S.C. House, to arrange the crucial committees to their liking and to ensure the passage of a bill releasing the state's lien on the road. This accomplished, they took out a second mortgage on the road and sold the resulting bonds.[56]

Perhaps the most cynical of all the frauds was the corruption of the Land Commission, the organization conceived by the Constitutional Convention of 1868 to provide small farms on credit to the poor of both races. It was apparently begun with the hope of benefiting the party as well as the poor. For example, white Republican R. J. Donaldson wrote to Governor Scott from Chesterfield County that his goal was to "introduce enough of settlers to this Co[unty] from North Carolina to control the Co. & add a large number to the State's republican majority."[57] Unfortunately, the Land Commission was to prove an embarrassment, not a benefit, to the party.

Under the leadership of the first land commissioner, Charles P. Leslie, the agency was riddled with corruption. It became common practice for members of the commission's Advisory Board to act in collusion with local agents of the commission, buying tracts of land at one price and selling them to the state at another, much greater price. As a result, the Land Commission, which was intended to be very nearly self-sufficient, overspent its entire appropriation and by 1870 needed another bond issue just to pay due bills. Certain black leaders in the legislature refused to grant the new issue until Leslie was replaced with a man of their race.[58] Leslie, however, refused to resign quietly unless he was paid forty-five thousand dollars, which necessitated another round of fraudulent purchases to raise the money. (The fact that the board agreed to this extortion, of course, strongly suggests that all or most of the members engaged in the plunder.) Once Leslie had been bought off, Governor Scott replaced him with Robert De Large, a member of Charleston's "colored aristocracy." The legislature then relented and issued five hundred thousand dollars' worth of bonds to pay the commission's bills.[59]

But if some Republicans showed a propensity to commit frauds, others were quite willing to expose them. All the frauds mentioned were originally exposed by Republicans, not Democrats. To place the Republicans' achievements in this regard in the proper context, however, it is necessary first to evaluate the steps taken by Democrats to reform the government.

After the defeat of the Reform Party at the polls, the most important Democratic response was the reign of terror described in the last chapter. Simultaneously, though, they began to organize and exert their power in more legitimate ways as well. At the end of March 1871, the Charleston Chamber of Commerce made an announcement that no new South Carolina bonds should be bought, "as they will be held null and void by us."[60] The chamber also called for a Taxpayers' Convention, which met in Columbia in early May 1871, at precisely the time historian Richard Zuczek has identified as the peak of Klan terrorism.[61] Under such circumstances, it is easy to doubt the motives of the Democratic leaders who gathered to protest Republican policies. Nevertheless, it is only fair to them to point out that the taxation during Reconstruction was much more than South Carolinians were accustomed to.

In the antebellum period, planters and especially small farmers had paid far less than their share of a tax bill that was, in any case, light. During Reconstruction, they would pay a much greater share of a much greater tax bill.[62] The total state taxes in the antebellum era might be as low as one mill on the dollar; by 1871, the total taxes amounted to eleven mills—and that does not take into account Democrats' charges that the property in the state was assessed at twice its real value. The number also does not take into account the county taxes or, in Charleston, city taxes, which could be high as well.[63] There is much evidence that the increased taxes were onerous, especially in 1871, when the legislature attempted to collect the taxes due for 1870 as well as for 1871 in the same year.[64] According to one leading Democrat, in some counties as much as one-sixth of the land was forfeited for nonpayment of taxes.[65]

There were suggestions that the Republican government intentionally made taxes exorbitant in order to get more land away from its owners. The idea was that if it was financially impossible to own land without cultivating it, then planters would have to hire freedmen at good wages, or sell them the excess land, or lose it to the state for nonpayment of taxes, whereupon the state could sell the land to the freedmen. Such proposals had been made as early as the 1868 Constitutional Convention. Richard B. Carpenter reported that Republican speakers used such rhetoric in the 1870 election campaign as well.[66] And in 1872, when the Republican Party split, a delegate to the bolting convention warned the Democrats not to try to take advantage of the split by running their own ticket: "If you Democrats attempt to hold a convention, your land is gone, for we will tax you to death."[67] Whether such a plan was ever government policy or merely campaign rhetoric is difficult to determine. If it was policy, it was surely not a wise one. Higher taxes would probably lower agricultural wages, not raise them, and if white planters could not pay their taxes, freedmen would be unlikely to be able to pay them either. Perhaps some Republicans agreed with the logic of Capt. Felix Torbell of the U.S. Infantry, who, frustrated with white violence in Union County, wrote to a superior, "I see no remedy for the State Government except to tax the land so high that that class of persons will be compelled to sell out and leave the county themselves."[68]

With the Republican victories in the election of 1870, it became clear that electoral politics did not hold the solution to the hard-pressed farmers' problems. Upcountry newspapers joined the Charleston Chamber's call for action against unreasonable taxes; suggestions ranged from county meetings to discuss the issue to an immediate taxpayer strike. Eventually the former course of action received widespread favorable comment, and in May 1871, South Carolina taxpayers, representing almost every county, met in convention in Columbia.[69] In addition to their complaints about taxes, the delegates devoted much of their attention to the debt. Perhaps chastened by Republican accusations that Democrats were undermining the value of the bonds by their denunciations of Republican policy, delegates carefully avoided any statements that would have a tendency to lower the value of existing state bonds. They reiterated, however, that no new bonds would be honored.[70]

The convention's potentially most useful work was an investigation of the state's debt. This investigation, however, was less than meticulous, if not an outright whitewash.[71] Rather than doing the useful work of auditing the state's finances, the convention spent most of its time attempting to remedy what it saw as the underlying problem: democracy. Because the principle of "mere majority rule" was "defective," it was proposed to inaugurate a system of cumulative voting or proportional representation by which a minority of the population, instead of having no or very little representation, would have representation proportional to its numbers. Once again, this innovation was induced not by any particular political theory but by the simple fact that these men, the Democrats, were out of power and the system must therefore be "defective." Perhaps more in the spirit of the old aristocracy, former governor J. L. Manning dismissed the proposal because "we, by this cumulative voting, shall be confined to one-third the power which we are entitled"—that is, all the power.[72]

A far more important investigation was conducted in the same year, 1871, by Republican legislators. The leader of this effort was Christopher Columbus Bowen, one of the most colorful characters in the Reconstruction government. He had moved from Rhode Island to Georgia before the war and had fought for the Confederacy. He ended the war, however, in a Charleston prison, charged with murdering the commanding officer who had had him court-martialed. Freed by Union troops during their occupation of Charleston, Bowen became one of the founding members of the South Carolina Republican Party. He threw himself wholeheartedly into the work of party building. In 1867 he wrote to Charles Sumner requesting funds "to send men into every district, and if need be, upon every plantation in each district" to convince the freedmen to vote Republican.[73]

Bowen's long-running conflict with Governor Scott began in 1867, when Bowen was a lawyer in the provost courts and Scott was the general in charge of the Freedmen's Bureau. Apparently, Scott had Bowen arrested on charges of defrauding freedmen of money.[74] The disposition of the case is unclear, but Bowen continued to be actively involved in Republican politics, winning election to Congress in 1868 for the Charleston district. In 1869 he gained a measure of revenge against Scott by joining with Senator Frederick A. Sawyer to replace Scott's friend, Albert Gallatin Mackey, with their own ally, George Clark, as the collector of customs at Charleston Harbor. The Custom House employed, at any one time, about thirty men, and although Custom House employees were officially appointed by the federal government, the collector seems to have had great latitude in hiring his work force. The jobs ranged from boatmen, who earned six hundred dollars a year, up to assessors and auditors, who earned eighteen hundred dollars a year or more.[75] By comparison, the plum county offices of treasurer and auditor paid twenty-five hundred and one thousand dollars a year, respectively.[76] The patronage provided by the Custom House thus allowed Sawyer and Bowen to build a political machine to rival Scott's, at least in Charleston.[77]

In 1870 Scott used all the powers of his office to secure the defeat of Bowen's congressional reelection bid. When the Land Commission fiasco came to a head and Scott was under pressure to replace Commissioner Leslie with a black man, he chose Robert De Large of Charleston, allegedly to allow De Large to steal enough money to run against Bowen. And as the election approached, Scott gave Chief Constable John Hubbard orders "to appoint as many constables as De Large and his friends may ask, for Bowen must be defeated, no matter what it costs."[78] Finally, there were reports that Republican election managers altered ballots by replacing Bowen's name with that of De Large.[79] Although initial returns indicated that De Large had won, Bowen contested the election and turned up enough evidence of irregularities that in 1873 De Large lost his seat.[80]

In 1871 Bowen, now in the state legislature, again tried to exact revenge on Scott, this time by investigating the governor's handling of the state's finances. The committee on which Bowen served was appointed in February and did not report until December. (The committee of the Taxpayers' Convention appointed to do the same job worked for three days.) The report of the committee was greatly anticipated for much of the year, not only among South Carolinians but also in the nation's financial community. A Connecticut broker wrote to Governor Scott in October that he had been "buying for customers quite largely of your securities" and asked whether there was any question of their legality. A New York banker who owned bonds with a face value of $170,000 wrote that "constant rumors in the newspapers in regard to these bonds . . . have caused me considerable suspense." Samuel Edmonds of Baltimore, owner of three hundred thousand dollars in bonds, had purchased them at 62 to 68 percent of face value; he reported to the governor that their "price this afternoon is 31" percent of face value.[81]

As uncertainty caused South Carolina bonds to decline in value, individual investors too began to flood the governor's office with questions and concerns. Some of these letters were poignant. A Massachusetts day laborer, who had "saved a little by economy & hard work," had heard that some of South Carolina's black legislators talked of repudiating bonds,[82]

> which seems hard. I have sent the freedmens beauro from five to thirty dollars at a time, & by some help have made my daughter & one of my S[unday] School Schollars life members of the A[merican] M[issionary] Association, have sent their Magazine to ten different individuals the year round so as to enlist the sympathies of others in the cause. I hope if those bonds are to be repudiated they will first take a look at the case of honest people who are no speculators & see that many who have always been their friends are to suffer severely by it.

Other erstwhile allies of the South Carolina Republicans were looking for answers as well; a Baltimore investor wrote that he not only owned South Carolina bonds but also had been defending them in print. A Connecticut apothecary, wondering how "a 6 per cent security can be selling at 40" percent of face value, complained that "no one seems to know anything definite about these—and large sales are constantly putting the price down."[83] Finally, the *New York Commercial and Financial Chronicle,* the leading financial paper of the time, on November 11 devoted considerable space to the question of "South Carolina and Her Financial Troubles." The paper rejected the evasions and "general vague statements" that state officials had provided thus far and demanded that "the forthcoming reports must be full and clear."[84]

The report of the committee, issued December 20, was devastating. It accused Governor Scott of diverting militia funds to his own reelection campaign, branded the Land Commission a "gigantic folly," and decried the sale of the state's railroad property "for almost nothing," a sale that "most certainly savors of 'a job.'" On the matter of greatest interest, the state bonds, the committee was "satisfied that the State has been defrauded by an over-issue of $6,314,000" and recommended that "this House take the necessary steps to hold accountable those persons who have violated the laws and ruined the credit of the State."[85] Accordingly, on December 18, as the Christmas recess approached, Bowen introduced impeachment resolutions against Scott and Parker.

The resolutions were defeated by bribery. Taking advantage of a law passed during the first wave of Klan terror, Scott drew three warrants on the Armed Force Fund and made them out to fictitious persons. The warrants were cashed by John J. Patterson, the architect of the Greenville and Columbia Railroad scheme. Patterson then systematically bribed exactly enough members of the state house of representatives to defeat the impeachment. With rumors flying around Columbia that a vote would kill impeachment, those favoring removal of Governor Scott scrambled for time. William J. Whipper, a black representative who favored impeachment, had the floor and intended to filibuster until the recess, during which the bribed men might be converted.

In order to defeat the filibuster, Scott and his allies had to purchase the aid of the Speaker of the House, Franklin J. Moses. Moses met with Scott's friends and informed them that he was opposed to the impeachment but that "it would be very difficult" to deprive Whipper of the floor in order to get a vote. Fifteen thousand dollars changed his mind, and he quickly devised a plan. As Moses later told the story,[86]

> I sent for S. J. Lee, a member of the House, and gave him a memorandum on paper of the successive points I wished him to make, on which I was to rule as Speaker, and told him how to meet any objections that were made. The points were made as I wished, and I made the rulings on them (in accordance with parliamentary law) by which Whipper was forced to yield the floor and the House was brought to a vote and the scheme for impeachment was defeated.

Thus the attempt to "hold accountable" those who committed frauds came to an ignominious defeat. As powerful a story as this instance provides, however, it is most unlikely that Scott would have been impeached on a fair vote. Many Republicans undoubtedly agreed with Treasurer Parker, who justified his role in bribing the legislature: "I thought at the time it would be a great calamity to have the Governor impeached as could occur—a much greater calamity than the expenditure of the money could be."[87] The legislators quoted in the Fraud Report testified, almost to a man, that they had no intention of voting to impeach, with or without bribes.[88]

The efforts of the investigating committee and the impeachers were not entirely in vain, though. Several of the major frauds of the Scott administration had been uncovered and set down in print, if not proven in court. The extent of the debt of the state was more accurately assessed, and the urgent need for reform in the Land Commission was highlighted. Perhaps most important, a coalition for reform was beginning to take shape within the Republican Party.

Nor was reform entirely defeated. The Land Commission was thoroughly overhauled, beginning in February 1872, when the office of land commissioner was abolished and the duties of that office given to the secretary of state. Under that officer, Francis L. Cardozo, the land reform program was conducted efficiently and honestly and did much good.[89] In addition, the election law Democrats had so loudly denounced, which the governor himself admitted was inadequate, was amended to prevent the easiest types of fraud.[90] Other reforms achieved in 1872 included the decision to pay members of the state legislature a yearly salary instead of a per diem, the abolition of the office of state auditor, and the repeal of the act giving the governor control of the Armed Force Fund—the fund Scott had drawn on to stave off impeachment. In addition, the Sterling Funded Debt, a new bond issue previously passed but not put into operation, was repealed.[91]

Clearly, however, fraud had in no way been stamped out in South Carolina. In particular, the impeachment debacle turned many defenders of the regime into strident critics. One of these was Senator Frederick A. Sawyer, who with Bowen controlled the customs patronage at Charleston but had attempted to maintain friendly relations with Scott as well. In mid-1871 he had given a strong defense of the South Carolina Republican Party on the floor of the U.S. Senate. He denied that misgovernment could in any way excuse Klan outrages. He affirmed that the state government was capable of punishing wrongdoing by Republicans, naming specific instances. Finally, he accused the white Democrats of the South of deserting their post. In refusing to participate in the Reconstruction governments, "they used every engine of social and moral power to crush the honest workers for reconstruction and restoration; they laughed to scorn the attempts made by men, forced into the positions they held, to do their difficult duty in the best manner under the circumstances."[92] The author of this thoroughgoing defense of the state party, one year later, was denouncing it and urgently demanding reform.

As the Republican nominating convention approached in August 1872, the word was out that the national party was demanding reform as well. The two main candidates for the Republican nomination were Moses, known to be corrupt, and Chamberlain, who had been near the bond frauds but steadfastly claimed his innocence. A third group, headed by former governor Orr and federal district attorney David T. Corbin, threatened to bolt from the convention and nominate a reform candidate. Rumor had it, however, that the national party and President Grant himself had decreed that a bolt was to be avoided and the nomination was to be Chamberlain's. This message was allegedly brought to the state by Senator Sawyer.[93] Comptroller Neagle, for example, supported Chamberlain in the convention because "he wanted a candidate who would be acceptable to the Republican party of the whole State and country."[94]

The perceived demands of the national party stirred resentment among many state Republicans. For example, when a delegate moved to allow Sawyer to speak, another delegate declared that "he asked nobody to come down from Washington to chalk in big letters on a blackboard for poor niggers to read the orders by which they should be governed."[95] On hearing rumors that Grant had accused him of stealing, Governor Scott remarked that he did not care if Grant was reelected and went on to assert that prior to 1868, Scott's family was ten times wealthier than Grant's and now it was the reverse. If Scott had gotten his money by stealing, he wanted to know how Grant got his.[96]

The Moses forces used such resentment of northern dictation in the service of their candidate. A more ominous argument of some Moses supporters was that the so-called reformers were as corrupt as Moses. The difference between the two was merely that "Chamberlain is the choice of the financial ring" and Moses "the choice of the lobbyists and the bribe-taking, thieving legislative crew." In this situation, Moses was to be preferred because, as the Democratic *Charleston Daily*

*News* sarcastically put it, he was “a Protectionist—in the sense that he requires that the stealing should be done at home, and the money be spent here.”[97]

Once Moses was nominated, Republicans who insisted on reform bolted and set up their own convention. The typical speech at either convention (the two met simultaneously) contained the following themes: Republicans have made mistakes, and we must have reform; the accusations against our man are patently false; and the other man is notoriously corrupt. Following the first theme, both regular Republicans and bolters acknowledged many mistakes in the past. Some speakers even candidly admitted their own personal wrongdoing. B. F. Whittemore, a carpetbagger who had been expelled from Congress for selling a cadetship at West Point but now an advocate of honesty and reform, admitted he had “committed one great blunder,” and he “hoped for mercy.” But he also hoped the Republicans would repent and reform as he had, for he felt “fear and trembling for the future of the party in South Carolina.”[98]

Speaking to the regulars after the bolters had left, native white John R. Cochran of Anderson pledged, “I myself have done wrong, but if I do wrong again, I hope that God will remove me from the face of the earth.”[99] Cochran also made a startling proposal regarding the Ku Klux Klan. Only four years earlier he had been busy fortifying his house in expectation of assassination attempts; now he suggested, “To the Ku Klux we must say, we have done wrong and you have done wrong, so we will shake hands and say no more about it.”[100] Cochran’s offer would at first appear to offer too much to Klansmen, who after all had committed violent crimes, including murder, whereas the Republicans had committed only property crimes. In fact, though, the offer presupposed that after any mutual amnesty, Republicans would remain in control of the state, a condition Democrats would never have accepted. At bottom, Cochran was admitting that the Republican government was unable to preserve law and order, a reality the Democrats knew well. Therefore, his proposal to “shake hands and say no more about it” was indicative not of magnanimity but of desperation.

For their part, the bolters played both sides of the Klan question. In a public letter asking the support of the people of the state, the bolters specifically denounced the existing government for failing to secure “the rights of person and property, which is the special function of good government to guard.”[101] On the other hand, they outdid Cochran in their rhetorical overtures to the Klan. The bolting nominee for governor, carpetbagger Reuben Tomlinson, claimed that he “did not justify Ku-Kluxism; but if the Ku-Klux had come to Columbia, taken the guilty officials and put them through, he could have forgiven them.” Senator Sawyer added, “If the Ku-Klux had extended their raids to Columbia and given the guilty ones thirty and nine lashes, or hanged them to the nearest lamp-post, every honest man would have said in his heart, although deprecating violence, ‘Served them right.’”[102] Whether Tomlinson and Sawyer intended by their words to sanction the death penalty as a punishment for stealing is unclear. Hard-line

Democrats, however, understandably interpreted these intemperate statements as admissions that they, and the Klan, had been right all along.

Also giving aid and comfort to the Democrats were speeches in each convention outlining the frauds committed by members of the other. Black congressman Robert Brown Elliott claimed the reformers had tried to bribe Moses to get him out of the way, and that "it was well understood that the Barnwell delegation was for sale." Scalawag Thomas J. Mackey accused Tomlinson of having "enriched himself at the expense of the State"; he called Whittemore a "thief" and said he "was a fit reformer on the principle admitted in medicine that to inoculate a patient you take the virus from the worst case you can find." Of the bolters in general, Mackey said, "Judge Orr was right in saying that the bolt is supported by tried Republicans. It is supported, indeed, by Republicans who have been tried and convicted."[103]

In general, delegates tarred the opposition without making any answer to charges against their own nominees. Accused of stealing from the Land Commission, carpetbagger Charles P. Leslie "said he could prove Moses was the first man in the State to make money out of the land commission." A caricature of these arguments was Cochran's claim that "one of those Bolters has signed as many pay certificates as Moses has."[104] The bolters did little better. Corbin said Mackey's charges against Tomlinson were "false as hell" and that the latter had "bought his phosphate stock with his own money." The last point is true, at least insofar as the evidence indicates. It should be noted, however, that Tomlinson's having bought the stock with his own money (as opposed to the state's money, provided by Kimpton, which other officials used) does not preclude his having profited from his position at the expense of the state.[105]

In the election itself, the bolters were crippled by the general suspicion that they were dupes of the Democrats. This suspicion was perhaps stronger among black Republicans than white Republicans. The *News* reported that the regulars intended "to give special attention to the low country, the only section of the State in which they are willing to admit that the Bolters have any considerable negro strength."[106] Indeed, a sampling of the bolters reveals a much higher proportion of scalawags than a comparable subset of the regular party, and the great majority of blacks who bolted represented the lowcountry.[107] In addition, only two years earlier, the "reform" issue had in fact been used by Democrats seeking to split the Republican Party. There were rumors that that was the case again. The Republican *Columbia Daily Union,* for example, reported allegations that the bolters promised to name Democrats treasurer and auditor of every county, and half the trial justices, if Democrats helped vote them in.[108] Finally, in national politics, the "Liberal Republican" Horace Greeley opposed the reelection of President Grant, who was enormously popular among South Carolina blacks. Although Orr and the other bolters denied having anything to do with the Greeleyites and in fact specifically endorsed Grant, the two movements may well have been linked in many voters' minds.

Election returns indicate that neither Moses nor Tomlinson excited the electorate. Turnout of voters was the lowest of any gubernatorial election year during Reconstruction, despite the fact that 1872 was a presidential election year as well. In addition, Moses drew only 69,838 votes, meaning that, alone among Republican nominees for governor during Reconstruction, Moses polled fewer votes than did the rest of his ticket. Of seven other statewide officers, all but one outpolled Moses, as did President Grant. Every other regular Republican who ran for governor during Reconstruction polled at least 10,000 votes more than Moses. Nevertheless, Moses's election was never in doubt, as Tomlinson polled only 36,553 votes, falling more than 15,000 short of the second lowest polling opposition candidate during Reconstruction.[109]

These numbers suggest that Democrats found the gubernatorial candidates distasteful as well. Doubtless most Democrats viewed the choice as one between a "black dog and a monkey," as the *Chester Reporter* put it.[110] Tomlinson did run ahead of the rest of the statewide bolters' ticket, and in fact ran 14,000 votes better than Horace Greeley, the Liberal Republican candidate for president. However, Democratic counties polled many more votes for Democratic candidates than for the bolters. In Oconee, for example, Democratic congressional candidate Benjamin F. Perry received 1,201 votes, Tomlinson got 1,078, and Greeley actually lost that heavily Democratic county with only 393 votes. These figures indicate that the bolters derived most of their voting strength from Democrats; only in Charleston does it appear that more than a few dozen Republicans voted for Tomlinson.[111]

The Tomlinson campaign can fairly be seen as a test of moderate strength in South Carolina. Those who voted for the bolters' ticket were either Republicans who rejected the worst excesses of their party or Democrats willing to cooperate with avowed Republicans in the interest of good government. As such a test, however, it was not promising. The bolting ticket of 1872 was the least successful full slate of candidates in the entire Reconstruction period. In order to win Democratic support, any reform candidate would have to make many more concessions to them than did Tomlinson, but by appealing to Democrats, such a candidate would lose Republican votes. The trap seemed inescapable; the only possible reform had to come from within the regular Republican Party.

In addition to the defeat of the reform candidates, the significance of the 1872 election was the lengths to which it carried Republican factionalism. Although Republicans had been fighting among themselves ever since the organization of the party in South Carolina, these fights were largely local in nature, resulting from personal rivalries and not united by any ideology. In Charleston the supporters of Bowen fought the supporters of Mackey. In Beaufort the contest pitted the Whipper group against the Smalls group. In Greenville the factions were headed by James M. Allen and William E. Earle. Edgefield saw conflict between P. J. Eichelberger and Lawrence Cain. Lexington was divided between Simeon

Corley and Elliott S. J. Hayes. The list could be extended indefinitely. The point is that these were rivalries over power, rarely involving ideology. When one contestant was white and the other black, race could become an issue, as it did in Edgefield. But there was nothing to unite the various county factions across the state.

To some degree, the 1872 campaign changed that. In almost every county, the leaders of the faction out of power bolted. As Robert Brown Elliott, a regular, pointed out, it was "misleading to say there were 50 bolters, as only ten of the 124 members of the regular convention left it." Most of those in the bolters' convention were defeated aspirants to delegate status.[112] This meant not only that county rivalries became briefly oriented around the statewide issue of reform but also that only those candidates who supported the winning side would benefit from patronage. Thus the losing side would remain out of county office and be more likely to bolt the next time, with the result that factionalism became at least somewhat entrenched.

That this hardening of factionalism occurred over the issue of corruption was important because of its usefulness to Democrats. The fact that bolting movements often included prominent Republicans gave weight to Democratic charges, and so they can be seen as detrimental to Republican efforts. Such was, indeed, the view of the regular Republicans at the time. A perspective that blames the bolters for the failure of the Republican Party, however, would get the matter backward. It was the corrupt politicians, not those who sought to expose them, who weakened the party. There were many reasons for the decline in northern support for Reconstruction, but an especially important one was southern Republican corruption.

Nevertheless, when the possibilities of reform within the party opened up, first with Governor Scott's impeachment and then with the bolters' efforts, Republicans overwhelmingly turned their backs. (Perhaps disgusted with the outcome of his efforts, Judge Orr resigned his position and accepted Grant's appointment as ambassador to Russia.)[113] Had reform been wholeheartedly and immediately embarked upon by the new governor and legislature, much of the subsequent history of Reconstruction in South Carolina might have been different. Republicans did at least make another attempt to secure to the government a monopoly on the use of force, as Governor Scott's militia, disbanded in 1871, was reconstituted under Governor Moses.

If South Carolina's Republicans were content (or resigned) to depend upon the federal government for protection, the most important priority then was rooting out corruption and extravagance. One positive step in this regard was the restructuring of the state debt in 1873. Most southern governments borrowed excessively during Reconstruction, with the damage mitigated by debt restructuring only after Redemption. In South Carolina, Republicans undertook this work themselves.[114] The Consolidation Act, passed on December 22, 1873, repudiated outright almost $6 million in bonds that had been issued illegally; it also scaled the remaining debt by inducing bondholders to exchange their bonds for "consolidation bonds" of lower face value. This was accomplished by providing for a tax to pay the consolidation bonds and vowing never to levy a tax to pay the old bonds. Given this inducement, and the fact that by the end of 1873 South Carolina bonds were selling for fifteen cents on the dollar, bond holders had little choice but to exchange their bonds.[115]

Unfortunately, the useful and necessary work of debt restructuring was compromised by the profligate legislature's appetite for cash. By any measure of legislative excess, the Moses years were the worst of Reconstruction. For example, the public printing had cost $173,000 at its most expensive during Scott's administration. In 1873 it cost $450,000, and in 1874, $385,000, by far the largest such outlays during Reconstruction.[116] Moses himself made frequent use of the governor's contingent fund, on one occasion to bribe a committee investigating that very fund. He also was said to have sold pardons to criminals, and although evidence for such a charge is lacking, his total of 421 pardons in two years was an impressive feat.[117] On one occasion in 1874, when Moses owed a debt to another white Republican named Andrews, they conspired to get the money by using an invalid warrant on the contingent fund. Andrews nominated, and Moses appointed, a black man named Humbert as county treasurer of Orangeburg, Andrews's home county; Humbert then cashed the warrant. When Humbert was later arrested, Moses's part in the scheme became known, and a bench warrant for his arrest followed. Moses, however, called out the newly reconstituted state militia to prevent his arrest.[118]

Yet the emblematic episode of the Moses years was one in which the governor himself did not play an important part: the election of John J. Patterson, carpetbagger from Pennsylvania and architect of several of the frauds aforementioned, to the U.S. Senate in December 1872. At that early date, all hope of reform from the new legislature was quashed as one of the most notorious men in the state achieved high office through open bribery. Unable to buy off his main rival, black congressman Robert Brown Elliott, Patterson bribed enough members of the legislature to defeat him, as well as the other aspirants, outgoing Governor Scott and the incumbent, Senator Frederick A. Sawyer. Testimony, both of those bribed and of those doing the bribing, is detailed in the Fraud Report of 1877. Even at the time, though, it seems to have been no secret that money was being used by Patterson. In endorsing Elliott, the leading Republican newspaper of the state charged that Patterson "has rendered no service to the party in this State which calls for such eminent recognition as he demands, and the people will regard his election as a direct bargain and sale."[119] Nevertheless, Patterson easily won the election. Elliott was the only other candidate to receive more than a few votes.

The national significance of the election of Patterson was not only the open secret of his having bought the election but also in his replacing Sawyer, whom President Grant trusted as a conservative and honest Republican and whom he had specifically endorsed for reelection.[120] Patterson soon justified the abhorrence with which many honest Republicans had viewed his election. His nickname, "Honest John," supposedly alluded to the fact that if he promised a bribe, he would pay it. Nevertheless, apparently taken by surprise at the cost of his seat in the Senate, Patterson began haggling with those who had supported him. At one point he was said to have remarked that "the damned election had cost him more than it was worth." He must have reconsidered, though, as he allegedly refuted another Republican's assertion that reform was necessary with the famous prediction that "there are still five years of good stealing in South Carolina."[121]

Even the reorganization of the state's finances was compromised by continued corruption. The estimate of $5,965,000 in illegal bonds was considerably lower than the actual amount, because interest coupons clipped from bonds, which should have been cancelled, had been resold to third parties and funded into consolidated bonds.[122] In combination with continued high expenses, these frauds raised the tax rate for 1874 to twelve mills, the highest rate yet. The results of this corruption, extravagance, and high taxation were another Republican-led investigation, another Democrat-sponsored Taxpayers' Convention, and the near abandonment of the state Republican Party by the Grant administration.

# FIVE

## Moderation in Pursuit of Justice

The events of 1874–76 in South Carolina were marked by irony. Although Daniel H. Chamberlain, elected in 1874, was surely the most honest Republican governor of the state's Reconstruction period, it was during his administration that President Grant and the national party abandoned South Carolina Republicans to their fate, largely because of the corruption issue. Furthermore, although Chamberlain did far better than either of his predecessors in winning the support of Democrats, it was when he ran for reelection that they nominated the first avowed Democratic candidate for governor in eight years. Finally, it was during the period of most responsible and efficient Republican government that the party was defeated and removed for almost a hundred years from the state's politics.

Although these ironies are compelling, they obscure the continuing realities of the Republicans' dilemma. First of all, the Chamberlain administration did significantly reform the state's government, but by then the damage had been done. Reports of corruption under previous administrations (as well as in other southern states) had led many northerners to conclude that good government was incompatible with the presence of blacks in positions of authority. (The experience of the Civil War, in which blacks had helped save the Union, had led only to a temporary muting of northern racism, not to its eradication.) Although northern Republicans supported Chamberlain's reforms, they did not consider him truly representative of the Republican Party of South Carolina, an entity they continued to regard as an embarrassment.

The second irony, that the governor who came closest to winning Democratic support was forced from office by Democrats, is easily explained as well. By the time Chamberlain entered office, all but four southern states had been "redeemed" (returned to Democratic control), and one of these, Mississippi, was soon to follow. The latter case is particularly important because of the precedent of the "Mississippi plan," by which that state's Democrats overthrew the Reconstruction government by force of arms—and the federal government did not intercede. These events were as important to South Carolina's fate as any of Chamberlain's acts. The success of Democratic force in Mississippi gave leverage to extremist Democrats in South Carolina, as against moderate Democrats who favored making common cause with Chamberlain. But perhaps more important, Chamberlain himself undermined his support with Democrats by deploring their violence in the "Hamburg massacre" of July 1876. A lone moderate, even if he was governor, could not by himself prevent extremists from dictating events.

Finally, although Chamberlain's administration was indeed much more responsible and efficient than those of previous Republican governors, he had no more success than they in solving the fundamental problem of Republican government in South Carolina: maintaining law and order. Put another way, he was unable to fulfill the single most important requirement of a government—that it have a monopoly on the use of force within its borders. Although the state's Republicans had always had superior political strength, the Democrats had superior military strength. Under those conditions, Chamberlain's success in reforming the government was merely a cosmetic improvement.

Chamberlain's failure to preserve order was not, as has been claimed, the result of massive defections of white Republicans. In reality, causation worked the other way: where they could safely do so, white Republicans held firm. In some counties, in fact, more whites voted Republican in 1876 than ever before. It was when Republicans faced grave physical danger that they abandoned the party. Thus the traditional view that moderate whites jumped at the chance to support Wade Hampton is mistaken. Many whites voted their approval of Chamberlain's course even when they had the chance, for the first time since Reconstruction began, to vote for a "Straight-Out Democrat." The Wade Hampton legend holds that he won because his personal history and character appealed to undecided voters. In reality, however, Hampton won because he was able to call forth the overwhelming military power of the Democrats in a way that earlier compromise candidates could not. In short, it was not Hampton's appeal to moderates that won him the governorship—it was his appeal to extremists.

In 1873 and early 1874, the Republican government of South Carolina endured its most devastating attack to date, the publication of James S. Pike's *Prostrate State*, one of the most influential, though not most accurate, books of the era.[1] Pike was a white New England Republican whose prewar opposition to slavery coexisted with intense racism.[2] He wrote the book as a series of articles for Horace Greeley, longtime editor of the *New York Tribune* and Grant's opponent in the 1872 presidential election. Greeley died shortly after the election, but his successor at the *Tribune*, Whitelaw Reid, also opposed Grant's administration and especially his Reconstruction policy. In addition to Pike's reports, the paper ran exposés on the Republican governments of Louisiana and Mississippi in 1873 and 1874. After appearing in the *Tribune* in the spring of 1873, Pike's indictment of the South Carolina Republicans was published as *The Prostrate State* in early 1874.[3]

In the book, Pike described a state misruled and despoiled. He was not the first to do so. What was new, at least for a northern Republican, was the bluntness of Pike's argument that blacks were the cause of South Carolina's sufferings. After admitting that carpetbaggers did in fact steal, he noted that the state "is mainly rescued from their clutches." Nor was the destruction of slavery the cause of white Carolinians' misfortune: "The best thinkers of the South to-day tell us they bless God for the war. It was necessary to get rid of slavery." It was, instead, the former slaves themselves who had ruined the state. This in turn was not because slavery had left them unprepared for their new roles; they would always be unprepared, because "the black is a child of vice and ignorance and superstition in South Carolina as well as in Africa." In general, "races of men exhibit the same general characteristics from age to age."[4]

These judgments were opposed not only to reality but also to Pike's own observations. As Pike's biographer Robert F. Durden has shown, the basis for Pike's assessments is not to be found in the notebooks he compiled during his trip through the state. In several instances, positive statements about blacks appearing in the notebooks are not found in the published book, and in other places comments condemning whites have been expurgated.[5] The effect of Pike's book was to place before the nation a description of misrule in South Carolina that identified inherent black inferiority as the sole culprit.

The response of the northern press was favorable. The *Atlantic Monthly*'s only complaint about the book was that it was not new: "It has for years been notorious that the ignorant negro rulers of that ex-Commonwealth had carried into their legislation and administration the spirit of the servile raid upon the plantation hen-roost and smoke-house."[6] The *Nation* went even further toward adopting Pike's perspective, claiming that the average intelligence among black South Carolinians was "so low that they are but slightly above the level of animals."[7] Again, northern racism was not new, but the general northern acceptance of Pike's fervently racist indictment of the Reconstruction laws must have emboldened southern Democrats. It is surely not coincidental that it was in early 1874 that South Carolina's white minority began to mobilize again.

In early 1874, leading Democrats, enraged by high taxes and press reports of record levels of fraud in the Moses administration, called for a second Taxpayers' Convention. The first, in 1871, had been largely ineffectual in its primary purposes—exposing government fraud and forcing a reduction of taxes—but it had had two salutary effects. It spurred the much more successful investigation of the state's finances by the Bowen committee, and it made politically impossible the planned issue of the Sterling loan bonds, which would have further increased the state debt. Perhaps even more important, however, it gave Democrats an unimpeachably legitimate organizational framework. The convention allowed them to come together and plan strategy, not on a political basis (and, of course, not on a military basis) but on an economic or policy basis. This device allowed them to stress their most legitimate grievance, that they paid the bulk of taxes but were not permitted a say in how heavily they were taxed or how the taxes were spent.

Of course, the issue of taxes, though meaningful, was secondary to the Democrats' main complaint: they did not govern. A government that taxed little, spent little, and was honest, but that did not include them, would have been just as objectionable. Therefore the convention spent most of its four-day existence in February 1874 not on issues of taxation but on a new and, to Democrats, exciting idea: immigration. The proposal, put forth by Confederate veteran Martin W. Gary, was to recruit white immigrants from Europe to settle in counties where the racial balance was fairly even. This would ensure white majorities in enough counties to take back the legislature. Gary had gone so far as to hire a recruiting agent in Germany.[8]

White immigration was the first part of a three-part plan agreed to by the convention. The second part was the organization of the Democrats into "tax unions" throughout the state. The third part of the plan agreed to by the convention was to present a memorial to the president and Congress seeking relief from what they again termed "taxation without representation."[9] None of these goals was achieved quite as Gary proposed, but all indirectly bore fruit for the Democrats. The immigration scheme never even got off the ground, but as historian Richard Zuczek points out, Gary's focus on race as the key to the whole issue certainly took hold among Democrats and was a first step toward the campaign of 1876.[10] The tax unions did not take any concrete steps toward alleviating the tax burden, but they did serve as an undeniably legitimate statewide organizational structure for Democrats to use in the upcoming 1874 campaign. But perhaps the most effective step taken by the Democrats was the one that seemed to have the least chance of success: the memorial to President Grant and Congress.

The memorial was first sent to Congress, where Republicans had it promptly tabled.[11] Grant, however, agreed to an audience with the South Carolina delegation in March 1874. The meeting was a failure. Grant, in fact, "lost his composure" in the meeting and angrily lectured the Democrats that their own recalcitrance had been the cause of their troubles. He further resented comments about himself allegedly made in a speech at the Taxpayers' Convention by Gary, calling the speech "a viler and more villainous slander than I have ever experienced before."[12] Nevertheless, if Grant had little patience with South Carolina Democrats, he also showed distaste for the state's Republicans, saying that it seemed to be the case that South Carolina was "badly governed and overtaxed" and that if that was so, it was "a matter very much to be deplored."[13]

After a meeting with leading South Carolina Republicans, who submitted in writing a thorough rejoinder to the Democrats' memorial, Grant retracted his comments of the previous day and pronounced himself satisfied that the rejoinder settled the matter.[14] Nevertheless, it would not be the last time Grant would waver in his support of South Carolina Republicans. The summer before the 1874 election, the president seems to have seriously considered endorsing a Democrat in the gubernatorial race.[15]

From early 1874 onward, South Carolina Republicans sounded out their northern backers and were dismayed at what they heard. Apparently the word had gone out from Washington that the national Republican Party, already saddled with an economic recession, could not afford to carry the scandal-prone southern wing of the party much longer.[16] One after another, leading South Carolina Republicans brought the message back to the state. In February, Congressman Robert Brown Elliott told his constituents that, in his experience, "to mention South Carolina is to merit the sneers of the Commonwealths of the North." He further warned them that the northern party considered South Carolina Republicans to be liabilities and that they would abandon them if reform were not implemented immediately.[17] This speech, "Plain Talk from a Black Congressman," as the *News and Courier* headlined it, was followed by others urging reform. The *Nation* reported that Congressmen Elliott, Rainey, Ransier, and Cain were telling Republican voters that "an educational qualification for electors" was being contemplated "unless these electors will go to the polls at the next election in a spirit of reform."[18]

In mid-1874, Governor Moses's term was drawing to a close, and the top priority for reform Republicans was to make sure he was not renominated. Moses's crimes were too numerous and too notorious for his protests to be heeded. Having been burned once, the party would not believe again that he was innocent. The leading Republican paper in the state, Columbia's *Daily Union-Herald*, catalogued his failings: "He has thwarted the efforts of the treasurer to bring to a strict accountability the treasurers. . . . He encouraged the extravagant and corrupt members of the legislature. He pardoned those convicted of fraud. He promised immunity to the dishonest but undetected."[19] The immediate cause for his falling out of favor with the party, however, was probably his being indicted for grand larceny. In March a grand jury reported a true bill against the governor for using state funds to pay his private debts. Accordingly, a bench warrant for his arrest was issued, but Moses refused to be arrested, calling out the militia to protect him. When the case came to trial, Moses did not put in an appearance, but his lawyers successfully argued that as chief executive of the state, the governor would have to be impeached before he could be tried. (Impeachment was not likely to be attempted, as Moses still had substantial support in the legislature.) As a result, the "Robber Governor," as he was now known, retained his office and fully intended to run for reelection.[20]

It was at this point, with a Moses renomination a distinct possibility, that the president apparently began to consider throwing over the South Carolina Republicans. The *Daily Union-Herald* reprinted a report to that effect: "Grant says if Moses is nominated, a Democrat shall be elected, or become Governor in some way."[21] (The ominous latter clause may have had a greater effect on state

Republicans than the threat of losing an election, which under normal circumstances was highly unlikely.) Moses, for his part, was perfectly willing to match threat for threat: "Moses says if he is not nominated he will, by virtue of his office, appoint Democrats to the office of Commissioners of Election, so that they may have things their own way. Accordingly he has already given a premonition by removing all the incumbents. He has not filled the vacancies, and he will not until after the convention."[22]

Incredibly, this was no idle threat. Moses really did intend to hand the election to the Democrats if he were not renominated. The scheme of appointing Democrats as election commissioners apparently had come up soon after the attempt to arrest Moses. At that time, Republican leaders thought they had concluded a deal whereby Moses would escape punishment if he declined to run.[23] Of course, Moses soon escaped prosecution on legal grounds and thus did not need the help of the party. Presumably he thus saw the deal, if it existed, as void. He was indeed a candidate for reelection.[24]

The opposition to Moses centered on Daniel H. Chamberlain, a Massachusetts carpetbagger who at the time was not in government. He had been attorney general during Governor Scott's administration, but since failing to receive the gubernatorial nomination in 1872, he had been engaged in the private practice of law. (He did not bolt from the party in that year, perhaps already planning for a second run at the office.) Chamberlain was universally conceded to be a man of great ability, but there were strong concerns as to whether he fit the description of a reform candidate. The *New York Times,* in an article generally favorable to his election, conceded that "he was connected, as Attorney General, with Gov. Scott's Administration, and some ugly rumors are circulated about certain financial operations in which he was said to have been engaged."[25] Some of these rumors were given added credence by a report, completed on June 14, 1874, on the state's bonded indebtedness. The findings of the report were certainly embarrassing to Chamberlain, as they showed with impressive clarity his failure to restrain the machinations of the "bond ring." The embarrassment of Chamberlain may well have been one of the report's purposes, as it was prepared by a committee headed by Thomas C. Dunn, an opponent of Chamberlain who would manage the campaign of Chamberlain's bolter opponent later in the year.

Dunn was a white carpetbagger born in Massachusetts who, after working in the lumber industry in Wisconsin, came in 1865 to Horry County, South Carolina. Not coincidentally, the major industry in Horry was timber, and Dunn rapidly established himself as a success; by 1870 his was the second largest lumber business in the state, exceeded only by that of Henry L. Buck. In politics, Dunn was a Republican, serving first as postmaster in his town of Little River in 1866, then as a member of Horry's board of registration in 1867. He ran for Congress in 1870 but lost the nomination to Darlington carpetbagger B. F. Whittemore. In 1872 he was successful in a race for the state senate. Because Horry held a large majority of white voters, Dunn's success can be taken as evidence that he had the confidence of the leading white citizens of the county. This conclusion is also supported by the fact that he later married the daughter of one of these leading citizens, the aforementioned Henry L. Buck.[26] Dunn has been described as "a member of the moderate wing of the Republican party," and his main concern seems to have been the economic development of Horry County.[27]

Dunn's report, by disclosing the ways in which the Financial Board under Scott had manipulated the state's finances, provided much ammunition to the opponents of Chamberlain, as he had served on that board.[28] As the report showed, the man who in 1874 sought election as a reform candidate had the chance to stop, or at least expose, one of the worst abuses of the Scott era, and he did not. He not only took no extraordinary measures to do so but also aided the "bond ring" at every step with legal opinions favorable to their (highly questionable) interpretations of laws. Few of these opinions seem to have been written (indeed, the Financial Board did not leave much in the way of written records at all), and in some cases Chamberlain could not recall having given them. Nevertheless, the report left Chamberlain with a shaky claim to the mantle of reform.

In fact, according to Francis Warrington Dawson, editor of the *Charleston News and Courier,* the difference between Moses and Chamberlain was "the difference between a footpad and a forger." The precise meaning of the idiom has unfortunately been lost in the mists of time, but it is clear from other statements that the editor thought one as corrupt as the other.[29] The paper therefore set out to expose Chamberlain, with articles appearing every day for a week in early August.[30]

As the 1874 state Republican convention approached, then, the leading candidates were a known corruptionist and a questionable character who, in some quarters both Democrat and Republican, was considered no better. It was at this time, apparently, that President Grant became involved in serious negotiations with prominent South Carolina Democrats about the possibility of Grant's siding with them in the 1874 gubernatorial election. The Democrats were considering running one of their own, Gen. James B. Kershaw, for the office; it would have been the first time since Reconstruction began that they had done so. What would have been Grant's role was left ambiguous. He certainly would have been expected to denounce Chamberlain, but whether he was actually to endorse Kershaw is unclear.[31] In any case, as late as September 3, Democrats expected Grant's cooperation. A few days later, on September 8, they got the bad news that "Grant is thoroughly committed to Chamberlain."[32] Without Grant's support, the Democrats apparently saw no use in running a candidate.

The administration's commitment to Chamberlain, of course, did not ensure his nomination. In 1872, after all, the national party had openly denounced Moses, but he was elected nevertheless. This time, though, Moses received no serious support. Various explanations have been offered for this change. Chamberlain's biographer writes that the party was serious about reform, editor Dawson claimed at the time that the Chamberlain forces were "using more money," and Congressman Elliott's biographer believes Elliott's role was crucial. Moses probably also hurt himself badly with his threat to appoint Democrats as election commissioners. He had, in fact, begun to do so by August 26, perhaps convincing some delegates, finally, that his only loyalty was to himself.[33]

As with so many issues related to Reconstruction politics, the difficulty here is to avoid both cynicism and naiveté. Peggy Lamson, Elliott's biographer, thinks Elliott and Chamberlain worked out a back-room deal with the ultimate purpose of reform. By this deal, Elliott would resign his seat in Congress, return to the state as Speaker of the South Carolina House of Representatives, and help Chamberlain clean up the party. As part of this plan he would of course help Chamberlain get elected in the first place. One appeal of this theory is that it accords with the facts (the scenario described in fact occurred). More important, perhaps, the theory takes the men involved at their word without prettifying the methods they used. Chamberlain and Elliott really did want reform, even if their motives were mixed. Chamberlain wanted the approval of South Carolina's elite whites, and Elliott knew that racial equality was contingent on federal support. At the same time, the methods used to advance the plan were certainly undemocratic and perhaps worse. Although Lamson finds Dawson's accusations of bribery implausible, it is not incompatible with her theory.[34] The two candidates opposing Chamberlain were men of better reputation for integrity than he, and it was still unclear that a triumph for Chamberlain meant a triumph for reform. Therefore, Republicans desiring to fend off reform (such as, perhaps, "Honest John" Patterson) might well have seen Chamberlain as their man and used their money accordingly. In any case, Chamberlain easily bested his two main opponents, John Winsmith of Spartanburg and Judge John T. Green of Sumter. Chamberlain received 72 votes to 40 for Green and 10 for Winsmith.[35]

As had happened in 1872, Republicans not satisfied with the nominee bolted the party; this time they supported Judge Green's independent candidacy. Green's bolt, however, was quite a different affair from that of 1872. In that year, substantial numbers of white Republicans had deserted the regular nominee, Moses. The 1872 bolt had affected both leading white Republicans and the rank and file; in white-majority counties, voting for the regular ticket plummeted between 1870 and 1872.[36] But the 1874 canvass was another matter entirely. Republican strength returned almost to 1870 levels, and in many counties, particularly white-majority counties, it surpassed that benchmark.

What statistics show for the rank-and-file white voter, anecdotal evidence illustrates for the more prominent white Republicans. The *Daily Union-Herald* ran an editorial comparing the two bolting movements, much to the disadvantage of the 1874 version. Although the earlier bolt had "the entire sympathy and moral support of the federal administration," the later one did not. Although the 1872 bolters had the backing of both U.S. senators, one congressman, several circuit judges, and "Judge Orr, a tower of strength in himself," the current bolters did not. And although the 1872 bolt had the support of five out of six Republican newspapers in the state, the current movement had the support of none.[37]

The paper also made a point of showing that the current bolt was a Democratic movement in disguise. It reported allegations that various county delegations had had their expenses paid by Democrats, that Democrats were supplying liquor to gatherings of bolters, and that in general the Democrats were backing the movement while simultaneously following a "possum policy" of keeping away from the proceedings so as not to arouse the suspicions of Republican voters. On October 17, an item quoted a Republican named N. B. Myers who had gone over to the Green movement but was disillusioned, finding it "only a white league ku klux possum."[38] Others agreed. With the exceptions of Thomas C. Dunn, Edmund W. M. Mackey, and of course Green himself, no prominent white Republicans went over.

Nevertheless, the election was much closer than either of the previous two. Chamberlain won by fewer than twelve thousand votes, whereas his two Republican predecessors had won by margins almost three times as large. One reason for this discrepancy is the Democratic vote. In 1870 and especially 1872, Democrats had stayed away from the polls, but by 1874 most returned and voted for Green.[39] But an even more important reason for the tightening of the margin was factionalism: the Republican Party continued to hemorrhage votes, with every election sending more Republicans into the bolters' camp.

As many as 10,000 Republicans who cast their ballots for Scott in 1870 and Moses in 1872 rejected Chamberlain in 1874, and 4,000 of these came from Charleston County alone. That county had long been riven by factionalism, but in 1870 both factions had gone for Scott, and in 1872 thousands had stayed home. Only in 1874 did the factional split in congressional voting, 11,278 for Mackey (bolter) and 8,673 for Buttz (regular), almost exactly mirror the split in gubernatorial voting—11,393 for Green, 8,727 for Chamberlain. Because Scott had won Charleston 13,000 to 7,000, this reversal in one county alone accounts for more than 4,000 of the 10,000 new bolters.

Add another 1,700 in Beaufort, Clarendon, Colleton, and Georgetown, and these lowcountry counties with heavy black majorities and a record of voting for Republicans contributed more than half the new bolters. Most of the rest came from Green's home county of Sumter. That county had gone for Scott and Moses by 2,000-vote margins but gave Green 4,091 votes to Chamberlain's 758.[40] All told, between 1870 and 1874, it is true that 7,000 previously abstaining Democrats came to the polls; but 10,000 previously voting Republicans—mostly blacks from the lowcountry—switched their votes. The Democratic strategy, or "possum policy," was working.

The results were actually even more encouraging for Democrats than the gubernatorial election would suggest. Unlike the 1872 bolters, the 1874 bolters had nominated a full slate of candidates, and many of these were Democrats. Combined bolter and Democrat strength in the new legislature was higher than it had ever been, with 53 out of 124 seats in the House and 15 of 33 seats in the Senate occupied by opponents of the regular Republican Party.[41]

The national elections were even more encouraging for Democrats. The congressional elections produced a breathtaking reversal; the Republican majority in Congress, which had been overwhelming throughout the Reconstruction period and in early 1874 stood at 110 seats, vanished. When the new Congress convened, it was the Democrats who formed a majority, with 60 seats to spare. The causes of this electoral earthquake include Reconstruction policy, corruption at all levels, and, probably most important, the depression of 1873. For South Carolinians of both parties, though, effects were more important than causes, and the most important effect was the creation of a federal government less likely than ever before to protect the state government from its armed white citizens.[42]

As Chamberlain took office in late 1874, he presided over a party much weakened by the three successive bolting movements. Not only had bolters such as Bowen and Dunn exposed the shady dealings of party regulars (including Chamberlain himself), but they had, by alliances with Democrats, substantially weakened the voting strength of the Republican Party. One might suppose that the incoming governor would attempt to heal the rifts within the party in order to avoid another costly bolt at the next election. Chamberlain, however, took a different tack. He attempted an overhaul of the government, focusing on honesty and competence, in an attempt at building a moderate coalition of honest Republicans and public-spirited Democrats. Feeling that honest Republicans would back him because they had nowhere else to go, he focused his efforts on winning over every Democrat who could conceivably support a Republican. This endeavor would create outrage within his own party, but for Chamberlain, so much the better: it illustrated that his efforts were sincere. Chamberlain also had personal reasons for attempting to win Democratic approval. He was well educated, cultured, and snobbish, and he naturally sought the company of similar men. By winning the political backing of leading Democrats, he could also join their society.[43]

The issue of race was also one that drew Chamberlain toward the idea of an alliance with moderate Democrats. Although he advocated racial equality before the law, he apparently remained skeptical about the actual equality of the races. He not only seems to have been less comfortable in integrated social situations than some white Republicans (especially former governors Scott and Moses) but also seems to have wanted to maintain white control over the Republican Party.[44] The clearest proof of this desire was his unfortunate comment that he would run for office "to keep the party from going over to *negroism*."[45] This comment may have been taken out of context, as he most likely was criticizing black voters for judging candidates by the color of their skin rather than the content of their character. (The comment was made when black South Carolinians were pushing for a larger share of Republican offices, much to the discomfort of some white Republicans.) Nevertheless, Chamberlain during his governorship was to find himself, on occasion, siding with white Democrats against black Republicans, and his framing of the issue on one of those occasions caused a severe break with his party.

From his inaugural address forward, it was clear that Chamberlain meant his promises to clean up the abuses of South Carolina's government. In that message, he provided not only general requests for honesty and frugality but also specific policies by which he expected to achieve these goals. He announced that taxes were too high, that many Republican officials were incompetent, and that the legislature had been profligate, if not larcenous, in spending money. To remedy the situation, he proposed to appoint only qualified and honest treasurers, auditors, and trial justices for the various counties, and he strongly urged the legislature to adopt a system of appropriations whereby taxes would be raised for specific purposes (he deplored the size of the state's "contingent funds") and appropriations would be made only up to the amount that had actually been raised specifically for the purpose. This recommendation strongly implied, if it did not frankly assert, that local officers and state legislators had abused the trust placed in them and could be trusted no further.[46]

The message, however, also contained much that was heartening for Republicans committed to reform. Chamberlain took care to point out that many of the most desperately needed reforms were already underway. After stating that assessments for property taxes were too high, he observed that a new assessment had been made that would "relieve the injustice of former assessments." After complaining of the large number of "subordinate officers and attachés of the General Assembly" and the expense thereby incurred, he announced himself "happy to speak in commendation" of an act by which the legislature had greatly reduced that number. On the subject of the public debt, a subject demanding "greater attention" and "wiser action" than any other, Chamberlain pronounced himself satisfied with the consolidation act previously passed, an act he considered "a final settlement." Finally, on the subject of public schools, the new governor had many suggestions but admitted that there had already "been steady progress since 1870, not only in the number of our schools, but in their efficiency and standard of instruction."[47]

All in all, Chamberlain's inaugural address announced a program of moderate Republicanism based on reform and retrenchment. In predicting this program's success, he pointed out that practically everyone in the state claimed to support it. He noted that he and his opponent in the election, Judge Green, ran on practically the same platform. As Chamberlain saw it: "The remarkable spectacle was thus presented, among a people hitherto considered most widely divided in their sympathies and aims, of an absolute identity of sentiment upon all the questions which were presented to the public by either party."[48] He predicted throughout his speech that this agreement on the proper policies would result in cooperation between Democrats and Republicans to achieve those policies. When the Democratic press praised his speech, he judged that their support "betokens a practical unification, in its best sense, of our two races."[49]

Chamberlain's inaugural and the program of moderation it laid out won the immediate support of the Democratic press, as historians have often noted.[50] Less well known is the appreciative response from moderate Republicans. These Republicans, many of them native whites, had found their connection to the party increasingly distasteful and embarrassing in recent years. Many had bolted in 1872; some had even opposed Chamberlain. But his attempt to redefine the party fired their enthusiasm for "Republican principles" anew. For example, A. C. Hawthorn was a prewar Unionist from Abbeville who joined the Republican Party but "believed we have had the past few years a great many unworthy men in position." Hawthorn commended the governor: "Your administration thus far, is the praise of every one." William Perry, a factory owner from Anderson, told Chamberlain, "You are gaining friends up here daily . . . as you ought to be." And Thompson H. Cooke wrote from Greenville "to express my very high appreciation for your course as Governor."[51]

A more dramatic example involved Simeon Corley of Lexington County. Corley, the prewar abolitionist who corresponded with Thaddeus Stevens and Charles Sumner, had become disillusioned with his party. He bolted the Republican convention in 1872 and opposed Chamberlain in 1874. When the new governor began to hand out the patronage, Corley's Republican rivals in Lexington made sure Chamberlain was aware of Corley's apostasy. Rollin Kirk, a Corley opponent, sent numerous sworn statements to Columbia proving that Corley advocated the election of Judge Green. He had told one deponent that "Green was a better man than Chamberlain"; he had been overheard by another to say that "though Chamberlain was his special friend he thought Green would make a better Governor than Chamberlain" because the latter "belonged to the ring." Kirk wrote the governor another letter to report that during the campaign Corley had "openly charged in a Lexington meeting that your nomination had been bought, and that he would not support you."[52]

Chamberlain knew all this as he made his nomination for county treasurer, but he was not swayed. Perhaps he found Corley's suspicions of him reasonable. Perhaps he was impressed with Corley's own letters to him: "Whatever the mistakes of the Republican party in this State have been, you and I are held responsible for them, whether justly or not, and we cannot shirk the responsibility."[53] But the greatest factor in Corley's favor was probably one mentioned by James Sharp, a Corley supporter: "I believe that if Mr. Corley is appointed to the treasurership of the county it will give general satisfaction to the Democrat party more so than any other man belonging to the Republican party."[54] Corley was appointed.

For the auditorship of the same county, Chamberlain chose C. E. Leaphart, a Republican of recent vintage. Elliott S. J. Hayes, who since 1870 had been

Republican boss in Lexington, said Leaphart "can only trace his Republican ancestry back to the election of 1872, and even then . . . he voted the bolter's ticket."[55] Again, though, Chamberlain was probably more impressed by the comment of Lexington's Democratic state senator, John Christian Hope, who considered Leaphart "strongly indorsed by the citizens of Lexington, both by the colored—& many tax paying whites, friends of mine at that."[56]

Hope, like James Sharp, was speaking Chamberlain's language. Acceptability to the Democrats was the first requirement for a patronage aspirant; acceptability to the leading Republicans was secondary at best. Historians have written of Chamberlain's "wholesale removal of corrupt officers" or his replacement of black officials with whites who were "frequently" Democrats.[57] In terms of numbers, these are overstatements. In appointing county treasurers and auditors, the two most sought-after appointed positions, Chamberlain probably removed fewer than one in four of these officials.[58] This percentage was certainly far smaller than the truly wholesale removals that occurred after the Democrats gained control. But it is also likely that Chamberlain made fewer removals in his first year in office than did Moses.[59]

As for the racial component of the argument, it is misleading to state that Chamberlain "removed many black trial justices," because (outside of Charleston County) there were so few black trial justices to begin with.[60] (The same is true for treasurers and auditors, who were also overwhelmingly white.) Chamberlain stated in his inaugural that the law at that time allowed for 347 trial justices in the state, and that the number actually existing was even higher. Meanwhile, Eric Foner in his directory of black officeholders during Reconstruction lists 32 black judges in the state during all of Reconstruction.[61] Foner's list is not complete, but it seems certain that the percentage of trial justices during Reconstruction who were black was less than 5 percent. For example, two black-majority counties, Abbeville and Colleton, each had 1 black trial justice nominated by Governor Scott; neither was retained by Moses. Anderson, a white-majority county, seems never to have had a black trial justice.[62] Considering that each of these counties had 20 or more trial justices at any given time, the overall percentage of Reconstruction-era judges who were black must have been small. The number of these who were removed by Chamberlain would then be exceedingly small. Foner lists only one, Plato C. Fludd of Darlington County.[63]

The effect of the policy Chamberlain followed was not so much to replace black officials with white ones, or to replace Republicans with Democrats, or to replace corruptionists with honest men, so much as it was to replace incompetent white Republicans with competent white Republicans. For any given office, Chamberlain seems to have looked for a competent black Republican first, then a competent white Republican, then an independent or moderate, and only as a last resort a Democrat. Corley, for example, wrote in reference to the removal of Lexington's auditor, "You expressed a desire to appoint a competent colored man in his stead. I then thought that Mr. Jacob Moorer would be competent for the position but from further inquiry, I learn that such is not the case. . . . Therefore a white man must be had . . . unless you import a colored man for the occasion."[64] A Colleton County party leader added to his nomination of a trial justice, "I would myself prefer a Colored Republican if I could find one capable of filling the position But up to date I do not know of any."[65]

On at least one occasion, Chamberlain despaired of finding any suitable candidate. In Lancaster County, a poor and rural county in the upstate, there were few Republicans of either color who met Chamberlain's standards of competence, and few Democrats sufficiently moderate to merit a nomination. When the new governor set about replacing the incompetent auditor, he had difficulty finding a candidate. The solution to the dilemma was suggested by Chamberlain's former law partner, Samuel W. Melton: import a man from Columbia. Charles P. Pelham Jr., wrote Melton, "is quite capable, and is a live, working and earnest young Republican. His family came from Lancaster, and is most respectably and widely connected in the county. . . . There is a lamentable dearth in that county of Republican material to fill the offices; and Mr. Pelham's residence there will give valuable strength to the party organization in Lancaster."[66]

Formerly, the key to appointive office was influence in the local Republican Party. Under Chamberlain, however, the highest priority was competence. This change in priorities infuriated white Radical Republicans no less than it did black Radicals. Elliott S. J. Hayes, the former Lexington boss, wrote to Chamberlain in outrage at his displacement: "As long as I was fought by such men as Simeon Corley and C. E. Leaphart, I felt comfortable, because I had no thought that your Excellency would remove a faithful and capable public servant" for one who joined "his influence with every bolting movement, as has been the case with Mr. Corley. Nor did I fear that you would remove a veteran . . . for a raw recruit who has not yet learned the party drill, as is the case with Leaphart." Hayes demanded a meeting with Chamberlain: "Let me, at least, have an opportunity to show you that I am no Craven, and that this Irish blood in my veins is yet warm, and that if I must die, I will die like a man."[67]

Hayes was far from alone among Republicans frustrated with Chamberlain's appointments. June Mobley, a black Union County Republican boss, wrote that he was "surprised to see you have appointed that man John H. Williams Trial Justice who have been arrested as a KKK and . . . was a bitter Democrat. My Reason for writing to you concerning the matter because I have ben controlling the appointments for this county. . . . You promisted me the Pattonige of this county."[68] The Folgers, a large family of white Republicans who dominated the party in upstate Pickens County, wrote in response to a rumor that a Democrat would be named county census taker: "We respectfully enter this our protest against the same. We who bore the social ostracism of Democrats in 1868 and passed through the days of Ku Klux terrorism . . . think we have a right to be heard." In other words, Chamberlain should take advice from them, "not from those who plotted your assassination in 1868 and 70 and would annihilate your body politic today."[69] J. H. Derham of Horry, a heavily Democratic county, wrote to point out to Chamberlain that "not a Republican holds a position of any kind in this County the writer excepted." He proposed naming as census taker a moderate Republican, one who had held office before the Civil War and who, in 1874, "did not vote our ticket throughout." Even this, Derham suggested, "would cheer up the Republicans of this county" who "think your Excellency has not remembered them sufficiently."[70]

Moderates (such as Derham) found Chamberlain's policy of appointing only competent men unobjectionable. Their complaint was that he too often allowed Democrats to define "competence." (The man Derham suggested for census taker was not appointed; the position instead went to a Democrat.) John R. Cochran succeeded only through strenuous effort in getting the position of Anderson County jury commissioner for Samuel Johnson, a black property owner and advocate of educational causes. In his first letter on the subject, Cochran included Johnson in a list of recommendations, casually remarking, "I am satisfied the appointments will give satisfaction to our party and will not prove objectionable to the opposition." The latter prediction was mistaken. Prominent Anderson Democrats wrote to the governor opposing the choice. "We most positively assure your Excellency that the appointment will not suit the people of our county," insisted one; another added, "Johnston [*sic*] is totally unfit for the position, and his appointment will not be acceptable to our people." Cochran, however, put the matter forcefully, insisting that the only objection to Johnson concerned his race, and that the party could not expect to receive the votes of blacks without recognizing their contributions. In the end, Cochran was victorious: Samuel Johnson was appointed jury commissioner.[71]

On another occasion, a Chamberlain confidant advocated racial inclusiveness in office holding, only to fail. Even before Chamberlain took office, John C. Winsmith, son of the Spartanburg planter who survived being shot seven times by Klansmen, complained to the governor-elect that "in the distribution of offices the claims of the colored people have been most shamefully overlooked here." He strongly advocated the appointment of Joseph M. Young Jr., "a colored man of good education," as county auditor.[72] The attempt failed. Winsmith then attempted to get Young the position of census taker. He failed in that as well, as Chamberlain gave that appointment to a white Republican named P. Orr Miller.[73] Miller was a recent addition to both the Republican Party and Spartanburg County. (He announced his Republicanism at a party rally on July 31, 1874, and had moved from Abbeville just before that.)[74] Spartanburg Republicans who survived the Ku Klux Klan's reign of terror between 1868 and 1871 may be forgiven for begrudging Miller his rapid rise to office. His appointment instead of Young's also prevented what Winsmith called "a just appreciation of the efforts of the colored voters in this County."[75]

The symbolism of Chamberlain's appointments, then, was likely to alienate many black voters—and, in at least a few of the above cases, to alienate county bosses who saw their control over patronage slipping away. Chamberlain cannot be said to have drastically reduced the number of black officeholders or to have appointed an unusual number of Democrats. (Cochran and Winsmith presented the slighting of blacks as a preexisting problem that they hoped Chamberlain would remedy; Derham was pointing to a longstanding dominance of Horry judgeships by the Democrats.)[76] If conventional wisdom holds that Chamberlain replaced blacks with whites in his judicial appointments, then, the numbers do not seem to bear out that view.

But it was symbolism that was important, and there was one high-profile incident that has colored the perception of Chamberlain's administration in this regard; in fact, it may be almost solely responsible for that perception. The incident was a two-part drama over a judicial appointment. The first part was the December 1874 election by the legislature of a circuit judge to fill a vacancy in the first judicial circuit (there were eight circuits in the state). The judge elected in that special election would hold office for a year. The second part of the drama was the election in December 1875 of a judge to fill out the full term. In both cases, Chamberlain sided with the Democrats in the legislature against the majority of Republicans. The first round of the fight confirmed him in Democratic eyes as a reformer; the second round led to the lowest ebb of Republican unity yet seen.

The election was a three-way contest with William J. Whipper as the leading candidate. He was black, and the entire circuit bench was white.[77] He had bolted in 1872 and was an advocate of reform. Nevertheless, he probably engaged in corruption at least to some degree, and Chamberlain was strongly opposed to his election.[78] Elihu Baker, a carpetbagger from Massachusetts, seems not to have enjoyed much support. Chamberlain's candidate, Jacob Pinckney Reed, was a white native from a distinguished Anderson County family who had recently begun to call himself a Republican.

Although the decision belonged to the legislature, Chamberlain took the irregular step of attending the debate and offering his views of the candidates (expressed as those of "a simple member of the Republican party," not the official views of the governor). He endorsed Reed, saying of Whipper that "in point of ability and legal learning he was not equal to the position." He went on to charge that Whipper's connection with the sinking fund "required explanation." Yet this point appears to have been secondary in Chamberlain's mind to the questions about Whipper's ability. It was, however, the implication of corruption that set off an uproar, and the question has often been portrayed by historians as one of honesty versus corruption. The meeting broke up without a vote, but when the legislators reconvened, they chose Reed by a margin of 103 to 40. Almost all observers gave Chamberlain credit for defeating Whipper. A more important factor may have been the legislators' willingness to defer to the delegation from Charleston, who voted unanimously for Reed and whom Reed would in fact be serving. Henry J. Maxwell, a black senator from Marlboro, for example, stated during the debate that "he was not in favor of making any nomination or supporting any on the question of color" and that "he wished the Charleston delegation to make their own nomination."[79]

Nevertheless, Chamberlain received the credit from the press for defeating Whipper. The Republican *Daily Union-Herald* called the vote "a general endorsement of the administration." The Democratic *News and Courier* asserted that "there is not an honest man in South Carolina who has not a higher opinion of Governor Chamberlain than he had a week ago."[80] But the vote predicted a split in the Republican Party that would widen over the next year. Democrats and white Republicans had voted overwhelmingly for Reed, whereas black Republicans had voted two to one for Whipper.

An even worse portent for Republican prospects was an armed confrontation in Edgefield County. This military engagement, often referred to as the "Ned Tennant riot," began when an extralegal white militia in that county (calling themselves a "rifle club") sought to arrest Ned Tennant, a leader of the all-black local militia, for arson.[81] Tennant called out the militia, and Matthew C. Butler, one of the leading Democrats, called out his vigilantes, numbering in the hundreds. Tennant somehow managed to escape, leading his men unharmed to the commander of the Edgefield militia, Lawrence Cain, to whom Tennant surrendered his company's weapons.[82]

Chamberlain sought an explanation of these events, the latest in a series of disturbing incidents in Edgefield in the past year. He received two reports on which he based his response. One report was from Thomas J. Mackey, a white Republican judge who had thrown himself wholeheartedly into the cause of reform, even to the extent of participating in a brawl with allegedly corrupt legislators during the 1874 campaign. The other was written by Col. Theodore Parmele, a U.S. officer. Both reports were remarkable for refusing to place blame on white vigilantes. Parmele offered a balanced account of the situation in Edgefield that claimed most of the county's citizens were peaceful and industrious but that among the blacks there were "some who do not wish to labor and are known as habitual thieves" and among the whites there was "a class of young men who hold life at little value, being as reckless in risking their own, as they are heartless in taking the lives of others."[83] In other words, the colonel blamed, seemingly in equal proportions, blacks who stole and whites who murdered.

Mackey's analysis placed the blame even more squarely on Republicans. He "reported that the county authorities had been guilty of gross abuses and exactions which the people resisted, and, further, that the difficulties were aggravated by the lawless behavior of the colored militia." He advised Chamberlain to disarm the Edgefield militia, which the governor did. This action was popular with not only the local Democratic press but also the national Republican press.[84] It was another public relations victory for Chamberlain, but it created even more concern within his party than his previous gestures toward moderation. More significantly, it signaled to rifle clubs in Edgefield and elsewhere that the governor had no good options for dealing with them.

The two gravest dangers for Republicans since the start of Reconstruction in the state were factionalism and Democratic violence. The former had come close to costing the Republicans control of the state through legal means, and the latter had cost Republicans control in other states through illegal means. But the key point was that Republicans had no margin for error. If they lost control once, they were not likely to regain it. Despite Chamberlain's dream of a "day which finds all our people so united in their regard for the public weal that the advent to power of any political party shall not endanger the liberties or the material interests of any class of our fellow-citizens," that day was not near at hand.[85]

The rest of 1875 and early 1876 saw the rift between Chamberlain and some Republicans widen while moderate Democrats became outright supporters of the governor. Robert Brown Elliott, who according to observers at the time and modern historians led the anti-Chamberlain group, made his move in March 1875. As Speaker of the state house of representatives, Elliott engineered the introduction of resolutions demanding that Chamberlain remove from office the mulatto state treasurer, Francis L. Cardozo, an ally of Chamberlain in his attempts at retrenchment. If successful, the resolutions would have put the governor in a difficult spot: he would have to fire an ally or appear to be protecting a corruptionist.[86]

If this was in fact the idea, Elliott underestimated how much progress the governor had made in winning over leading Democrats. Chamberlain took the bait, supporting Cardozo very strongly. He used the *Union-Herald,* the Republican daily in which he owned an interest, in Cardozo's defense, and he supported his ally in an extensive interview with the Democratic *Charleston News and Courier.* But instead of announcing its disillusionment with Chamberlain, the Democratic paper endorsed his position. In an editorial following the interview, the paper reserved judgment on Cardozo's case but gave "great weight" to the governor's defense of him: "We are profoundly impressed, we frankly admit, by Governor Chamberlain's words." Chamberlain was competent ("ranks with the first of the foremost lawyers in the state") and honest ("has stood like a wall of adamant between the public robbers and the honest and law-abiding people of the state"). In sum, the editorial concluded that those opposing Cardozo only did so "because he has been faithful and capable, and has jealously guarded the treasury."[87] Instead of turning on Chamberlain for his defense of Cardozo, the leading Democratic paper in the state defended Cardozo because of his association with Chamberlain! Elliott must have been in disbelief. With the support of the national press and South Carolina Democrats, Chamberlain was able to convince enough Republicans in the legislature to vote against the resolutions that they were defeated.[88]

The explanation for the *News and Courier*'s stand was simple: Chamberlain's plan to create a coalition with moderate Democrats was working. By this time Chamberlain had developed a friendship with Francis Warrington Dawson, editor of the Democratic paper, who wrote favorably of him and saw to it he was invited to elite social events.[89] Nor was Dawson alone in his newfound appreciation for Chamberlain. A. P. Aldrich, one of the staunchest opponents of change in the 1865 convention, now advocated standing by a Republican governor. He quoted favorably a Republican's assessment that if anything, the governor "was going too fast" and risked alienating his own party.[90]

Chamberlain was clearly delighted with this development and found it a challenge to live up to his own advice to Dawson: "We must not be *too* good friends."[91] He lent his support to Dawson when the latter was indicted for criminal libel; Chamberlain secured the extradition of an important witness from Georgia, and the resulting mistrial saved Dawson the loss of reputation, not to mention money.[92] Less concrete, but more public, evidence of Chamberlain's flirtation with the Democrats came from his ingratiating letters to various elite organizations when he was invited to attend their meetings.[93]

Although the prospect of an alliance between Chamberlain and the Democrats was of great concern to many Republicans, the party at last had a leader who could command some respect in white society and in the country at large. Chamberlain also divided Republicans by his policies. His messages had laid out a series of reforms, among them election of county treasurers, auditors, and trial justices; reduction of services provided by the state mental hospital; and institution of a convict-lease system.[94] The legislature rejected all these changes, but a minority of Republicans sided with the governor on each. White Republicans in particular were often divided on such issues. Conservative Republicans such as Stephen D. Russell of Charleston usually voted with the Democrats, but white liberals such as Melvin J. Hirsch of Williamsburg usually voted with the majority. Most resembled Lemuel Guffin of Abbeville or Joel Copes of Fairfield, who often voted conservatively when party was not made an issue (as on a bill to enact a fence law) but toed the party line when it was squarely made the issue.[95]

Precisely such a case—when party was made squarely the issue—provided the occasion for Chamberlain's break with his party. In December 1875, when the governor was away from the capital to award prizes to successful students of classical Greek, Elliott, as Speaker of the House, took up the issue of judicial elections. Apparently having arranged a vote ahead of time, he took the opportunity to ensure the election of Whipper to replace Reed as judge of the first circuit and of former governor Moses to replace the Democrat Shaw in the third. In the former case, Elliott announced that he would measure the Republicanism of each and every member by whether or not he voted for Whipper.[96] Most Republicans, including most white Republicans, followed their party. In the House, only three of twenty white Republicans opposed Whipper; in the Senate, three of eight opposed him.[97]

The results of the elections were the victories of Republicans in each circuit, including Whipper, Moses, and P. L. Wiggins, who ousted the Democratic judge of the second circuit. The reaction of the Democratic press was one of outrage, and Chamberlain himself was apoplectic. The *News and Courier* said of the legislative majority, "Their plan is to Africanize the state and to put the white man under the splay foot of the negro and hold him there." Of the judges, Chamberlain added, "I look upon their election as a horrible disaster." Asked to predict the consequences of the events, he responded, "One immediate effect will obviously be the reorganization of the Democratic party within the State, as the only means left, in the judgment of its members, for opposing a solid and reliable front to this terrible crevasse of misgovernment and public debauchery."[98]

It is interesting to note that the strongest outrage was focused on the election not of Moses, who was easily the least honest of the three, nor on Wiggins, who had replaced a more competent man and a Democrat to boot, but on Whipper. It is difficult to resist the judgment made by Elliott that the main objection to Whipper was racial. As Elliott's biographer puts it, from the Democratic point of view, "the judge who sat on the First Circuit would exercise dominance over the Broad Street clique. For an office of such significance and power to fall to a black was insupportable."[99] The day of the elections was thenceforth known as "Black Thursday," and the pun cannot have been unintentional. Chamberlain spoke, more mutedly, in a similar way. He declined an invitation to attend the annual meeting of the New England Society of Charleston, warning, "*The civilization of the Puritan and the Cavalier, of the Roundhead and the Huguenot, is in peril.*"[100]

The moderate governor followed up extreme words with extreme actions. He refused to sign the commissions of Whipper and Moses, even though his position did not entitle him to veto the actions of the legislature in the matter at hand. (His excuse—that the incumbents' terms were not yet up—did not prevent him from signing the commissions of the other six judges.) The Democratic press called his action what it was, a coup d'état, and lavished praise on him for it.[101]

Chamberlain's feverish reaction to the judicial election and his extraordinary actions in response might be contrasted with his response to an incident three months previous. Joseph Crews, member of the South Carolina General Assembly from Laurens and generally thought of as the boss of the Republican Party in that county, was gunned down by assassins on September 7, 1875. Recalled one Democratic leader, "It was understood that they intended to put an end to his leadership."[102] A reward was offered for the murderers, a halfhearted case was assembled and dismissed, and Crews's seat was left open for the remainder of the term.[103] If Chamberlain ever made mention of the incident in public, the speech has not survived.

In the wake of the judicial elections, Chamberlain's standing among moderate whites was higher than ever; on the other hand, his prediction of the reorganization of the Democratic Party proved accurate, and hard-line Republicans seemed to have become unalterably opposed to his leadership. The strategy of moderation Chamberlain had undertaken was becoming more challenging. What he probably envisioned was a struggle for supremacy over the Republican Party between himself and hard-liners such as Elliott in which Democrats would hold the balance of power. Such a scenario had been widely employed in county elections in 1874. In Richland County, for example, there had been a struggle between two black leaders, W. B. Nash and Charles Minort, which Nash had won by offering a legislative seat and the office of probate judge to the Democrats in exchange for their support.[104]

Chamberlain, through the *Union-Herald,* had approved this practice during the campaign; in fact, he may even have instigated it. The paper announced the Republican nominees from Richland, all African Americans, then editorialized, "It is time to have at least one white man in the Legislature from this county."[105] By November, the ticket included John T. Sloan Jr., a Democrat from Columbia. Other counties elected mixed delegations in 1874 as well; black-majority counties such as Colleton, Marlboro, Union, and York sent one or two Democrats to the legislature. In Charleston and Marion, Republican bolters combined with Democrats to beat regular Republicans and then divided legislative seats evenly.[106]

The concept, of course, was not new. In the early days of Reconstruction, some counties had put together compromise, or "general consent," tickets. At that time, however, extremists were able, in short order, to defeat the plan by forcing a confrontation. Moderates—those nominated by "general consent"—were then forced to take sides. Those who remained in office became Republicans; those unwilling to do so resigned and joined the Democratic opposition. Notwithstanding the failure of previous efforts at compromise, it seems that such a combination ticket was what Chamberlain had in mind for 1876. In his prediction of the revitalization of the Democrats in the wake of Black Thursday, he expressed the hope that they would not "find it impossible, because they are organized as Democrats, to give their help to whomsoever shall be best able to undo the wrongs of last Thursday."[107]

He seems even to have looked for the institutionalization of such a moderate course—not through a third party but through the mechanism of minority representation. This idea had been proposed by the Taxpayers' Convention in 1871 and roundly ignored by most Republicans. Several possibilities had been discussed, including proportional representation and cumulative voting (whereby each voter would have as many votes as there were positions to be filled; he could then vote a full slate, give all his votes to one candidate, or otherwise disperse his votes). Republicans, of course, had seen no need to dilute their voting strength through such measures. Chamberlain, however, endorsed the idea and recommended that the legislature pass a bill proposed by Senator Cochran to begin implementing it on a small scale.[108] Cochran was perhaps a model for Chamberlain. He was, after all, a Republican who consistently won reelection to the legislature from a white-majority county, largely because white residents of Anderson tended toward independent politics and respected Cochran's service to the community.[109]

As naive as such hopes appear in retrospect, events in early 1876 seemed favorable to Chamberlain's plans. If Republicans were divided on whether to support Chamberlain, so were Democrats. Furthermore, Democrats could be divided by personal rivalries (and the desire for position) as well as Republicans could. In Democratic Lexington, for example, state senator John C. Hope discovered in March 1876 that "our members in the House are forming combinations to put me out, and make room for themselves." His response was to form a combination of his own—with Republican county auditor C. E. Leaphart. He planned to secure the support of all the county's Republicans for a ticket composed mostly of moderate Democrats.[110]

The cooperationist leanings of Senator Hope and editor Dawson were one possible response to the deep division in the Republican Party; they hoped to continue to chip away at the Republican majority in the legislature through the use of "common consent" slates of candidates that included both Democrats and Republicans in the various counties. But they were also engaged in a power struggle with hard-liners in their own party, who took a different view of the Whipper-Moses affair. In their view, that incident proved not only that Republicans were unrepentant, not only that reform had been a sham. What it really proved was that most whites in the state were more receptive to a message of outrage than they were to a message of moderation, conservatism, and precise accuracy in distinguishing good Radicals from bad Radicals.

The hard-liners' belief that a Straight-Out Democratic ticket would draw white voters to the polls better than a fusion ticket was, for them, the key to the entire issue.[111] It is important to keep in mind the stakes involved in national elections during the Civil War and Reconstruction era. There was perhaps a greater difference between the two national parties in those years than ever before or since. A Democratic victory in the presidential election of 1860 would likely have produced no Civil War, and a Democratic victory in 1864 would probably have ended the war with the Confederacy an independent nation. After the war, the stakes were still high. A Democratic president, Andrew Johnson, had done all he could to limit the scope of Reconstruction. He had failed, but only because the Republicans had a large enough majority in Congress to override his vetoes. Now, with Congress in Democratic hands, a victory in the presidential election of 1876 would instantly end Reconstruction. The way events actually transpired has obscured the fact that in 1876 it was universally assumed that a Republican president would continue Reconstruction, whereas a Democrat would end it. Thus for both parties the presidential election was all-important.

Cooperationist and Straight-Out Democrats debated each other through half the year; at that point, one event turned the tide. Just as violence had precluded moderation and bipartisanship in the early days of Reconstruction, so the

Hamburg massacre foiled Chamberlain's best efforts and ultimately brought down Reconstruction itself. The events in Hamburg, a heavily black town in Aiken County next door to Edgefield, began with a July 4 parade through town by the county's company of the state militia. Two white men evidently felt aggrieved by their celebration—July 4 was a holiday celebrated by very few white southerners —and they tried to ride a buggy through the militia's lines. After a standoff, the militia allowed the men through, but they swore out a complaint against the militia leader anyway for blocking the road. He countersued them for disrupting his drill. Four days later, the court date would provide the pretext for a military confrontation.[112]

Stephen Kantrowitz's biography of Benjamin Ryan Tillman demonstrates that the events of July 8 and 9 did not happen by chance; people such as Tillman made them happen. As the future statesman himself later wrote, the leading citizens of Edgefield were determined "to provoke a riot" in which the whites could "demonstrate their superiority" over black men "by killing as many of them as was justifiable."[113] When the two white men arrived in Hamburg, they were at the head of several dozen members of white rifle clubs. The black militiamen barricaded themselves in an upstairs room; a siege followed, with some of the whites sending for reinforcements from Georgia. At some point the whites began firing. When a white man was killed by return fire, the rifle clubs brought out artillery and demolished the militiamen's refuge. As they ran, at least one was killed by the rifle clubs' gunfire and many were captured. The captives were held for several hours before the whites began to choose captives, one at a time, to be shot through the head in cold blood. After five such murders, the remaining captives were turned loose, although one was shot down as he fled. As for the rifle club men, Tillman later remembered, "We were all tired but more than satisfied with the result."[114]

The result was to define politics in such a way that bipartisanship was impossible. Although respectable Democratic opinion did not condone the Hamburg massacre, it did hold that the killings were the work of a few lawless men who in no way represented most white citizens. More important, Democratic opinion held that Chamberlain should not seek federal aid in bringing the perpetrators to justice. The *News and Courier* summarized, "We have supported Governor Chamberlain's reform measures, and we have frankly expressed our opinions of the Hamburg riot, but we must protest against any move that wears the appearance of taking advantage of a local disturbance to prop up the waning fortunes of South Carolina Republicanism."[115]

On the one hand, Chamberlain's call for the federal government to "exert itself vigorously to repress violence in this State during the present political campaign" drew the ire of Democrats, giving Straight-Outs an advantage over Cooperationists that they never relinquished. On the other hand, Chamberlain's pleas to President Grant went largely unheeded. All that was left for the governor to do, then, was to fulminate impotently against the perpetrators. The message to the Democrats was clear. Chamberlain, like Scott and Moses, was willing to prop up his government with federal bayonets. Unlike them, however, he had few of those bayonets at his disposal.[116]

Cooperationism as a policy option was dead. The Democrats would nominate a full ticket and would not seek compromises with any Republican faction. In terms of votes, this was poor strategy, as simple arithmetic showed that the Democrats could not hope to win anything like a fair fight. But votes were only incidental to Democratic plans. While the patrician Wade Hampton III appealed for black support, men such as M. C. Butler and Ben Tillman organized the state's rifle and saber clubs into a coordinated organization, known by their uniforms as the Red Shirts, in order to win the election by any means necessary.

Part of this strategy relied on direct force (as well as fraud) at the polls on election day, but Democratic efforts began well before then. As they had in 1868, they tried to apply economic pressure to prevent blacks from voting. The Democrats' unofficial "Plan of the Campaign" required that every Democrat "feel honor bound to control the vote of at least one negro" in any manner he chose. Specific efforts were made to prevent whites from voting Republican as well. Every attempt was made to convince or coerce white Republicans to "cross Jordan," as it was called when one joined the Democrats. Democrats put scalawags on notice that they would be held responsible for any outrages committed by blacks. Social ostracism was also to be employed. Former governor B. F. Perry, for example, urged his followers to "stop all social intercourse with any man who is base enough to be a radical."[117] Abbeville County leader and white Republican J. R. Tolbert later told investigators that although he had previously been popular with Democrats, once the campaign began, "men who used to be friendly with me in church, and in business, and in the office, and all that sort of thing, now refuse to speak to me when I would hold out my hand and greet them."[118]

Ostracism was far from the worst that Republicans suffered. The most prevalent Democratic tactic was that of "division of time," whereby Democrats with guns would appear at Republican rallies in overwhelming numbers; they would then demand the opportunity to respond to Republican speakers. In truth, Republican speakers rarely had the chance to speak at all before Democrats drowned them out with charges of lying. Often shots were fired or brawls broke out. Eventually, according to Chamberlain, "you could not get quiet, peaceable Republicans to come out and expose themselves to such treatment."[119]

Although in some counties Democrats contented themselves with breaking up Republican gatherings, Democrats in other counties did much more. In at least some parts of the state, Republicans in 1876 operated under conditions they had not seen since 1871, if ever. A group of black residents of Laurens County drew the distinction explicitly: "Laurens of '76 is not Laurens of '72. No sir; it is not; for then a black man, and the poor white man not excepted, could dare to say who he would cast his ticket for without being starved, whipped, or shot to death." They were writing to Chamberlain to ask his protection from "men in the democratic party, who are bent upon coercing us against our wishes to vote with them to our detriment."[120]

A few days later, the mayor of Hamburg, where the July riot and massacre had occurred, wrote to the governor declaring his "inability to protect the lives and property of the citizens" from "the lawlessness existing daily in this town and its vicinity." From Blackville came reports that Democrats "have killed colored men in seven precincts. . . . The whites are telling the colored men that you [Chamberlain] can't protect them, and that they will [protect them], if they join their [Democratic] clubs." In Union County, the site of numerous political murders during the Klan's reign of terror, Republicans informed the governor that local Democrats had agreed that "guns should be carried and secreted at the polls on the night before the election, and if the negroes would not vote with them, or they lost the election, to make a promiscuous slaughter."[121]

The worst instance of violence took place in the swamps near Ellenton in Aiken County (the same county in which the Hamburg massacre occurred). There a contingent of at least three hundred, and possibly over a thousand, Red Shirts attacked a black militia unit of one hundred men. Casualties included three whites and at least thirty blacks, including at least one prisoner—Republican state senator Simon Coker—who was murdered in cold blood. Further slaughter was prevented only by the arrival of federal cavalry. A federal officer reported hearing a Red Shirt mutter that he would have "given five hundred dollars if we had been an hour late."[122]

Such a climate is the necessary context for understanding the defection of white Republicans to Hampton. Historical legend holds that white Republicans flocked to Hampton's banner. In fact, reports of scalawag desertion were highly exaggerated when applied to leaders of the party. Among rank-and-file white Republicans, who had less of a stake in the party's success and were more vulnerable to Democratic threats, the desertion rate was much higher. Even here, though, the key point is that it was Democratic violence (and the lack of any impressive counter to it) that persuaded white Republicans to "cross Jordan."

Democratic propaganda sought to portray a mass exodus of whites from the Republican Party during the campaign. The *News and Courier* began periodically displaying the "Roll of Honor," a list of prominent white Republicans who intended to vote for Hampton. In fact, several of these men were not prominent, or not white, or not Republican.[123] Apparently the roll did not impress, and it was discontinued in favor of periodic items naming converts to the Democrats.[124] Most leading scalawags, however, held firm. Congressman Alexander Stuart Wallace vowed to speak in rural Lancaster even "if he dies in the attempt"; he made the speech and lived to tell about it.[125] J. F. G. Mittag of Lancaster, even though he had called his black neighbors "an ungrateful class of people," remained a Republican.[126]

Democrats were more successful in deterring rank-and-file Republicans from staying in the party. A report from upcountry Pickens County on October 10 claimed that of that county's three hundred scalawags, only twenty remained Republicans.[127] Another dispatch cited unnamed Lancaster scalawags who intended to give up the fight.[128] Anderson County Republicans did not even field a full ticket, and it was alleged that John Cochran was the only white man left in the party.[129] The real proof of Democratic efforts, of course, was the actual vote on November 7.

On election day, Democrats engaged in a wide array of frauds in addition to the usual threats of violence. Some of these frauds included distributing false ballots, stuffing ballot boxes, importing voters from neighboring states, and repeat voting.[130] Violence prevented many Republicans from voting in Abbeville, Edgefield, and Barnwell Counties. Usually the Democrats' overwhelming superiority in firepower prevented outright conflict (because Republicans ceded the field), but the day after election day there was serious violence in Charleston, where a riot cost two whites and one black their lives.[131]

These differences among counties led to differences in Republican voting among counties as well. Some counties that had produced reliable Republican majorities went Democratic in 1876, whereas others produced higher Republican majorities than ever before. What was true for Republicans in general was true for white Republicans in particular. In Darlington County, for example, carpetbagger B. F. Whittemore reported that whereas in previous elections between two and three hundred white residents voted Republican, in 1876 he did "not suppose there were over twenty white Republicans." On the other hand, in white-majority Lexington and Chesterfield, where the election was carried off peacefully, Republicans polled more votes than they ever had before.[132] Finally, in Charleston, where Republican numbers could hold their own against the Democrats' firepower, there may have been as many as one thousand white Republican votes for Chamberlain.[133]

Too much should not be made of the election returns, as fraud was rampant. In Edgefield, for example, returns showed more votes than eligible voters.[134] The result of the massive Democratic effort was an extremely close election, at least as measured by the official returns. The Republican-dominated State Board of Canvassers determined that on the face of the returns, Hampton had received 92,261 votes to Chamberlain's 91,127. Republicans immediately challenged the returns, and Democrats challenged the board's authority to do anything more than count votes. After taking almost ten days, the legal limit before it would cease to have any official existence, the board announced that fraud was so massive in Edgefield and Laurens that their returns should be excluded entirely. If those counties were excluded, Chamberlain would win by a count of 86,216 to 83,078.

Laurens County no doubt saw massive fraud. A U.S. Senate committee reprinted seventeen pages of affidavits testifying that Republicans were intimidated into voting the Democratic ticket or not at all, that Democrats voted multiple times, that Democrats from other counties or even states voted, and that the county election commissioners signed the returns only under duress.[135] Nevertheless, the Laurens returns at least added up to the correct sum; in Edgefield, 8,081 voters cast 9,374 votes.[136] Unlike an excess over the census figures, which could be explained by a great increase in Edgefield's population between 1875 and 1876, this discrepancy in the counting of votes was irrefutable proof of a badly flawed election—with no need of an investigating committee. Furthermore, throwing out the Edgefield returns alone would have given Chamberlain the victory. Why, then, did the Republican board make the issue more complicated by including Laurens County? Why not ask simply for Edgefield's obviously fictitious returns to be thrown out?

The answer is that although excluding only Edgefield's vote would give Chamberlain the victory, that decision was not the board's to make. The state constitution provided that disputed elections be settled by the board—except elections for governor and lieutenant governor, which would be settled by the state house of representatives. And there, Democrats on the face of the returns held a six-seat edge, a majority that would not be eliminated with the exclusion of Edgefield alone but would be overcome if representatives from Edgefield and Laurens were excluded.[137]

The evidence that the board's motive in including Laurens was political—to ensure the victory of Republican candidates—is circumstantial but compelling. They could hardly fail to know what body would determine the next governor, considering the publicity given to the process in the state press and indeed the national press. Furthermore, it would clearly have been easier and less controversial to eliminate only the counties where fraud was obvious from the numbers themselves and did not require proof; but this would have eliminated only Edgefield and Williamsburg Counties, the latter of which sent *Republicans* to the assembly. Given the ubiquity of fraud, the board might have considered invalidating the entire South Carolina election, but this would have given the presidency to the Democrat Tilden. Hayes, the Republican, needed South Carolina's electoral votes, which on the face of the returns he won, in order to be elected. A final piece of circumstantial evidence is that the members of the board were in no way indifferent to the result. Three of the five members—Secretary of State Henry Hayne, Treasurer Francis L. Cardozo, and Comptroller Thomas C. Dunn—were themselves candidates for reelection. The board thus needed to throw out the votes of a second county, and they chose Laurens over the other counties where protests arose—for example, Barnwell and Abbeville—because it was the one where Democratic intimidation had the most obvious effects. In Laurens over one thousand blacks failed to vote Republican, the most of any county.[138]

Democrats, of course, were furious and demanded that the South Carolina Supreme Court countermand the board's decision. The court issued certificates of election to the Edgefield and Laurens representatives, but they arrived at the first session of the legislature to find the U.S. Army inside the state capitol, refusing entry to anyone not possessing a certificate signed by the board. This coup had been achieved by Chamberlain, who had taken advantage of the chaotic situation to effectively assert control over federal troops. Once the situation became known, higher military authorities demanded that the troops leave the capitol and resume their original function of preventing violence. The Republicans had already organized by electing E. W. M. Mackey as Speaker. Outraged Democrats, in order to prevent a quorum, walked out and organized their own legislature, with W. H. Wallace as Speaker, in a nearby building.[139]

Democrats quickly thought of a better plan. Those Democrats possessing certificates from the board reentered the capitol, en masse, with the Laurens and Edgefield Democrats in their midst. In the crush of humanity, Republicans could not separately exclude the disputed delegates, and they were able to push their way in. The "Mackey House" and "Wallace House," as they became known, now existed simultaneously in the same hall, each trying to conduct business over the din of the other. Chamberlain wanted the contested delegates removed, and Democrats reluctantly complied. (Chamberlain was still unquestionably the governor, and to resist his order might bring the federal troops back into play.) However, not merely the contested delegates but all Democrats again walked out and reorganized in the building they had occupied before.[140]

With the Democrats gone, the Mackey House judged the election to have been won by Chamberlain. He was duly inaugurated, his second term beginning on December 7, 1876. For their part, the Democrats in the Wallace House judged Hampton the victor, and he was inaugurated as governor on December 14. Each man attempted to exercise the powers of the office for the next several months. Hampton possessed several distinct advantages. First, he was recognized as the legitimate governor by the state supreme court. That body was not admitted by Chamberlain or the federal government to have the power to make that decision; nevertheless, the court's support proved useful to Hampton. Prisoners he pardoned were set free; prisoners Chamberlain pardoned were not. This at least gave Hampton a claim on the de facto governorship of the state.

Second, the same court prohibited the banks where state funds were deposited from making payments to support Chamberlain's government. Hampton could not get at these funds either—he was prevented by the Republican state senate—but he could ask his supporters to pay a "voluntary tax," and they willingly complied. The wealth of South Carolina's Democrats thus provided Hampton another advantage. Finally, Hampton commanded thousands of Red Shirts, several hundred of whom could appear at Columbia in a few hours' time in case of trouble.[141]

Against all this, Chamberlain's only support was the federal garrison that defended his government. It thus became a matter of great moment in late February 1877 how President Rutherford Hayes, recently awarded his own disputed election, would react to the situation in the South. Hayes summoned both Chamberlain and Hampton to Washington for interviews, and on April 3 he announced his decision: the troops would cease their defense of Chamberlain's authority a week later. When the troops left, Chamberlain yielded to the inevitable and resigned his office in an angry farewell address to his supporters: "To-day—April 10, 1877—by the order of the President whom your votes alone rescued from overwhelming defeat, the Government of the United States abandons you, deliberately withdraws from you its support, with the full knowledge that the lawful government of the State will be speedily overthrown."[142] Reconstruction in South Carolina was at an end.

# Epilogue *White Republicans after Reconstruction*

After Reconstruction the Republican Party faded into irrelevance with astonishing rapidity. Democrats ousted most Republican officeholders except those from overwhelmingly black lowcountry counties. The Republican Party did not field a statewide ticket in 1878 or, indeed, until 1884—and even in that year only one candidate, D. A. Straker, the black nominee for lieutenant governor, actually remained in the race until election day. The state party existed solely for federal patronage, and it had no effect on statewide politics for almost a century after the end of Reconstruction. It has been argued that the party had an indirect effect on the state's politics in that it forced whites to unite in the Democratic Party, thereby stifling reform movements such as the Greenbackers and the Populists. But in reality, it was the continuing presence of a numerically superior black population that created white one-party orthodoxy; this would have been the case even if the Republican Party ceased to exist.[1]

Yet although the Republicans did not factor in state politics for ninety years after Reconstruction, it is not true that the party vanished. It continued to send delegates to the National Republican Convention well into the twentieth century, and individual Republicans continued to receive patronage benefits. A few even held local or county office, usually on "common consent" tickets. White Republicans reacted to such dramatically changed circumstances in different ways. Some continued to be active in party politics; some ceased to be active in politics at all; some became Democrats.

Historian Joel Williamson's contention that "most scalawags simply disappeared from public life"[2] is true enough if "public life" means office; few Republicans of either race held office after Reconstruction ended. But if it means participation in the political process, the truth of the assertion is unclear. Many scalawags continued to affiliate with the Republican Party. One of the most impressive examples of persistent Republicanism is that of John R. Cochran of Anderson County. After the Democrats took control of the state legislature in 1877, they appointed the investigating committee that produced the Fraud Report, an enormous compendium of Republican crimes. Cochran chaired this committee, causing one historian to label him "the tool of the Redeemers."[3] Whatever his motives were in 1877–78, however, Cochran remained a Republican to the end of his life in 1923. He served as a delegate to the National Republican Convention in 1892, and in 1909 he traveled to Augusta, Georgia, to meet President-elect Taft.[4] Even more remarkable, his Republicanism passed to the next generation in his son Ernest Ford Cochran. The latter, who became a federal judge and a pillar of the Anderson community, did so despite his "staunch and sustained" Republicanism. (He was a delegate to the 1900, 1904, and 1916 national conventions.) Historian David Duncan Wallace, writing in 1934, explains that Cochran "is an outstanding Republican, but has not made his partisanship of an offensive character."[5]

It is important to note, however, that the most elevated positions that the younger Cochran occupied were federal positions: U.S. attorney, U.S. commissioner, and U.S. district judge. He no doubt received the esteem of his community —he also served as city attorney in Anderson from 1898 to 1900, was a member of fraternal and church organizations, and was an active and prominent member of the local bar—but state office was not a possibility for a Republican.[6]

This pattern of local acceptance and possible federal office, but no possibility of state office, was typical for white Republicans after Reconstruction. Thomas J. Coghlan, the Sumter blacksmith and mill owner who proposed criminalizing the use of racial epithets, continued to represent Sumter in state Republican conventions after Reconstruction ended. He was not ostracized for this, but the only office he held afterward was that of federal census taker in 1880.[7] James Earl Hagood, a Republican from a prominent Pickens County family, served after Reconstruction as clerk of U.S. circuit court, U.S. commissioner, and special master in U.S. circuit court.[8] Robert M. Wallace, son of Congressman Alexander Stuart Wallace, held a variety of federal positions as well as enjoying business ties with South Carolina's elite Democrats, but as an active Republican he never ran for elective office.[9]

Georgetown and Beaufort Republicans continued to enjoy a share of county offices for two decades after Reconstruction's end, usually on common consent tickets. This arrangement was designed to provide some representation for black residents in these overwhelmingly black counties. White Republicans, however, rarely won election under this office-sharing system. In Georgetown County, for example, R. O. Bush was the only white Republican to hold an office after Reconstruction. (He served as probate judge until replaced by a black candidate in 1894.)[10]

Although black Republicans enjoyed a distinct advantage over scalawags in compromise ticket nominations, white Republicans won most of the higher offices within the appointment of Republican presidents. The position of U.S. district attorney for South Carolina, for example, was always held by a white man after Reconstruction—first Lucius C. Northrup, a carpetbagger whose selection and performance came in for criticism, then Samuel W. Melton, a native whose work was praised by South Carolina Republicans and by his superiors in Washington.[11]

E. A. Webster of Orangeburg, a carpetbagger who remained a Republican and in fact chaired the state party's executive committee in 1892, served after 1889 as U.S. collector of internal revenue. He also attended the national conference of the Methodist Church in a leadership role. Despite earning the "respect and good will of his [political] opponents," however, opponents they remained, and Webster was never elected to any office.[12] Friends and neighbors could forgive Republicanism in an otherwise good and public-spirited man; they would not, however, elect a Republican.

The fate of those white Republicans who had "crossed Jordan" in 1876 was somewhat different. Williamson writes that "those men like T. J. Mackey and T. J. Robertson who were allowed to come back into the conservative fold soon found themselves laboring under informal but inflexible political disabilities."[13] In fact, this was not always the case. Mackey and Robertson are not really appropriate case studies; Mackey, after continuing to serve as a state circuit judge until 1882, moved to Washington, whereas Robertson was by 1876 already in poor enough health that his retirement from public life should not be seen as the result of Democratic ostracism.[14]

Other white Republicans who declared for the Democrats provide clearer examples. R. J. Donaldson, a Chesterfield Republican who "changed his political allegiance in 1876," went on to serve as a state Democratic executive committeeman, among other lesser offices.[15] Elliott S. J. Hayes, rival of Simeon Corley for control of the Lexington County Republican Party, supported Hampton in 1876 and was appointed commissioner of elections for Lexington in 1880.[16] James M. Smith, Republican of Barnwell, became actively involved in Democratic politics beginning early in 1876. Having moved to Columbia, he ran for alderman in that city in 1888 as a Democrat. Other Democrats, "unhappy over his Republican past," ran a candidate against Smith. He won, though, and he later held other offices as well.[17]

Persecution against persistent Republicans seems to have been slight, except for those who continued to campaign. Carlos Stolbrand, for example, was an immigrant from Sweden who affiliated with the Republican Party during Reconstruction and after. According to the memoirs of Edwin McCravy, a Democratic politician and Red Shirt, Stolbrand was campaigning in 1880, "the last bold stand made by the 'Carpet Baggers,'" when he was set upon by a group of armed, mounted Red Shirts. These men violently pushed their way through the crowd—some "negroes undertook to resist, but their heads were promptly cracked and they were soon subdued"—and seized Stolbrand. At that moment, according to McCravy, Stolbrand made some sort of masonic gesture, after which two Democrats told the Red Shirts that if they released him, Stolbrand would leave the state and never return. Both ends of the bargain were upheld.[18] Less fortunate was Pembroke Guffin, one of a family of white Republicans in Abbeville County. In a case that drew national attention, former sheriff Guffin, running for election to his former office, was assassinated in a billiard hall on September 27, 1880. The perpetrators were acquitted by a Democratic jury.[19]

It was undoubtedly this kind of treatment that South Carolina Republicans sought to avoid by declining to campaign in most post-Reconstruction elections. In 1880 tried-and-true white Republicans counseled against running a statewide ticket. Among them were men whose courage was not to be doubted: Simeon Corley, who publicly advocated abolition of slavery before the Civil War, and John Winsmith, who at age sixty-eight entered a gunfight with Klansmen and received seven bullet wounds as a result. Nevertheless these men and the party in general declined to make the campaign. The party's strategy, best articulated by Robert Brown Elliott, was to "attack the enemy in detail," that is, focus on local offices. The reasons for this plan seem to have been threefold: (1) local nominations would not stir the Democrats to violence, (2) local nominations would not embarrass the national party, and (3) local nominations would not require the expenditure of money that Republicans had no way of getting.[20] (As should be obvious from Pem Guffin's murder, however, the first assumption was highly questionable.)

Corley, therefore, declined the party's nomination for lieutenant governor and concentrated on Lexington County politics, advertising a local Republican gathering as "for the most part respectable looking and well behaved," and assuring Democratic readers that "there was none of that blood and thunder talk that the Radicals of Newberry are pouring forth to their deluded followers."[21] From one who formerly had rhetorically pummeled the Democrats as vigorously as any Radical in the state, this timid and polite campaigning was certain evidence that the sun had set on Republican politics in South Carolina. Corley himself soon gave up active campaigning but remained a Republican until his death in 1902.[22]

Although some white Republicans did leave public life, others, such as E. A. Webster, J. L. Breeden of Marlboro, and the Tolberts of Abbeville, combined a continuing commitment to Republican politics with good reputations in their communities and even close relationships with Democratic neighbors. Alonzo M. Folger retained his position as patronage boss of Pickens County because of help from an unexpected source: strident Democrat and former Red Shirt Edwin Parker McCravy. The story, as the latter tells it, began in the late 1890s, when South Carolina Democratic senator John McLaurin broke with his party organization and made a deal with the Republican McKinley administration. Excommunicated from the state Democratic Party but now in control of federal patronage in South Carolina, McLaurin attempted to build up a "lily-white" Republican Party that could compete with the Democrats. By 1908, he had established his control of patronage, displacing "the old Black and Tan Party, headed by the Tolberts."[23]

At this point, McCravy recalls receiving a call on the telephone—which by now existed—asking if he would accept the position of postmaster in his hometown of Easley. He discerned in this offer that the lily whites "were trying to sandbag

Mr. A. M. Folger, who was a life-long Republican and a mighty good man he was. Mr. Folger had been consistent in his politics. He was a Republican from principle and choice." McCravy, who had participated in the terrorist campaign that ended Reconstruction, responded with a long letter declining the post "and endorsing Mr. Folger as strongly as it was possible to do. I told them that Mr. Folger had been a consistent Republican all his days, that he had reared a fine family, that he had made a good postmaster and I thought that he was entitled to hold it." Folger retained the position and his family and McCravy's became lifelong friends: "While we have differed in politics, we have never allowed this to affect our friendship and loyalty to each other."[24] As the last passage suggests, Folger's children, too, remained Republicans, including his son Clarence Mendenhall Folger, whose success in institutional finance earned him an entry in D. D. Wallace's 1934 directory of notable South Carolinians.[25]

The idea of a lily-white Republican Party apparently came up more than once after Reconstruction, but it was usually proposed by Democrats disaffected with their party's leadership; old-line white Republicans saw biracialism as central to their party's identity. So when J. Hendrix McLane, a disaffected Democrat, explored such a possibility, leading white Republicans showed no interest.[26] Even after the 1895 Constitutional Convention disfranchised most black South Carolinians, white Republicans do not seem to have been tempted by racial exclusivity.[27] McLaurin's 1898 movement was in opposition to the regular white Republicans, and another lily-white movement that attempted to take advantage of the Bull Moose bolt in 1912 also failed to gain ground. The regular party, under the control of the Tolberts, expelled from the party any Republican not supporting the regular nominee, President Taft.[28]

Of course, not all Reconstruction-era white Republicans showed the tenacity of the Folgers, Tolberts, and Cochrans. Some left the state entirely. As early as 1880, black Republican T. E. Miller castigated those Republicans who "had left the State and deserted the party in the time of its reverses."[29] Y. J. P. Owens was one of these. The former Laurens senator fled prosecution in 1877 and died in Baltimore in that year.[30] Former governor Moses, the best-known scalawag of all, also fled prosecution by South Carolina Democrats (only to spend time in prison for various misdemeanors in the North) and eventually died in Massachusetts.[31]

But leaving the state was a course easier for carpetbaggers than for scalawags.[32] White carpetbaggers who left included Aiken politician and editor Henry Sparnick, who moved to Denver in 1878. According to Mrs. R. M. Wallace, who toured the west with her husband in 1883, Sparnick had "established himself & has made a good reputation of which he is proud—Has succeeded in business." He had also been "made County Clerk of Court. He drinks no more nor plays cards & is a reformed gentleman & a polished Society man." Showing the same ambition that had taken him to South Carolina, Sparnick hoped to run for sheriff then eventually "step from that office to be Member of Congress at Washington."[33] Former

Newberry senator Henry Corwin moved to Topeka, Kansas, after Reconstruction ended.[34] The most interesting case is that of former governor Chamberlain, who returned to the North in 1877. For some years he defended his party and scathingly criticized the "betrayal of 1877." Eventually, however, he became a convert to the doctrine of white supremacy and looked back on his task as governor as a hopeless one: "With a preponderating electorate of negroes, it was never within the bounds of possibility to keep up a bearable government." With this acceptance of racism, he became much more sympathetic toward white southerners: their burden was "greater than was ever before put on white men."[35]

For scalawags, though, South Carolina remained home, and they accommodated themselves to the new order as best they could. Still, many remained resentful at their treatment by the national party. John R. Cochran, unsuccessful in his attempts to win federal patronage, pinned the blame for southern Republicanism's demise on the national administration's preference for carpetbaggers over natives: "Every step taken in that direction strengthens the democracy and convinces native republicans that they have been upon a 'Fools Errand,' in advocating and sustaining a party that refuses to recognize any merit amongst the natives."[36]

Cochran was too optimistic; the game was up as soon as the Democrats gained control. But he was right that Republicans in 1876 were making considerable progress in reforming their government and attracting more and more native whites to their party. The process was cut short by Democratic violence, a problem for which Republicans never found a solution. But it is possible that a few more years of support from the federal government could have given the party space to win over enough whites to be able to maintain itself financially and militarily. The more time Republicans had to achieve effective government, the longer they controlled jobs in a depressed economy, and the longer blacks enjoyed equal rights without Democrats' dire predictions of a "war of races" coming true, the better chance there was that the state would develop a competitive two-party system. Even as early as 1876, Republicans almost held on, despite minimal federal help.[37]

Of course, one can only speculate what South Carolina Republicans would have done with more time, but even with the time they had, they proved one important point. White supremacy was not the natural state of affairs in South Carolina. It was not even supported by all whites. For its imposition it required the largest and most successful terrorist campaign in American history, a massive program of electoral fraud, and a narrowing of the bounds of politics that lasted almost a century. White Republican E. W. M. Mackey analyzed the issue in 1881:[38]

> Thousands of white voters in South Carolina . . . are too ignorant to have a single political idea save what they imbibe from some crossroad politician, who, in turn, generally gets his information from some fourth or fifth-rate country newspaper, edited by some Democrat, who, ten chances to one,

> never travelled beyond the limits of the town in which he was born. The ignorance of such voters makes them intolerant, and to them free thought and free speech are crimes. . . . In this condition has the Democratic party of South Carolina kept the white voters of the State for the past sixty or seventy years; and hence, except at intervals, there never has been but one political party in this State. This is a disgraceful fact, to be attributed only to the death and extinction of free thought and free speech.

Mackey and the other Reconstruction-era white Republicans would be long dead, and the memory of their actions buried under volumes of hostile propaganda, before free thought and free speech returned to South Carolina politics.

# APPENDIX A

## *South Carolina White Republicans—A Preliminary Compendium*

*Abbeville*

William Ashley
George Dusenberry
Charles W. Guffin
Lemuel Guffin
Pembrook Guffin
A. C. Hawthorn
John A. Hunter
Hiram W. Lawson
James Martin
George McCalla
T. B. Milford
Jacob Miller
James Rogers Jr.
W. H. Taggart
E. L. Tolbert
Thomas N. Tolbert

*Aiken*

S. W. Beard
James F. Harling
James A. Major
John Woolley

*Anderson*

Alexander Campbell
John R. Cochran
Dr. J. L. Crumley
B. D. Dean
G. W. Hammond
James Lawrence Orr
James A. Major
B. A. McAllister
Nathan McAllister
N. A. McCully
James McLeskey
John Scott Murray
N. J. Newell
S. M. Pegg
William Perry
Jesse Pickrell
Elvin I. Pinson
Jacob Pinckney Reed
William Telford
James Webb
W. D. Wilkes
John Wilson
R. N. Wright

*Barnwell*

William E. Armstrong
Benjamin F. Berry
Arthur D. Cooper
John C. Dowling
W. H. Duncan
Conrad Erhardt
Abram Knopf
John J. Maher
William Joyce Mixson
James M. Smith
G. E. Steadman
J. N. Teague
N. G. W. Walker

*Beaufort*

J. W. Collins
Henry M. Fuller
Dan H. Towles
Alfred Williams
William Wilson

*Charleston*

C. C. Bowen
William J. Brodie
George Cannon
Michael Caulfield
James Cosgrove
G. I. Cunningham
Louis Dunneman
Julius Flaum
George W. Heriot
J. P. Howard
Francis Lance
Fleetwood Lanneau
Orlando R. Levy
Albert Gallatin Mackey
T. J. Mackey
Michael McLaughlin
P. L. Miller
Stephen D. Russell
Frederick A. Sawyer
E. B. Seabrook

*Chester*

M. H. V. Bird
James M. Brawley
B. G. Cannon
R. N. Culp
T. M. Graham
W. M. McDonald
C. D. Melton
W. M. Nickelson
John L. West

*Chesterfield*

Thomas S. Cavender
R. E. Evans
T. L. Weston

*Clarendon*

Thomas W. Arladge
M. M. Benbow
W. R. Burgess
William J. Clark
Elias E. Dickson
Wm. H. Dickson
R. F. Fielden
Joseph W. McCloud
John Plowden

*Colleton*

John W. Burbidge
J. J. Klein
R. J. LaRoche
George F. McIntyre
Thomas Messeroy
John C. Raysor
L. Shuman
John K. Terry
Dr. A. E. Williams

*Darlington*

A. Baruch
J. M. Brown
Barry Ellis
H. A. Francis
G. Holliman
H. Hymes
Philip Lewenthal
Joseph A. Moss
F. A. Thomas
Aaron Weinberg
Michael Welsh
Zachariah Wines
J. Wright
J. A. Wright

*Edgefield*

Dr. John A. Barker
H. N. Boney
George R. DeMeddis
Philip A. Eichelberger
Jono. C. Harris
William N. Heath
James W. Heyward
Levi Hill
John H. McDevitt
C. L. B. Marsh
William Parkman
W. D. Ramey
Andrew Ramsay
James A. Richardson
Truman Root
A. W. Turner
David L. Turner
Hardy Wall

*Fairfield*

S. B. Clowney
J. H. Cook
Joel Copes
A. K. Craig
Dr. James D. Cureton
M. G. Dunlap
Lewis W. Duvall
Martin Hall
Robert Hawthorn
D. B. Kirkland
Warren Marshall
W. M. Nelson
William Place
Charles L. Refoe
James N. Rutland
John S. Scott
S. M. Smart
Henry A. Smith
John T. Wilson

*Georgetown*

John F. Beckman
R. O. Bush
Franklin F. Miller
Christian Nielson

*Greenville*

James M. Allen
Wiley A. Bishop
Absalom Blythe
C. P. Dill
William E. Earle
Daniel Holland
Edward Hooker
J. B. Hyde
William B. Johnson
Dr. J. P. Latimer
Rev. James Lenderman
William Lenderman
Josh Pruitt
James M. Runion
John P. Scruggs
J. Mimms Sullivan
Samuel Tinsley

*Horry*

Henry M. Anderson
James C. Bryant
Joseph H. Derham
E. T. Lewis
C. P. Townsend

*Kershaw*

J. P. Boswell
John A. Boswell
Solomon G. W. Dill
Allison W. Hough
John S. Mewney
Columbus Shiver
James F. Sutherland
James L. Thompson
John C. Williams

*Lancaster*

Dr. W. C. Armfield
James Blackmon
Joseph Clark
R. W. Cousart
John Bratton Erwin
J. F. G. Mittag
C. P. Pelham Jr.
Thomas S. Riddle
D. C. Wolfe

*Laurens*

Joseph Crews
Wade R. Henderson
Thomas Owens
Young J. P. Owens
E. Thompson

*Lexington*

Lemuel Boozer
Lemuel H. Boozer
F. C. Caughman
Simeon Corley
J. J. Derrick
Geo P. Drafts
W. M. Drafts
James W. Harman
Joseph F. Harman
Bolivar J. Hayes
Dr. Elliott S. J. Hayes
J. H. Hendrix
B. E. Hutto
Chas Hutto
Rollin Kirk
C. E. Leaphart
James Sharp
S. M. Simons
James H. Taylor
G. W. Wingard

*Marion*

J. S. Barr
Daniel F. Berry
P. P. Bethea
William S. Collins
Arthur Eagerton
W. E. Finklea
Sandy Ford
James Graham
Eben Hayes
B. F. Hays
M. K. Holloway
H. H. Jackson
E. L. McConnell
G. W. Offley
C. Columbus Smith
Louis F. Spencer
E. M. Stoeber

*Marlboro*

Thomas W. Allen
J. L. Breeden
Joel I. Easterling
John P. Green
J. H. Jones
Dudley P. McLaurin
John Wesley Smith
George W. Waddill

*Newberry*

Alfred Denson
B. Odell Duncan
Mordecai Foot
J. W. Girardeau
W. P. Harris
Dr. John N. Herndon
Charles W. Montgomery
Summerfield Montgomery
John T. Peterson
D. R. Phifer
Jesse C. Smith
William Summer
T. A. Thompson
Z. L. White

*Oconee*

Dr. B. W. Bell
Augustus Brenake
Alexander Bryce Jr.
Alexander Bryce Sr.
M. H. Bryce
W. N. Craig
R. A. Frasier
H. A. H. Gibson Jr.
H. A. H. Gibson Sr.
W. O. B. Hiott
J. W. Holleman
Edward Honea
J. M. Hunnicutt
Elias Jenkins
Dr. L. B. Johnson
J. R. W. Johnston
G. P. Kirkland
Lucius B. Lee
T. L. Lewis
H. B. Schroder
J. R. Sloan

*Orangeburg*

Thaddeus C. Andrews
George Boliver
A. J. Browning
H. Powell Cooke
Francis DeMars
A. B. Knowlton
E. W. M. Mackey
Lucius C. Northrop
John H. Phillips
W. H. Reedish
E. T. R. Smoake
James Van Tassel
F. W. Vogt
E. A. Webster

*Pickens*

Luke Ariail
E. H. Barton
W. B. Bramblett
J. M. Cox
M. Day
Alfred M. Folger
Alonzo M. Folger
J. Frank Folger
Orlando C. Folger
William F. Gary
R. J. Gilliland
A. D. Goodlett
S. D. Goodlett
James E. Hagood
Elias Kennemore
W. A. Lesley
Jeremiah Looper
M. Mauldin
Alfred McCrary
Perrin O'Dell
Jeremiah Trainum

*Richland*

John Agnew
John Alexander
B. F. Boone
Jacob Boozer
W. A. Carr
George W. Davis
John T. Dent
Phineas Frazee
Edwin F. Gary
William K. Greenfield
Benjamin F. Griffin
Thomas E. McPherson
S. W. Melton

Daniel B. Miller
J. J. O'Connell
Robert John Palmer
Charles P. Ramsen
Thomas J. Robertson
Philip Schwartz
John C. Seegers
William Shiver
T. M. Wilkes

### *Spartanburg*

Jason Blackwell
Tench Blackwell
William Bright
Dr. Javan Bryant
Reuben Bryant
W. G. Bryant
J. P. F. Camp
Peter Quinn Camp
James Casey
William Champion
E. P. Clement
E. F. Davis
Rufus Erwin
John Genobles
John S. Gentry
Matthew F. Gossett
H. H. Grambling
Joseph Harvey
Edmund Hawkins
Henry Henderson
Middleton Henderson
James Henley
Eli Hood
William Irwin
C. J. Lockwood
P. Orr Miller
W. F. Parker
John Payne
Green Pearson
Louis N. Poole
E. H. Price
Perry Price
James Ray
George A. Setsler
Alfred Tolleson
J. B. Tolleson
George W. Tuck
C. C. Turner
T. O. P. Vernon
Thomas Westbrook
J. C. White
S. F. White
John Winsmith
John C. Winsmith

### *Sumter*

Thomas J. Coghlan
H. D. Corbett
J. N. Corbett
T. J. Duncan
J. J. Fleming
J. D. Graham
John T. Green
C. M. Hurst
William Lewis
John H. Livingston
F. I. Moses Sr.
Franklin J. Moses Jr.
G. W. Reardon
J. M. Tindall

### *Union*

Robert Beaty
Charles Bolt
Henry Cannon
James Carlisle
T. J. Coleman
P. J. Davis
Jacob W. DePass
Abel Farr
Abram Farr
Willard Farr
D. D. Goings
James H. Goss
A. A. Hammett
James George Hunter
John Caldwell Hunter
David Johnson
Charles McGurchin
J. J. Mabry
Jerry Miller
J. S. Mullens
A. B. Owens
J. H. Runkle
J. C. Simpson
A. Smith
James W. Vinson
John Laurens Young

### *Williamsburg*

James P. Barrineau
William Darrington
Louis Donath
H. W. Ferris
Philip Heller
M. J. Hirsch
Louis Jacobs
Charles M. Olsen

### *York*

Hiram Alexander
James Bynum
Daniel Carroll
John R. Ferris
William Z. Kell
S. B. Hall
Michael O'Connell
Patrick J. O'Connell
James B. Porter
William E. Rose
R. L. Simmons
Alexander S. Wallace
John R. Wallace
R. M. Wallace

# APPENDIX B

## *Known Republicans Who Joined the 1872 Bolting Movement*

(Source: *Columbia Daily Union*, September 4, 17, 19, 26, 27, October 3, 9, 1872.)

*White*

Charles Bolt (Union)
C. C. Bowen (Charleston)
B. F. Briggs (York)
Dr. Javan Bryant (Spartanburg)
Alexander Bryce Jr. (Oconee)
James Carlisle (Union)
L. C. Carpenter (Richland)
S. B. Clowney (Fairfield)
Thomas J. Coghlan (Sumter)
T. J. Coleman (Union)
J. H. Cook (Fairfield)
David Corbin (Charleston)
Simeon Corley (Lexington)
Dr. James D. Cureton (Fairfield)
C. P. Dill (Greenville)
William E. Earle (Greenville)
Abel Farr (Union)
Abram Farr (Union)
J. J. Fleming (Sumter)
Edwin F. Gary (Richland)
D. D. Going (Union)
John T. Green (Sumter)
Martin Hall (Fairfield)
A. A. Hammett (Union)
Daniel Holland (Greenville)
Tim Hurley (Charleston)
C. M. Hurst (Sumter)
J. B. Hyde (Greenville)
Charles McGurchin (Union)
John Scott Murray (Anderson)
James L. Orr (Anderson)
S. T. Poinier (Spartanburg)
Joshua Pruitt (Greenville)
A. C. Richmond (Charleston)
B. L. Roberts
Frederick A. Sawyer (Charleston)
John P. Scruggs (Greenville)
S. M. Smart (Fairfield)
A. Smith (Union)
Reuben Tomlinson (Richland)
B. F. Whittemore (Darlington)

*Black*

Macon B. Allen (Charleston)
Byrd Arnold (Greenville)
G. W. Barber (Fairfield)
B. A. Bosemon (Charleston)
B. Byas (Charleston)
P. E. Ezekiel (Beaufort)
Simon Farrow (Union)
Sanders Ford (Fairfield)
S. E. Gaillard (Charleston)
J. N. Hayne (Barnwell)
Henry Jacobs (Fairfield)
W. R. Jervey (Charleston)
Samuel Johnson (Anderson)
S. Lee (Sumter)
Alf. Moore (Fairfield)
W. M. Nelson (Fairfield)
Edward Petty (Charleston)
Joseph Quash (Aiken) (recanted)
S. W. Swails (Williamsburg)
W. J. Whipper (Beaufort)
J. H. White (York) (recanted)

# NOTES

### *Introduction*

1. *Columbia State,* November 8, 1998.

2. Joel Williamson argued that, in addition, Hampton's administration did not end the frauds begun during Reconstruction. Joel Williamson, *After Slavery: The Negro in South Carolina during Reconstruction, 1861–1877* (New York: W. W. Norton, 1965), 414. William Cooper, however, disagrees. See William J. Cooper Jr., *The Conservative Regime: South Carolina, 1877–1890* (1968; repr., Columbia: University of South Carolina Press, 2005), 49n17.

3. Whether prewar immigrants who became white Republicans should be classified as scalawags or carpetbaggers is an open question. A case can be made that northern birth and upbringing sufficiently explain later Republicanism and that, therefore, such migrants should be called carpetbaggers. In my view, however, prewar immigrants had chosen to be southerners, had established roots in the state before the war, and had been put in the position of sorting out conflicting loyalties during wartime. If Confederates, they should obviously be considered southerners. If Unionists, they experienced the war not as their northern countrymen had but as southern-born Unionists had. I therefore hold that a scalawag is any white Republican who lived in South Carolina or a bordering area at the time of the 1860 census.

4. Quoted in the *Nation* 7, no. 165 (August 27, 1868): 1.

5. Richard Zuczek, *State of Rebellion: Reconstruction in South Carolina* (Columbia: University of South Carolina Press, 1996).

6. In all probability, James S. Pike's work, *The Prostrate State: South Carolina under Negro Government* (New York: D. Appleton, 1874), a rabid denunciation of South Carolina's Republican government, actually helped turn northerners against the Reconstruction governments. Traditional accounts include Pike, *Prostrate State;* John Schreiner Reynolds, *Reconstruction in South Carolina, 1865–1877* (Columbia, S.C.: State, 1905); Henry T. Thompson, *Ousting the Carpetbagger from South Carolina* (Columbia, S.C.: R. L. Bryan, 1927); William Watts Ball, *The State That Forgot: South Carolina's Surrender to Democracy* (Indianapolis: Bobbs-Merrill, 1932); Alfred Brockenbrough Williams, *Hampton and His Red Shirts: South Carolina's Deliverance in 1876* (Charleston, S.C.: Walker, Evans & Cogswell, 1935); William Arthur Sheppard, *Red Shirts Remembered: Southern Brigadiers of the Reconstruction Period* (Atlanta: Ruralist Press, 1940); Hampton M. Jarrell, *Wade Hampton and the Negro: The Road Not Taken* (Columbia: University of South Carolina Press, 1950).

7. Francis B. Simkins and Robert H. Woody, *South Carolina during Reconstruction* (Chapel Hill: University of North Carolina Press, 1932), 26, 92. The book was termed "revisionist" by Terry Seip and Edmund Lee Drago. See Seip, *The South Returns to Congress: Men, Economic Measures, and Intersectional Relationships, 1868–1879* (Baton Rouge: Louisiana State University Press, 1983), and Drago, *Hurrah for Hampton! Black Red Shirts in South Carolina during Reconstruction* (Fayetteville: University of Arkansas Press, 1998), 139–40. Joe Gray Taylor praises the book for "challenging some of the verities" of the older accounts his essay "The White South from Secession to Redemption," in *Interpreting Southern History: Historiographical Essays in Honor of Sanford W. Higginbotham,* ed. John B. Boles and Evelyn Thomas Nolen, 162–98 (Baton Rouge: Louisiana State University Press, 1987); quotation on page 183.

8. For examples of the latter, see the traditional accounts listed above or the county histories listed below.

9. Spartanburg Unit of the Work Projects Administration in the State of South Carolina (SUWPA), *A History of Spartanburg County* (Spartanburg, S.C.: Band and White, 1940), 148; William Willis Boddie, *History of Williamsburg* (Spartanburg, S.C.: Reprint Company, 1980), 447.

10. SUWPA, *History of Spartanburg County,* 146, 147, 160; U.S. Congress, *Report of the Joint Select Committee to Inquire into the Condition of Affairs in the Late Insurrectionary States,* 13 vols. (Washington, D.C.: Government Printing Office, 1872) (hereafter cited as *Late Insurrectionary States*), 4:676, 929, 934; *Charleston Daily Courier,* August 3, 1868, p. 1; Robert H. Woody, *Republican Newspapers of South Carolina* (Charlottesville, Va.: Historical Publishing, 1936), 44.

11. Allen W. Trelease, *White Terror: The Ku Klux Klan Conspiracy and Southern Reconstruction* (New York: Harper & Row, 1971; Baton Rouge: Louisiana State University Press, 1995), 359; A. S. Wallace to Robert M. Wallace, October 29, 1868, Governor Robert K. Scott Papers (hereafter cited as Scott Papers), South Carolina Department of Archives and History, Columbia, South Carolina (hereafter cited as SCDAH). See appendix A for a partial list of white Republicans by county. It is true that only a few of these lived at the court house town, but many more than two did. In any case, the authors clearly intended to create the impression that the court house was typical of the rest of the county in lacking white Republicans.

12. Julian Stevenson Bolick, *A Laurens County Sketchbook* (n.p., n.p., 1973), 208. Another obfuscatory technique is to misidentify white Republicans as black. I know of no case when a black Republican was misidentified as white.

13. W. W. Sellers, *A History of Marion County, South Carolina, from Its Earliest Times to the Present, 1901* (Columbia, S.C.: R. L. Bryan, 1902), 95.

14. Alrutheus Ambush Taylor, *The Negro in South Carolina during the Reconstruction* (Washington, D.C.: Association for the Study of Negro Life and History, 1924).

15. Williamson, *After Slavery,* 374.

16. Ibid., 374–75, 397.

17. Thomas Holt, *Black over White: Negro Political Leadership in South Carolina during Reconstruction* (Urbana: University of Illinois Press, 1977). See especially chapter 5, "White Domination or Black Control: The Dynamics of Power."

18. Zuczek, *State of Rebellion,* 53, 72; Lou Falkner Williams, *The Great South Carolina Ku Klux Klan Trials, 1871–1872* (Athens: University of Georgia Press, 1996), 93.

19. Even South Carolina's black Democrats were written about first. See Drago, *Hurrah for Hampton!*

20. Eric Foner, *Reconstruction: America's Unfinished Revolution, 1863–1877* (New York: Harper and Row, 1988), 297–300; quotation from 297. See also Kenneth M. Stampp, *The Era of Reconstruction, 1865–1877* (New York: Alfred A. Knopf, 1969), 160–65, and Carl N. Degler, *The Other South: Southern Dissenters in the Nineteenth Century* (Boston: Northeastern University Press, 1982), 191–229.

21. Foner, *Reconstruction,* 300, 317.

22. Degler, *Other South,* 202–3.

23. On the upper South, see James Alex Baggett, "Origins of Upper South Scalawag Leadership," *Civil War History* 29, no. 1 (1983): 53–73; Thomas B. Alexander, "Whiggery and Reconstruction in Tennessee," *Journal of Southern History* 16 (August 1950), 291–305; and James L. Lancaster, "The Scalawags of North Carolina, 1850–1868" (Ph.D. diss., Princeton University, 1974).

24. Ted Tunnell, *Crucible of Reconstruction: War, Radicalism, and Race in Louisiana, 1862–1877* (Baton Rouge: Louisiana State University Press, 1984), quotation on page 9; Michael Fitzgerald, "Radical Republicanism and the White Yeomanry during Alabama Reconstruction, 1865–1868," *Journal of Southern History* 54, no. 4 (November 1988): 565–96; Sarah Woolfolk Wiggins, *The Scalawag in Alabama Politics, 1865–1881* (University: University of Alabama Press, 1977); Margaret deMontcourt Storey, "Southern Ishmaelites: Wartime Unionism and Its Consequences in Alabama, 1860–1874" (Ph.D. diss., Emory University, 1999); Carl H. Moneyhon, *The Impact of the Civil War and Reconstruction on Arkansas: Persistence in the Midst of Ruin* (Baton Rouge: Louisiana State University Press, 1994), 243.

25. David Donald, "The Scalawag in Mississippi Reconstruction," *Journal of Southern History* 10 (November 1944): 447–60.

26. Allen Trelease, "Who Were the Scalawags?" *Journal of Southern History* 29 (November 1963): 445–68; Donald's criticism of this argument, and Trelease's reply, are in "Communications," *Journal of Southern History* 30 (May 1964). On the Whigs, see Michael F. Holt, *The Rise and Fall of the Whig Party: Jacksonian Politics and the Onset of the Civil War* (New York: Oxford University Press, 1999). Holt adds an interesting nuance to the debate about "persistent Whiggery" by speculating that old Whigs became, during Reconstruction, leaders of both the Republican and Democratic Parties. See Holt, *Rise and Fall of the Whig Party,* 984.

27. One historian, adopting a more precise methodology, sided with Donald. See Warren A. Ellem, "Who Were the Mississippi Scalawags?" *Journal of Southern History* 38, no. 2 (1972): 217–40. Another, in turn, disputes *his* findings: William C. Harris, *The Day of the Carpetbagger: Republican Reconstruction in Mississippi* (Baton Rouge: Louisiana State University Press, 1979), 469.

28. Baggett, "Origins," 73.

29. For list of scalawags, see appendix A. All but Edward Hooker, J. B. Hyde, A. G. Jimison, and James Lenderman were probably Confederate veterans. For Confederate service, see Janet B. Hewett and Joyce Lawrence, *South Carolina Confederate Soldiers, 1861–1865,* vol. 1, *Name Roster* (Wilmington, N.C.: Broadfoot, 1998).

30. See the discussion in Walter Edgar, *South Carolina: A History* (Columbia: University of South Carolina Press, 1998), 358–60.

31. James Alex Baggett, *The Scalawags: Southern Dissenters in the Civil War and Reconstruction* (Baton Rouge: Louisiana State University Press, 2003), appendix table 3. Baggett does show South Carolina scalawags as having the highest percentage of secessionists in their ranks of any state group, but he still argues that only 26 percent favored secession. I believe that figure is explained by the fact that his sample of forty-seven South Carolina scalawags is a fairly elite group—officeholders—who would be expected to be more Unionist than rank-and-file scalawags. Their status might give them the latitude to take an unpopular position, for example. In any case, Baggett agrees that even of his sample, most (55 percent) were Confederate veterans.

32. See, for example, Steven A. Channing, *Crisis of Fear: Secession in South Carolina* (New York: W. W. Norton, 1974).

33. For an example of this type of rhetoric, see Simeon Corley, "To the Voters of the Third Congressional District," April 4, 1868, in Manuel Simeon Corley Papers, South Caroliniana Library, University of South Carolina, Columbia (hereafter cited as Corley Papers).

34. Jeffrey J. Crow, "Thomas Settle Jr., Reconstruction, and the Memory of the Civil War," *Journal of Southern History* 62, no. 4 (November 1996): 689–726.

35. Degler, *Other South,* 220–22; quotation on 222.

36. Ibid., 231; see also Williamson, *After Slavery,* 349, and Foner, *Reconstruction,* 303.

37. For examples from South Carolina, see A. G. Mackey, *The Political Treason of Senator F. A. Sawyer, and Representative C. C. Bowen: Speech of the Hon. A. G. Mackey; Before a Mass Meeting of the Republican Party, at Charleston, S.C., on 28th July, 1869* (Charleston, S.C., 1869), 2; and William J. Armstong, *Speech of William J. Armstrong, delivered at Columbia, July 25, 1867* (n.p., n. d.), 5. Both are pamphlets in South Caroliniana Library, University of South Carolina, Columbia (hereafter cited as SCL).

38. W. E. B. Du Bois, *Black Reconstruction* (New York: Harcourt, Brace, 1935); Armstead L. Robinson, "Beyond the Realm of Social Consensus: New Meanings of Reconstruction for American History," *Journal of American History* 68 (September 1981): 276–97, especially 287; Fitzgerald, "Radical Republicanism and the White Yeomanry," 565–96; J. Mills Thornton III, "Fiscal Policy and the Failure of Radical Reconstruction in the Lower South," in *Region, Race, and Reconstruction: Essays in Honor of C. Vann Woodward,* ed. J. Morgan Kousser and James M. McPherson (New York: Oxford University Press, 1982).

39. See James L. Orr, *Southern Politics: Ex-Governor Orr's Reasons for Joining the Republican Party in South Carolina* (Columbia, S.C., 1870), 2. This is a pamphlet in SCL. Thomas Holt also chronicles Republicans' many attempts to woo elite whites; see *Black over White,* 102–3.

40. Corley, "To the Voters."

41. For the former, see Corley, "To the Voters," and Armstrong, *Speech;* for the latter, see Orr's *Southern Politics.* The quotation is from Albert Gallatin Mackey, a wealthy Charleston merchant who became a Republican, from his speech to the 1868 Constitutional Convention; see S.C. Constitutional Convention (1868), *Proceedings of the Constitutional Convention of South Carolina, Held at Charleston, S.C., Beginning January 14th and Ending March 17th, 1868* (Charleston, S.C.: Denny and Perry, 1868) (hereafter cited as *1868 Convention*), 6.

42. Paul D. Escott, "White Republicanism and Ku Klux Klan Terror: The North Carolina Piedmont during Reconstruction," in *Race, Class, and Politics in Southern History:*

*Essays in Honor of Robert F. Durden,* ed. Jeffrey J. Crow, Paul D. Escott, and Charles L. Flynn Jr. (Baton Rouge: Louisiana State University Press, 1989), 5.

43. Baggett, *Scalawags,* appendix table 3.

44. Trelease, "Who Were the Scalawags?" 458, 456.

45. Williamson, *After Slavery,* 349.

46. *Columbia Daily Union-Herald,* August 18, 1874.

47. See Drago, *Hurrah for Hampton!* 43, 153n213, which refers the reader to Williamson, *After Slavery.* Williamson refers to a Republican estimate of five thousand white Republicans but judges that figure too high.

48. *Columbia Daily Union-Herald,* August 18, 1874. Not all Democrats would have agreed, especially those writing after the fact. Reynolds, whose 1905 work *Reconstruction in South Carolina* is strongly anti-Republican, claims that 99 percent of whites were Democrats (100).

49. See *Late Insurrectionary States* 3:7.

50. On the other hand, at least one Democrat indicated that as many as 25 percent of whites might support Reconstruction. See letter by "Cato" to *Columbia Phoenix,* April 14, 1868.

51. Williamson, *After Slavery,* 375.

52. Ibid., 375n35.

53. *Charleston News and Courier,* November 30, 1876.

54. On Laurens, see John A. Leland, *A Voice from South Carolina* (Charleston, S.C.: Walker, Evans & Cogswell, 1879); Williams, *Great South Carolina Ku Klux Klan Trials,* 16, 25. On Edgefield, see Orville Vernon Burton, "Ungrateful Servants? Edgefield's Black Reconstruction: Part 1 of the Total History of Edgefield County, South Carolina" (Ph.D. diss., Princeton University, 1975), and Zuczek, *State of Rebellion,* 174. One exception to this trend is J. C. A. Stagg's article on Klan violence in the upcountry, which focuses on the uses of violence for labor discipline. See Stagg, "The Problem of Klan Violence: the South Carolina Up-Country, 1868–1871," *American Studies* 8, no. 3 (December 1974): 303–18.

55. Louise Ayer Vandiver, *Traditions and History of Anderson County* (Atlanta: Ruralist Press, 1928), 255–56, 303–5; Moore, *Columbia and Richland County: A South Carolina Community, 1740–1990* (Columbia: University of South Carolina Press, 1993), 222–23.

56. Foner, *Reconstruction,* 381.

57. *Charleston Courier,* April 16, 1868.

58. Ibid., April 21, 1868.

59. William Henry Trescot to Gov. Robert K. Scott, October 24, 1868, Scott Papers.

60. Foner, *Reconstruction,* 302–3. See also Harris, *Day of the Carpetbagger,* 465.

61. Williamson, *After Slavery,* 349.

62. Fitzgerald, "Radical Republicanism and the White Yeomanry," 596; Thornton, "Fiscal Policy," 391.

63. Peter Kolchin, "Scalawags, Carpetbaggers, and Reconstruction: A Quantitative Look at Southern Congressional Politics, 1868–1872," *Journal of Southern History* 45, no. 1 (February 1979): 76. Of course, as Kolchin notes, scalawag *votes* were always desirable, in the greatest numbers possible.

64. Harris, *Day of the Carpetbagger.*

65. Kolchin, "Scalawags, Carpetbaggers, and Reconstruction," 64, 73.

66. Williamson, *After Slavery,* 361.

67. Ibid., 360.

68. Michael Edwin Thompson, "Blacks, Carpetbaggers, and Scalawags: A Study of the Membership of the South Carolina Legislature, 1868–1870" (Ph.D. diss., Washington State University, 1975), 135.

69. Thompson, "Blacks, Carpetbaggers, and Scalawags," 153–56.

70. Seip, *South Returns.*

71. John R. Cochran to William Henry Trescot, January 21, 1881, William Henry Trescot Papers, SCL (hereafter cited as Trescot Papers).

72. John R. Cochran to William Henry Trescot, January 21, 1881, Trescot Papers.

73. Holt, *Black over White,* 3–4.

74. Thornton, "Fiscal Policy," 350.

75. Williamson, *After Slavery,* 381.

76. Michael Perman, *The Road to Redemption: Southern Politics, 1869–1879* (Chapel Hill: University of North Carolina Press, 1984), 34, 147. Quoted passage is on 34.

77. Williamson, *After Slavery,* 413.

78. Simkins and Woody, *South Carolina during Reconstruction,* 498.

79. Zuczek, *State of Rebellion,* 210.

80. Richard H. Abbott, *The Republican Party and the South, 1855–1877: The First Southern Strategy* (Chapel Hill: University of North Carolina Press, 1986); William Gillette, *Retreat from Reconstruction, 1869–1879* (Baton Rouge: Louisiana State University Press, 1979).

81. Seip, *South Returns.*

82. The theme of northern racism has been touched on by practically every work on national Reconstruction, but perhaps the most devastating catalog is C. Vann Woodward's "Seeds of Failure in Radical Race Policy," in *New Frontiers of the American Reconstruction,* ed. Harold M. Hyman (Urbana: University of Illinois Press, 1966), 125–47.

83. Quoted in Tunnell, *Crucible of Reconstruction,* 140.

84. The best work on South Carolina's Republicans after 1876 remains James Welch Patton, "The Republican Party in South Carolina, 1876–1895," in *Essays in Southern History: Presented to Joseph Gregoire de Roulhac Hamilton, Ph.D., LL.D., by His Former Students at the University of North Carolina,* ed. Fletcher Melvin Green (Chapel Hill: University of North Carolina Press, 1949), 91–111. Also useful are Cooper, *Conservative Regime,* and George Brown Tindall, *South Carolina Negroes, 1877–1900* (Columbia: University of South Carolina Press, 1952).

85. *Sumter News,* March 28, 1868; *Charleston Courier,* July 21, 1868; *Late Insurrectionary States* 5:1439–40.

### *1. Origins of the Scalawags, 1865–1867*

1. An article in the *New York Times* on July 31, 1867, describes the first Union Republican Convention in South Carolina, reporting that two-thirds of the delegates were black.

2. Michael Perman, *Reunion without Compromise: The South and Reconstruction, 1865–1868* (Cambridge: Cambridge University Press, 1973), 337–47.

3. Roger P. Leemhuis, *James L. Orr and the Sectional Conflict* (Washington, D.C.: University Press of America, 1979), 16, 33–34. On one other issue Orr's attitude was

more Whig than Democratic: the rights of the Indians. As chairman of the House Committee on Indian Affairs, Orr, atypically for a Democrat, admitted that the United States had dishonored itself in its treatment of the Indians. Leemhuis, *Orr,* 45–46; Beth Ann Klosky, *The Pendleton Legacy: An Illustrated History of the District* (Columbia, S.C.: Sandlapper Press, 1971), 90. On the principles and policies of the Whig Party, see Daniel Walker Howe, *The Political Culture of the American Whigs* (Chicago: University of Chicago Press, 1979), and Holt, *Rise and Fall of the Whig Party.*

4. Leemhuis, *Orr,* 24, 49, 71; quotation on 71. Orr made this statement on August 16, 1860.

5. Ibid., 48–54.

6. William F. Russell of New York, quoted in ibid., 56.

7. Ibid., 71–72. Such talk was common even among opponents of secession in the state. Unconditional Unionists were exceptionally rare in South Carolina; Lacy Ford counts, among prominent men, only one in 1860: the often-quoted Charleston lawyer James L. Petigru ("South Carolina is too small for a republic and too large for a lunatic asylum"). There were not many more in 1850; Unionist B. F. Perry estimated that there were five unconditional Unionists in the state legislature. See Lacy K. Ford Jr., "James Louis Petigru: The Last South Carolina Federalist," in *Intellectual Life in Antebellum Charleston,* ed. Michael O'Brien and David Moltke-Hansen (Knoxville: University of Tennessee Press, 1986), 152–85; and William H. Pease and Jane H. Pease, *James Louis Petigru: Southern Conservative, Southern Dissenter* (Athens: University of Georgia Press, 1995), 68–76, 156–64.

8. Leemhuis, *Orr,* 76–77.

9. Ibid., 82; CSA Congress, *Journal of the Congress of the Confederate States of America, 1861–1865,* 7 vols. (Washington, D.C.: Government Printing Office, 1904–5), 1:844, 849; CSA Congress, "Proceedings of the Confederate Congress," *Southern Historical Society Papers* 45:250–53, 48:187–90.

10. See Bill G. Reid, "Confederate Opponents of Arming the Slaves," *Journal of Mississippi History* 22 (1960): 249–70.

11. Leemhuis, *Orr,* 90.

12. Quoted in ibid., 93–94.

13. Simkins and Woody, *South Carolina during Reconstruction,* 33–34.

14. Quoted in Sidney Andrews, *The South since the War* (Boston: Houghton Mifflin, 1971), 96.

15. S.C. Constitutional Convention (1865), *Journal of the Convention of the People of South Carolina, Held in Columbia, S.C., September, 1865* (Columbia, S.C.: J. A. Selby, 1865), 61 (hereafter cited as *1865 Convention*).

16. Some delegates openly expected compensation for the loss of property occasioned by abolition; of these, some sought to deny the validity of uncompensated emancipation by stressing the extraconstitutional method of its achievement. McGowan's avowed motive was to tell "the whole truth." His proposed resolution read, "The emancipation of slaves having actually taken place, slavery shall not be re-established in this state." See Andrews, *South since the War,* 58, 60, 66. Dan T. Carter's assessment of southern actions on secession and slavery is that they "revealed the postwar southern leadership at its most inept: prideful, arrogant, and blinded by the constitutional dogmatism of the past." See Dan T. Carter, *When the War Was Over: The Failure*

*of Self-Reconstruction in the South, 1865–1867* (Baton Rouge: Louisiana State University Press, 1985), 70.

17. S.C. General Assembly, *Statutes at Large of South Carolina* (Columbia, S.C.: Republican Printing, 1875), 13:269–85.

18. Andrews, *South since the War,* 96; Jarrell, *Wade Hampton,* 8–15. Even so, Hampton almost won the election; Orr defeated him by a scant eight hundred votes out of nineteen thousand cast.

19. See Jarrell, *Wade Hampton,* 8; Simkins and Woody, *South Carolina during Reconstruction,* 43; Leemhuis, *Orr,* 102–3. Diehard Confederates saw Orr as untrustworthy, a half-hearted Rebel. See Andrews, *South since the War,* 96.

20. William Henry Trescot, "Letter of William Henry Trescot on Reconstruction in South Carolina, 1867," *American Historical Review* 15, no. 3 (April 1910): 574–75; R. Nicholas Olsberg, "A Government of Class and Race: William Henry Trescot and the South Carolina Chivalry, 1860–1865" (Ph.D. diss., University of South Carolina, 1972).

21. John Hammond Moore, ed., *The Juhl Letters to the Charleston Courier: A View of the South, 1865–1871* (Athens: University of Georgia Press, 1974), 19–23, 82–83.

22. *Anderson Intelligencer,* August 24, 1865.

23. Carter, *When the War Was Over,* 83; Andrews, *South since the War,* 60.

24. See Perman, *Reunion without Compromise,* 343.

25. Carter, *When the War Was Over,* 230–31; Moore, *Juhl Letters,* 53, 63.

26. Weatherly remained a Democrat but was willing to work with Republicans and retained a high enough reputation with the Republicans of black-majority Marlboro County that in 1874 they placed him on their slate of candidates as a state representative. See *Columbia Daily Union-Herald,* October 10, November 21, 1874.

27. Eric L. McKitrick, *Andrew Johnson and Reconstruction* (Chicago: University of Chicago Press, 1960), 470–71.

28. "Ex-Governor J. L. Orr," in *Cyclopaedia of Eminent and Representative Men of the Carolinas of the Nineteenth Century,* vol. 1, *South Carolina,* ed. Samuel A. Ashe and Edward McCrady Jr., 115 (Madison, Wis.: Brant and Fuller, 1892); Andrews, *South since the War,* 89.

29. Martin Abbott, ed., "James L. Orr on Congressional Reconstruction," *South Carolina Historical Magazine* 54, no. 3 (July 1953): 141–42.

30. Abbott, "James L. Orr," 142; Leemhuis, *Orr,* 136.

31. Vandiver, *Traditions and History of Anderson County,* 256. Another historian of Anderson County considerably softens the picture of that county's feelings toward Orr; see Frank A. Dickson, *Journeys into the Past: The Anderson Region's Heritage* (published by the author, 1975), 138.

32. Anne King Gregorie, *History of Sumter County* (Sumter, S.C.: Library Board of Sumter County, 1954), 308; *Columbia Daily Phoenix,* December 11, 1867.

33. *Nation,* October 1, 1868.

34. Quoted in Leemhuis, *Orr,* 145.

35. Quoted in ibid., 100.

36. *Late Insurrectionary States* 4:1189.

37. Quoted in Leemhuis, *Orr,* 129.

38. Ibid., 144–45; *New York Herald,* February 21, 1867; *New York Times,* February 28, 1867.

39. Lilian A. Kibler, "Unionist Sentiment in South Carolina in 1860," *Journal of Southern History* 4 (August 1938): 346ff.; Williamson, *After Slavery,* 349. Another center of Unionism was Lexington County. Lexington, while geographically in the Midlands (an area of high slaveholding), was demographically more like the upcountry, having a very large white majority. Furthermore, like the upcountry counties (but unlike its neighboring counties) Lexington was relatively recently settled. For purposes of this discussion, then, Lexington will be treated as an upcountry county. See Edwin J. Dreher, "A Brief but Interesting History of Lexington County," *Lexington Dispatch,* July 2, 9, 1902; Nancy F. Wingard and Clayton B. Kleckley, *Brief History of Lexington County and Schedule for Lexington County Tricentennial Activities* (Lexington, S.C.: Lexington County Historical Society, 1970); Edwin J. Scott, *Random Recollections of a Long Life, 1806–1876* (Columbia, S.C.: Charles A. Calvo Jr., 1884); and Merlene Hutto Byars, *South Carolina Scrapbook: Learn about Your Heritage with the Saxe Gothans* (Cayce, S.C.: Saxe Gotha Historical Society, 1994). A full-length history of Lexington County would be a welcome addition to the historiography of South Carolina.

40. For events leading to the compromise, see Rachel N. Klein, *Unification of a Slave State: The Rise of the Planter Class in the South Carolina Backcountry, 1760–1808* (Chapel Hill: University of North Carolina Press, 1990).

41. See William A. Schaper, "Sectionalism and Representation in South Carolina," *Annual Report of the American Historical Association for the Year 1900,* 2 vols. (Washington, D.C.: Government Printing Office, 1901); George Michael Briggs, "South Carolina Reapportionment, 1776–1978" (master's thesis, University of South Carolina, 1978); Philip M. Hamer, *The Secession Movement in South Carolina, 1847–1852* (Allentown, Pa.: H. Ray Haas, 1918).

42. Kibler, "Unionist Sentiment," 346–66.

43. Ella Lonn, *Desertion during the Civil War* (New York: Century, 1928), 62–79; James T. Otten, "Disloyalty in the Upper Districts of South Carolina during the Civil War," *South Carolina Historical Magazine* 75 (1974): 95–110; Charles Edward Cauthen, *South Carolina Goes to War, 1860–1865* (Chapel Hill: University of North Carolina Press, 1950), 174–77.

44. In some areas of upcountry South Carolina, the proportions of desertion overwhelmed the resources the Confederacy allocated to addressing the problem. See J. A. Keller to John M. Obey, March 16, 1865, SCL. For South Carolina as the only southern state not to provide a white company, see Richard N. Current, *Lincoln's Loyalists: Union Soldiers from the Confederacy* (Boston: Northeastern University Press, 1992), 107.

45. Dreher, "Brief but Interesting History." The piece continues, "I will venture the assertion that there were more sincere Union men in Lexington county than in any other county in the State. Notwithstanding this fact Lexington county furnished her full quota of troops for the deplorable and disastrous war that followed; and her soldiers were as gallant and brave, and her people as zealous and self-sacrificing in their devotion to the 'Lost Cause' as those of any other county in South Carolina."

46. Andrews, *South since the War,* 74. In fact, Frost did become a Republican, and of the few other members of the convention who even hinted at support for the political rights of the freedmen, most would join Frost. Andrews quotes the following delegates as expressing some degree of support for the rights of the freedmen to vote and/or serve on juries: Frost, Orr, J. G. Thompson, T. N. Dawkins, Robert Dozier, and C. D. Melton.

*South since the War,* 88–89. Frost, Orr, Thompson, and Melton became Republicans. Dawkins cooperated with the moderates through 1866, but it is unclear what course he pursued afterward. I predict that he became a Democrat; in the Convention he is cited as one who favored civil rights for blacks but was afraid to vote that way without consulting his constituents. I would imagine that after he did so, he changed his course. See *Late Insurrectionary States* 5:1425. I have been unable to determine the later politics of Dozier. See John Calvin Bradley Jr., "The Political Reconstruction of Spartanburg County, 1865–1868" (honors thesis, South Carolina College, 1983), 13.

47. Quoted in Leemhuis, *Orr,* 130.

48. Quoted in John P. Hollis, *The Early Period of Reconstruction in South Carolina* (Baltimore: Johns Hopkins Press, 1905), 57.

49. Quoted in *New York Times,* January 4, 1866. For a modern version of the argument, see Vincent Harding, *There Is a River: The Black Struggle for Freedom in America* (New York: Harcourt Brace Jovanovich, 1981), 225–35.

50. Leemhuis, *Orr,* 130.

51. Jarrell, *Wade Hampton,* 16–17; James L. Roark, *Masters without Slaves: Southern Planters in the Civil War and Reconstruction* (New York: W. W. Norton, 1977), 188–89.

52. Quoted in Andrews, *South since the War,* 73.

53. Quoted in ibid., 86–87; Leemhuis, *Orr,* 100, 143; Daniel Walker Hollis, *University of South Carolina,* vol. 2, *College to University* (Columbia: University of South Carolina Press, 1956), 46. Orr suggested instead that the Citadel, which had not reopened after the war, be used as a separate college for blacks. It will be recalled that Citadel cadets had fired on the ship *Star of the West* to inaugurate hostilities at Fort Sumter.

54. *1868 Convention,* 47.

55. Leemhuis, *Orr,* 151; J. P. M. Epping to Orr, May 14, September 23, 1867, and Benjamin Odell Duncan to Orr, May 25, 1868, all in Governor Orr Papers, SCDAH (hereafter cited as Orr Papers); *Late Insurrectionary States* 3:21; Orr, *Southern Politics.*

56. Blacks who did not vote "we hold as harmless." Jonesville Democratic Club, quoted in Allan D. Charles, *The Narrative History of Union County South Carolina* (Spartanburg, S.C.: Reprint Company, 1987), 220.

57. S.C. General Assembly, *Evidence Taken by the Committee of Investigation of the Third Congressional District, under Authority of the General Assembly of the State of South Carolina, Regular Session, 1868–'69* (Columbia, S.C.: John W. Denny, 1870) (hereafter cited as *Third District Investigation*), 624. On Wright as trial justice, see *Columbia Daily Union,* April 30, 1872; and John R. Cochran to Daniel H. Chamberlain, February 4, 1875, and Petitioners from Honea Path, Anderson County, to Daniel H. Chamberlain, February 5, 1875, Governor Chamberlain Papers, SCDAH (hereafter cited as Chamberlain Papers).

58. *Late Insurrectionary States* 4:758–59; Bradley, "Political Reconstruction," 12–13, 15, 26. One historian has said of Cannon that during the antebellum years, he "was probably the most reactionary upcountry politician in the state." I have found no evidence that Cannon deserves this dubious distinction. See Olsberg, "Government of Class and Race," 91.

59. Bradley, "Political Reconstruction," 12–13, 15; quotation on page 13.

60. Ibid., 12–14; quotation on page 14.

61. Ibid., 23.

62. See Olsberg, "Government of Class and Race," 21, 202.

63. See Anonymous to Orr, December 3, 1866, and Farrow to Orr, March 16, 1867, Orr Papers.

64. Quoted in Bradley, "Political Reconstruction," 13.

65. Farrow to Orr, June 8, 1867, Orr Papers.

66. On planters' efforts to woo black votes, see Bradley, "Political Reconstruction," 20–22.

67. Farrow and Cannon, for example, did so. See ibid., 26. Bradley says that they moved "back into the Republican party," but the context makes it clear that the phrase should read "back into the Democratic party."

68. In the context of 1865, this meant that the three (Wylie, Frost, and J. G. Thompson) opposed the idea of Black Codes and thought race should not enter into the justice system. Voting, then considered a privilege rather than a right, was a different matter. See testimony of Alexander P. Wylie in *Late Insurrectionary States* 5:1425, and Andrews, *South since the War,* 88–89.

69. *Late Insurrectionary States* 5:1434, 1428, 1439–40.

70. Ibid. 5:1434.

71. Ibid. 5:1439–40.

72. Ibid. 5:1436.

73. Ibid. 4:780. I have put the most favorable construction on Cannon's speech, taking him at his word in his explanation of it to a Republican-dominated examining committee. He insisted that his words constituted a prediction, not the threat it appeared to be, and that he spoke to them as a friend who wished to help them avoid the result he spoke of, not as one who would carry it out. However he meant it, though, the point remains the same: he at first advocated and practiced moderation but found that course unsustainable.

74. Ibid. 4:781–83. This system was common all over the state. For examples from Abbeville, Anderson, Edgefield, and Newberry Counties, see *Third District Investigation.*

75. Ibid. 4:782.

76. See Bradley, "Political Reconstruction," 14; *Late Insurrectionary States* 4:626; S.C. Convention (1852), *Journal of the State Convention of South Carolina; Together with the Resolution and Ordinance* (Columbia, S.C.: Johnson & Cavis, 1852), 19. Bradley calls Winsmith a secessionist, but Winsmith himself flatly denied favoring secession. He admitted, though, that once secession occurred he "contributed more for the support of the war than any other man in this district." See *Late Insurrectionary States* 4:621–22.

77. *Late Insurrectionary States* 4:620–23.

78. Winsmith to Chamberlain, December 7, 1874, Chamberlain Papers.

79. Unknown to Dr. Gerhard Muller, January 16, 1851, Gerhard Muller Papers, SCL.

80. Perry to Benson J. Lossing, September 2, 1866, B. F. Perry Papers, SCL.

81. It is still disputed whether the killing of Baylis Boozer more resembled a duel or an assassination. *Central Midlands Historic Preservation Survey* (Lexington, S.C.: Central Midlands Regional Planning Council, [1974?]), 196. This volume, available at the Lexington County Public Library, Lexington, South Carolina, calls the killing an ambush. In my discussion on January 4, 1999, with Horace Harmon, head of the Lexington History Museum, he indicated it was more like a duel. In any case, it could hardly have made much difference to Lemuel Boozer.

82. The description is by James D. Tradewell in S.C. General Assembly, *Proceedings in the General Assembly and Supreme Court of South Carolina, on the Death of Hon. Lemuel Boozer, Judge of the Fifth Judicial Circuit* (Columbia, S.C.: J. W. Denny, 1870) (hereafter cited as *Death of Boozer*), 25–26.

83. Claim of Albert M. Boozer and Lemuel H. Boozer, administrators of the estate of Lemuel Boozer, deceased, case 3205, RG 217 (General Accounting Office, 3rd Auditor's Office), Southern Claims Commission, South Carolina, NA.

84. Byars, *South Carolina Scrapbook,* 120; Harmon interview.

85. After Boozer's death in 1870, the Southern Claims Commission, charged with evaluating the claims of southerners to have been Unionists and to have had supplies seized by Union forces, reviewed his claim and allowed it. See claim of Boozer, Southern Claims Commission, NA.

86. *1865 Convention.*

87. *Death of Boozer,* 17; *Central Midlands Historic Preservation Survey,* 196; Harmon interview.

88. James D. Tradewell, in *Death of Boozer,* 28.

89. Andrews, *South since the War,* 75–82. Votes are confirmed by the convention journal but with little of the detail provided in Andrews's account. See *1865 Convention.*

90. Andrews, *South since the War,* 75–82.

91. Simkins and Woody, *South Carolina during Reconstruction,* 45–47; Robinson, "Beyond the Realm," 286.

92. The highest white Republican vote for any county for any election that I have found was the approximately 20 percent of white citizens of Oconee County who voted for Governor Scott in 1870. Estimate obtained from figures in S.C. General Assembly, *Reports and Resolutions of the General Assembly of the State of South Carolina,* 1870–71 and 1874–75 (hereafter cited as *Reports and Resolutions,* followed by the date).

93. Orr, *Southern Politics,* 3. Not coincidentally, the legislature he referred to was the last elected under the parish system.

94. See Olsberg, "Government of Class and Race," 56, 112.

### *2. The Republican Alternative*

1. Simeon Corley to Thaddeus Stevens, February 6, 1866, Thaddeus K. Stevens Papers, Library of Congress (hereafter cited as Stevens Papers).

2. Corley, "To the Voters"; Corley to Ben. Perlay Poore, December 31, 1868; Simeon Corley, "A Short Sketch of the Life of Simeon Corley"; all in Corley Papers. His lack of confidence in Johnson is clear from a private letter in which he apologized (quite unnecessarily) for his writing ability: "I am only a tailor you know, and since Andrew Johnson is one too, that is not saying much." Corley to Charles Lanman, July 28, 1868, Corley Papers.

3. Corley, "To the Voters," 1868, Corley Papers.

4. In his speech in Congress in 1869, he took a traditional ideology to its logical conclusion: "We need more of the moral element in politics, which may be had by the enfranchisement of woman." *Congressional Globe,* January 28, 1869, 40th Cong., 3rd sess., appendix, 94.

5. P. I. Rawl's recollections, in *Recollections and Reminiscences, 1861–1865 through World War I,* 1:56–72 (n.p.: South Carolina Division, United Daughters of the Confederacy, 1990); quoted passages on 1:71–72.

6. Corley, "To the Voters."

7. Ibid.

8. Ibid.

9. Ibid.; Corley to Ben. Perlay Poore, December 31, 1868, Corley Papers; Corley, "Short Sketch of the Life of Simeon Corley."

10. Corley, "To the Voters."

11. Corley, "Short Sketch of the Life of Simeon Corley."

12. *1868 Convention,* 207.

13. Corley, "A Short Sketch of the Life of Simeon Corley." Corley wrote that after his 1855 marriage to a woman from Vermont, he "adopted the vegetarian theory, toward which he had been tending for years." How much influence his wife, the former Martha A. Reynolds, had on Corley's views is unclear, but his abolitionism seems to have predated their meeting. It is also unclear how they met; the stridently Democratic *Charleston Mercury* charged that Corley had gone to the North to search for a wife at the suggestion of a phrenologist. See *Charleston Mercury,* February 24, 1868.

14. Corley to Stevens, February 6, 1866, Stevens Papers.

15. Such views were common in the North as well. The *New York Times* editorialized, "We shall eliminate the Indian—we shall not assimilate the Asiatic—but the African was imported, as we Europeans were imported, to become an American." See *New York Times,* July 30, 1867.

16. Simeon Corley to the Editor, *Lexington Dispatch,* October 7, 1874.

17. See Coghlan's signature on a "Petition to the General Assembly from citizens of Sumter, suggesting removal or enslavement of free Negroes," I.D. 0010 003 ND00 01873 00, Legislative Papers, SCDAH (hereafter cited as Legislative Papers).

18. *1868 Convention,* 205.

19. In 1872 Wallace wrote that his district had nine to ten thousand white majority. See Wallace to unknown, December 4, 1872, Alexander Stuart Wallace Papers, SCL.

20. Robert Nicholas Olsberg lists Wallace as one of a group of antebellum upcountry politicians who opposed the planter oligarchy and also supported "stringent race controls." See Olsberg, "Government of Class and Race," 56, 112. Wallace's name is found on an 1858 York County Grand Jury Presentment asking the state legislature to secure the removal of free blacks from South Carolina. See item 0010 015 1858 00042 00, Legislative Papers.

21. M. C. Butler told a congressional investigating committee, "I do not think Mr. Wallace, the present member of Congress, was a very humane man, from what I have heard of him. He is now a shining light, I believe." See *Late Insurrectionary States* 4:1212. It should be noted that Butler, one of the most extremist Democrats, was in no sense unbiased or trustworthy.

22. *Columbia Daily Union-Herald,* October 28, 1874; "Robert M. Wallace," in *Cyclopaedia of Eminent and Representative Men of the Carolinas of the Nineteenth Century,* vol. 1, *South Carolina,* ed. Samuel A. Ashe and Edward McCrady Jr., 387–88 (Madison, Wis.: Brant and Fuller, 1892).

23. *Yorkville Enquirer,* September 30, 1869.

24. Lacy K. Ford Jr., "One Southern Profile: Modernization and the Development of White Terror in York County, 1856–1876" (master's thesis, University of South Carolina, 1976), 79–80.

25. Ford, "One Southern Profile," 80.

26. *Yorkville Enquirer,* April 26, 1866.

27. This is shown by election results and mentioned in the testimony of Alexander P. Wylie in *Late Insurrectionary States* 5:1425.

28. *Yorkville Enquirer,* September 30, 1869.

29. *Late Insurrectionary States* 3:365–66.

30. John William De Forest, *A Union Officer in the Reconstruction* (Baton Rouge: Louisiana State University Press, 1997), 100–101.

31. *1868 Convention,* 638, 869.

32. George M. Fredrickson, *The Black Image in the White Mind: The Debate on Afro-American Character and Destiny, 1817–1914* (New York: Harper & Row, 1971), 172–74; quotation on 174.

33. Samuel Tinsley to Thaddeus Stevens, March 15, 1868, Stevens Papers.

34. John Wooley and John H. McDevitt to Gov. Scott, October 27, 1868, Scott Papers.

35. Samuel Tinsley to Thaddeus Stevens, March 15, 1868, Stevens Papers.

36. A. G. Hayes to Thaddeus Stevens, July 20, 1868, Stevens Papers.

37. Wm. M. Thomas to Thaddeus Stevens, May 9, 1868, Stevens Papers.

38. Eric Foner has noted the tendency of white Unionists to be the strongest advocates of disfranchising former Rebels. See Foner, *Reconstruction,* 323–24.

39. Corley to Stevens, February 6, 1866, Stevens Papers. The problem Corley referred to continued into the early part of congressional Reconstruction. White Republican George Dusenberry of Abbeville County sent a letter to the Republican governor by addressing it to the governor's secretary. He explained, "Had I directed it to the Governor, it is very doubtful whether he would have got it, as letters have been intercepted directed to prominent Republicans." See *Third District Investigation,* 532.

40. Solomon Breibart, "The Constitutional Convention of 1868" (master's thesis, University of North Carolina, 1938), 50, 53, 57, 59–60.

41. Simkins and Woody, *South Carolina during Reconstruction,* 86–88; quotations on 87.

42. If prewar immigrants to the state are considered scalawags and postwar immigrants carpetbaggers, then sixteen of fifty-one whites in the convention were carpetbaggers and thirty-five were scalawags.

43. Trescot made this judgment before elections to the convention were held, but since Republicans almost exclusively won election, he would doubtless have had the same opinion of the convention. See Trescot, "Letter of William Henry Trescot," 576.

44. Channing, *Crisis of Fear,* 187. Channing is writing of Trescot's prewar beliefs, but the phrase felicitously summarizes his Reconstruction attitudes as well. Trescot and his peers had, in this respect at the least, learned nothing and forgotten nothing.

45. Trescot, "Letter of William Henry Trescot," 579; Corley, "To the Voters."

46. *Charleston Daily News,* March 9, 1868.

47. *Charleston Mercury,* February 24, 1868; *1868 Convention,* 158. The cited issue of the *Mercury* contained a special section with "sketches" of all the delegates to the convention. Almost all were as unflattering as that of Mackey, and many if not most contain misleading or even libelous aspersions. The reporter for the paper was eventually expelled from the convention hall by the outraged members. See *1868 Convention,* 178.

48. *Charleston Mercury,* February 24, 1868.

49. *Charleston Daily News*, March 9, 1868.

50. *Charleston Mercury*, February 24, 1868.

51. See Michael Les Benedict, "Reform Republicans and the Retreat from Reconstruction," in *The Facts of Reconstruction: Essays in Honor of John Hope Franklin*, ed. Eric Anderson and Alfred A. Moss Jr. (Baton Rouge: Louisiana State University Press, 1991). Quotation on page 71.

52. Benedict, "Reform Republicans," 69.

53. Ibid., 70–71; *Nation*, October 1, 1868; *New York Times*, July 31, 1867, and January 23, 1868. See also Perman, *Reunion without Compromise.*

54. *New York Times*, January 23, 1868.

55. And neither profile was entirely flattering. See sketches of F. J. Moses Jr. and James Rutland in the *New York Times*, January 23, 1868.

56. *New York Times*, July 31, 1867, and January 23, 1868.

57. South Carolina Republicans clearly felt tremendous unwillingness to become a problem for the national party. On the necessity of southern Republicans to choose between party and section on economic measures, the best work is Seip, *South Returns.*

58. *1868 Convention*, 196, 375–76.

59. Ibid., 196, 376–78.

60. Ibid., 412.

61. Ibid., 438–39.

62. Ibid., 226, 227.

63. Ibid., 198. The courts eventually decided that the contracts for slaves could not be impaired; thus the ordinance passed by the convention was ruled unconstitutional. See Simkins and Woody, *South Carolina during Reconstruction*, 100.

64. *1868 Convention*, 198–99. He later called the former rulers "the most corrupt and damnable of all political leaders" and "the vilest traitors to the Union and humanity that ever cursed the soil of South Carolina" (493).

65. *1868 Convention*, 71.

66. *Charleston Mercury*, February 24, 1868.

67. *1868 Convention*, 595.

68. Ibid., 17.

69. Ibid., 49.

70. Ibid., 825–35. The two were Henry W. Webb, a white carpetbagger from Connecticut, and Thomas Williamson, a black Abbevillian who had been free (and a slaveholder) before the war. William J. McKinley, a black tailor from Charleston, had also supported the qualification but was absent for the final vote. See *Charleston Mercury*, February 24, 1868.

71. *1868 Convention*, 738.

72. See Simkins and Woody, *South Carolina during Reconstruction*, 39, 97.

73. See, for example, *1868 Convention*, 87, 101, 637, 649. These preferences may have been the results of frustration with the old leaders' success in governing with the least public accountability they could get away with, culminating in the refusal of the secession convention to submit their decision to a public vote.

74. Simkins and Woody, *South Carolina during Reconstruction*, 101; Martin Abbott, "County Officers in South Carolina in 1868," *South Carolina Historical Magazine* 60, no.

1 (January 1959): 30–40; Alexia J. Helsley and Michael E. Stauffer, *South Carolina Court Records: An Introduction for Genealogists* (Columbia: SCDAH, 1993).

75. Abbott, "County Officers," provides some evidence to support the supposition.

76. For discussion of school funding in antebellum South Carolina, see Thornton, "Fiscal Policy." The need for schools is mentioned in the 1865 convention journal on page 55, but no provision was passed by that body. See *1865 Convention.*

77. *1868 Convention,* 257.

78. See Corley, "To the Voters"; Armstrong, *Speech;* Orr, *Southern Politics;* and Daniel H. Chamberlain, *The Facts and the Figures: The Practical and Trutful* [sic] *Record of the Republican Party of South Carolina* (Columbia, S.C.: J. W. Denny, 1870), 15. All in SCL.

79. *1868 Convention,* 464–68. Proponents of the homestead accused Robertson and Rutland of opposing it on personal grounds: both were creditors rather than debtors and thus stood to lose money by the passage of the act. Robertson was in fact one of the largest creditors in the state. Rutland admitted to being a creditor but said he was nevertheless a poor man; this would seem to strengthen the case that he was self-interested in the debate. See 473, 495, 503.

80. Ibid., 493.

81. Ibid., 506.

82. Ibid., 785.

83. Ibid., 622, 788, 779. In fact, the legalization of divorce in South Carolina was not accomplished until the passage of a law to that effect by the legislature in 1872. Most of the opposition to the law came from upcountry whites of both parties. Seven years later, and two years after Reconstruction ended, Democrats repealed the law, and divorce was not allowed in the state until halfway through the twentieth century. For an insightful analysis of this history, see Janet Hudson, "From Constitution to Constitution, 1868–1895: South Carolina's Unique Stance on Divorce," *South Carolina Historical Magazine* 98, no. 1 (1997): 75–96.

84. *1868 Convention,* 785.

85. Ibid., 838. While Whipper was the only delegate to speak for women's suffrage at the convention, Simeon Corley did later address Congress on the subject, as previously mentioned.

86. Ibid., 72, 100, 353–56; Eric Foner, *Freedom's Lawmakers: A Directory of Black Officeholders during Reconstruction,* 2nd ed. (Baton Rouge: Louisiana State University Press, 1996), 175–76. Another interpretation is that Leslie was suggesting adding those words to the state constitution, but given his unwillingness to support antidiscrimination laws in this and other contexts, I believe he was disputing Randolph's contention that the races were created equal.

87. *1868 Convention,* 890–91. He also opined somewhat less persuasively that it was wrong to integrate "children, who are more prejudiced" than their parents.

88. Ibid., 894.

89. Ibid., 900–901.

90. Ibid., 901–2.

91. Ibid., 211, 310.

92. Ibid., 672–73, 897.

93. *Charleston Daily News,* March 9, 16, 19, 1868.

*3. The Democratic Counterattack*

1. Simkins and Woody, *South Carolina during Reconstruction,* 107–11.

2. *An Appeal to the Honorable the Senate of the United States, in Behalf of the Conservative People of South Carolina, against the Adoption, by Congress, of the New Constitution Proposed for South Carolina* (Columbia, S.C.: Phoenix Book and Job Power Press, 1868), 5. This document is a pamphlet held by Woodruff Library, Emory University, Atlanta (hereafter cited as *Conservative Appeal to the Senate*).

3. *Conservative Appeal to the Senate,* 4, 1.

4. Robert E. Shalhope, "Toward a Republican Synthesis: The Emergence of Understanding of Republicanism in American Historiography," *William and Mary Quarterly,* 3rd ser., 29 (January 1972): 49–80; Sylvia Frey, "Republicanism: Sources, Meanings, and Usages in American History," *Historical Journal* 35, no. 2 (1992): 471–85; James T. Kloppenberg, "Republicanism in American History and Historiography," *Toqueville Review* 13, no. 1 (1992): 119–36; Daniel T. Rodgers, "Republicanism: The Career of a Concept," *Journal of American History* 79, no. 1 (1992): 11–38; Lacy K. Ford Jr., *Origins of Southern Radicalism: The South Carolina Upcountry, 1800–1860* (New York: Oxford University Press, 1988), 351–65.

5. *Conservative Appeal to the Senate,* 2. The authors were no less distressed at the "representation without taxation" afforded to those who did not pay tax but served in government.

6. Foner, *Reconstruction,* 340–41, states flatly that the election was "the last presidential campaign to center on white supremacy."

7. U.S. Congress, *Papers in the Case of A. S. Wallace vs. W. D. Simpson, Fourth Congressional District, South Carolina,* 41st Cong., 1st sess., H. Rept. 5 (Serial 1403) (hereafter cited as *Wallace vs. Simpson*); U.S. Congress, *Papers in the Case of S. L. Hoge vs. J. P. Reed, Third Congressional District, South Carolina,* 41st Cong., 1st sess., H. Rept. 3 (Serial 1403) (hereafter cited as *Hoge vs. Reed*). In both reports, practically every witness testifies that many Republicans were prevented from voting by threats and intimidation. See also *Third District Investigation,* 339, 425.

8. *Third District Investigation,* 604–6.

9. Ibid., 682.

10. A. L. Hammond, M.D., to Gov. Scott, October 1, 1868, Scott Papers.

11. *Third District Investigation,* 658.

12. *Wallace vs. Simpson,* 37.

13. *Charleston Courier,* July 14, 1868.

14. R. J. Donaldson to Gov. Scott, September 3, 1868, Scott Papers.

15. *Third District Investigation,* 350.

16. Ibid., 429.

17. Ibid. 395.

18. Ibid., 613, 602.

19. Ibid., 681, 100–103.

20. *Hoge vs. Reed,* 29.

21. See John Hammond Moore, "South Carolina's Reaction to the Photoplay, *The Birth of a Nation,*" *Proceedings of the South Carolina Historical Association, 1963* (Columbia: South Carolina Historical Association, 1964), 30–40.

22. See Francis B. Simkins, "The Ku Klux Klan in South Carolina, 1868–1871," *Journal of Negro History* 12 (October 1927): 618.

23. See Zuczek, *State of Rebellion,* 60–61, 160, and Stephen Kantrowitz, *Ben Tillman and the Reconstruction of White Supremacy* (Chapel Hill: University of North Carolina Press, 2000), 57–59. The novelty of the Klan has also been questioned; Kantrowitz, for example, sees it as comparable to the prewar slave patrols. To the extent that their common purpose was white supremacy, the comparison is valid. But while slave patrols sought to keep blacks enslaved, the Klan sought to influence electoral politics through terrorism. As such it was a product of the new postwar political environment in which white supremacy had to be maintained through elections. The key point, one which fairly summarizes Zuczek's book, is that Klanism was one tactic that white Democrats employed in their continuing war against Reconstruction.

24. The foremost proponent of the latter thesis is Stagg, "Problem of Klan Violence."

25. Trelease, *White Terror,* xlvi–xlvii. Two recent studies confirm this judgment for South Carolina: Zuczek, *State of Rebellion,* 57–58, and Williams, *Great South Carolina Ku Klux Klan Trials,* 85–89.

26. For a "Ku Kluks" warning to white Unionists, see W. H. Phillips and others to Gov. Scott, August 19, 1868, Scott Papers. The notice warns Union "league Devvels" that they are "traitors to there Kuntry" and that "Hell is with out Doubt yore portion with out a speeddy change."

27. *Hoge vs. Reed,* 34.

28. *Third District Investigation,* 360–63.

29. Ibid., 667–71.

30. Ibid., 125, 664, 382.

31. Ibid., 103, 389, 393, 407, 420–23, 533.

32. *Hoge vs. Reed,* 39.

33. See, for example, *Third District Investigation,* 389.

34. *Wallace vs. Simpson,* 41.

35. *Third District Investigation,* 382.

36. Ibid., 393–94.

37. Ibid., 273, 418.

38. It is unclear why Republicans did not push for the use of secret ballots. As early as the summer of 1868, white Republican Benjamin Odell Duncan of Newberry had foreseen the need for "every polling box to be kept in a closed room." See B. O. Duncan to Gov. Scott, July 19, 1868, Scott Papers. Perhaps the expense and difficulty of such an arrangement prevented it, or perhaps it was simply tradition.

39. *Third District Investigation,* 25, 557.

40. Ibid., 547.

41. Ibid., 582.

42. Ibid., 71. Such sentiments were echoed by many others. T. J. Roberts, a fifty-year-old farmer who always voted Democratic, nevertheless would not attend the club meetings because he "was opposed to the manner in which they conducted the Club" (618). Sixteen-year-old John McCalla quoted his father as saying that "he couldn't belong to either party." The elder McCalla went about armed after a confrontation with a man named Briscoe, whom McCalla denounced for committing outrages against black Republicans (403).

43. Zephaniah Platt and others to Gov. Scott, October 19, 1868, Scott Papers. The petitioners presented themselves as a committee of four Democrats and four Republicans chosen to represent the respectable and peaceable people of the town.

44. Ibid., 228, 300–305, 341. Apparently such "general consent" tickets were not uncommon. For a similar situation in Darlington County, see Holt, *Black over White,* 103, and B. F. Whittemore to Gov. Scott, November 5, 1868, Scott Papers.

45. Vandiver, *Traditions and History of Anderson County,* 11–12; *Third District Investigation,* 664.

46. *Mercury,* February 24, 1868; *Third District Investigation,* 407.

47. Thomas H. Pope, *The History of Newberry County, South Carolina,* vol. 2, *1860–1990* (Columbia: University of South Carolina Press, 1992), 32–33; *Third District Investigation,* 120.

48. Vandiver, *Traditions and History of Anderson County,* 203; *Third District Investigation,* 673.

49. Mrs. John Cochran to Robert K. Scott, October 27, 1868, Scott Papers.

50. *Hoge vs. Reed,* 28–30; *Wallace vs. Simpson,* 33–36.

51. See, for example, the testimony of E. S. J. Hayes, a white Republican from Lexington, in *Hoge vs. Reed,* 28.

52. *Wallace vs. Simpson,* 57–58.

53. U.S. Circuit Court (Fourth Circuit), *Proceedings in the Ku Klux Trials at Columbia, S.C.* (Columbia, S.C.: State Printers, 1871), 178.

54. *Third District Investigation,* 673–74, 497.

55. Ibid., 350, 354, 671.

56. Most sources on South Carolina's Reconstruction mention Dill's assassination. I have relied for details on Thomas J. Kirkland and Robert M. Kennedy, *Historic Camden: Part Two, Nineteenth Century* (Columbia, S.C.: State, 1926), 201–2.

57. See, for example, the testimony of James L. Orr in *Late Insurrectionary States* 3:3.

58. *Third District Investigation,* 216, 170, 22, 205–6, 194.

59. Ibid., 39, 79, 102, 62, 312, 17, 246, 240.

60. Williamson, *After Slavery,* 260; *Third District Investigation,* 328, 376; Thompson, "Blacks, Carpetbaggers, and Scalawags," 213. Thompson incorrectly identifies Martin as a carpetbagger who arrived in South Carolina after the war.

61. Thompson, "Blacks, Carpetbaggers, and Scalawags," 85.

62. *Late Insurrectionary States* 3:447. Since Chesnut was only claiming to speak for his own county of Kershaw, this was a clear reference to Dill, who apparently made himself obnoxious by heading the Kershaw Union League.

63. *Late Insurrectionary States* 3:449.

64. *Third District Investigation,* 384.

65. *Late Insurrectionary States* 3:456.

66. *Third District Investigation,* 407–8, 530–33.

67. Quotations are taken from the comments of William Hill, H. S. Cason, and Matthew McDonald, Democrats elected to county offices on a "general consent" ticket, and H. W. Lawson, who did not join the Democratic club. See *Third District Investigation,* 328, 342, 346, 353.

68. *Third District Investigation,* 386; Nelson [Sassard] to [Arthur G.] Cud[worth], October 7, 1868, Arthur G. Cudworth Papers, SCL.

69. *Third District Investigation,* 377, 386, 487–91, 347. For example, she claimed to have heard Henry say that Milford was next on the group's hit list, a belief shared by many others, including Milford.

70. Zuczek, *State of Rebellion,* 47–63.

71. Hampton's message apparently was originally printed in the *Columbia Phoenix,* October 23, 1868, and reprinted in newspapers around the state. It is reproduced in *Late Insurrectionary States* 5:1248–49.

72. This is Zuczek's contention. See *State of Rebellion,* 60–61.

73. *Late Insurrectionary States* 5:1249.

74. Quoted in the *Nation* 7, no. 165 (August 27, 1868): 1.

75. Aiken was editor of the *Rural Carolinian,* a monthly magazine on agricultural improvements published throughout Radical Reconstruction. Simkins and Woody consider Aiken to have been "foremost among the leaders" of the agricultural reform movement. See Simkins and Woody, *South Carolina during Reconstruction,* 259.

76. *Third District Investigation,* 415, 391, 566–67, 585–86.

77. Ibid., 386–91; 396–97.

78. Ibid., 396–97.

79. J. A. Leland to Gov. Robert K. Scott, January 5, 6, 1869, Scott Papers. Moreover, an informant named Burton wrote to the governor asking for three hundred dollars in exchange for naming two of Martin's killers; he later named Joe Davis and William K. Talbert. Surely if he had known of the involvement of Logan and J. W. Talbert—not to mention more prominent citizens—he would have advertised the fact. See A. B. to Gov. Robert K. Scott, October 23, 1868, and A. Burton to Gov. Robert K. Scott, November 1, 1868, Scott Papers.

80. See Ransier to T. S. Tullock, October 19, 1868, and Scott to T. S. Tullock, October 20, 1868, William E. Chandler Papers, Library of Congress (hereafter cited as Chandler Papers).

81. *Third District Investigation,* 496, 529. I have quoted Hutson Lomax's account of the exchange, but his recollection is strongly supported by C. V. Hammond, the white conductor of the train. Furthermore, the same story is told by Aiken's admiring biographer, with the sole addition that Randolph had been making incendiary speeches. See Claudius Hornsby Pritchard Jr., "Colonel D. Wyatt Aiken, 1828–1887: South Carolina's Militant Agrarian" (master's thesis, Longwood College, 1965), 50–51.

82. Pritchard, "Colonel D. Wyatt Aiken," 50–51.

83. Virginia Carolina Smith Aiken Diary, vol. 1, SCL. See entries for April 3 and April 24, 1872.

84. The speaker in this instance was Simpson Bobo, a wealthy planter and industrialist in Spartanburg. See *Late Insurrectionary States* 4:797.

85. The phrase is from a newspaper article attached to Minute Book January 1869–March 1872, U.S. Circuit Court, District of South Carolina, National Archives, East Point, Ga.

86. *Third District Investigation,* 531, 674.

87. Remarks of Hon. S. Corley, *Congressional Globe,* January 28, 1869, 40th Cong., 3rd sess., appendix, 94–95. Corley made this appeal during a speech in support of the Fifteenth Amendment. He singled out the national Democratic Party for criticism: "While [t]his party inscribes upon its banner the glaring falsehood that the reconstruction laws

are 'unconstitutional, revolutionary, and void,' it but fires the rebel heart with hate to the Government, and murder to all who support and defend it."

88. *Late Insurrectionary States* 3:26–30.

89. W. O. B. Hiott to Scott, November 7, 1868, Scott Papers.

90. Testimony is found in *Third District Investigation* as well as *Hoge vs. Reed* and *Wallace vs. Simpson.*

91. Ishmael Powell to Gov. Scott, November 30, 1868, and John T. Henderson to Gov. Scott, November 30, 1868, Scott Papers.

92. James Perry to Gov. Scott, December 10, 1868, Scott Papers.

93. R. W. Cousart to Gov. Scott, December 9, 1868, and J. F. G. Mittag to Gov. Scott, December 23, 1868, Scott Papers.

94. W. F. DeKnight to William Stone, November 6, 1868, Scott Papers.

95. L. P. Wagner to Gov. Scott, February 4, 1869, Scott Papers.

96. P. J. O'Connell to Gov. Scott, April 4, 1869, Scott Papers.

97. Governor Scott's address quoted in *Charleston Courier,* July 10, 1868.

98. Richard Humbert to Gov. Scott, July 18, 1868, Scott Papers.

99. Robert L. Martin and H. W. Duncan to Gov. Scott, July 25, 1868; "Conservatives of Union County" to Gov. Scott, July 26, 1868; M. L. Bonham to Gov. Scott, August 19, 1868; and William Whaley to Gov. Scott, September 18, 1868; all in Scott Papers.

100. John B. Hubbard to Gov. Scott, September 3, 1868, Scott Papers. According to Hubbard, John Bates, the leader of this group, exercised great power over his fellow Union County blacks and used this power to provoke the whites, who were bitterly opposed to the federal and state governments in any case.

101. T. J. Mackey to Gov. Scott, September 16, October 10, 1868, Scott Papers.

102. Sebastian Kraft to Gov. Scott, August 5, 1868, Scott Papers.

103. Richard H. Cain to Gov. Scott, October 24, 1868, Scott Papers.

104. Robert K. Scott to T. L. Tullock, October 20, 1868, Chandler Papers.

105. Scott as quoted in Thompson, *Ousting the Carpetbagger,* 47.

106. F. J. Moses to Gov. Scott, February 20, 1869, Scott Papers.

107. Lem Guffin to Gov. Scott, January 22, March 31, April 5, 1869, all in Scott Papers.

108. Lem Guffin to Gov. Scott, March 31, 1869, and James W. Hayward to Gov. Scott, June 20, 1869, Scott Papers.

109. F. J. Moses to Gov. Scott, April 4, 1869, Scott Papers.

110. George W. Williams to Gov. Scott, April 3, 1869, and Lem Guffin to Gov. Scott, March 31, 1869, Scott Papers.

111. James N. Brisco to Gov. Scott, June 8, 1869, and P. A. Eichelberger to Gov. Scott, June 19, 1869, Scott Papers.

112. Quoted in Zuczek, *State of Rebellion,* 72. See also Julian Landrum Mims, "Radical Reconstruction in Edgefield County, 1865–1877" (master's thesis, University of South Carolina, 1969), 23–24, and Abbott, "County Officers," 32. It may be that McDevitt's frustration with his position poisoned him against the society he lived in as well as the state government, thus making it easier for him to rationalize corruption. In any case, in 1868 he was a young Citadel graduate whose neighbors had confidence in his character, but in 1875 he fled the state after the issuance of a warrant for his arrest.

113. Lem Guffin to Scott, July 22, 1869, Scott Papers. In fact, it may be that Abbeville Democrats would devise a less direct way of dealing with Guffin. The Guffins were one

of two prominent white Republican families in the county, and more than the other, they had "aroused the antipathy of the white population during this period." In 1871, when Lem's brother Pem Guffin served in the state legislature, and his other brother Charles was mayor of Abbeville, it was put out that the three had been involved in a robbery of the county treasurer's office. The evidence was circumstantial, and Lem asserted that there had been no robbery but that the money was taken by the treasurer, who was thought by Republicans to be "a man easily swayed by the factions around him"—that is, the vigilantes. All Guffins were acquitted, but the treasurer was not put on trial. See Lowry Ware, *Old Abbeville: Scenes of the Past of a Town Where Old Time Things Are Not Forgotten* (Columbia, S.C.: SCMAR, 1992), 121–25.

114. John Feriter to Scott, November 9, 1869, Scott Papers.

115. Charles, *Narrative History of Union County,* 225.

116. Capt. J. A. Walker to Gov. Scott, September 20, 1870, Scott Papers.

117. H. H. Wilson to John B. Hubbard, September 21, 1870, Scott Papers.

118. John B. Hubbard to Gov. Scott, September 21, 1870, Scott Papers.

119. Robert H. Woody, "The South Carolina Election of 1870," *North Carolina Historical Review* 8 (April 1931): 173, 180.

120. J. A. Leland to Gov. Scott, November 4, 1870. Leland, a professor and trial justice, frequently corresponded with Scott, and the governor may have trusted him more than was wise: Leland was later arrested for complicity with the Ku Klux Klan. Leland defends himself in his post-Reconstruction memoir, *A Voice from South Carolina.*

121. Boston, Scott, and Hutsin to Gov. Scott, October 24, 1870, Scott Papers.

122. Zuczek, *State of Rebellion,* 88–89.

123. J. L. Watson to Gov. Scott, December 9, 1870, Scott Papers.

124. William Magill Fleming to Gov. Scott, January 1, 1871, and Rev. W. J. Parker to Gov. Scott, October 2, 1871, Scott Papers.

125. Warren Diver to Gov. Scott, September 1, 1871, Scott Papers.

126. Capt. Felix H. Torbell to Maj. W. P. Carlin, commander U.S. troops in South Carolina, December 3, 1870, Scott Papers.

127. Zuczek, *State of Rebellion,* 92.

128. *Late Insurrectionary States* 3:25–30, 55–56.

129. Zuczek, *State of Rebellion,* 103–6, has shown that the violence subsided well before Grant's measures could have any effect, most likely because its aims had been achieved; Governor Scott had recalled the arms of many militia units, and many Republican officials had been frightened off. See 88–117, especially 103–6.

130. Javan Bryant to Gov. Scott, October 9, 1871, Scott Papers.

131. L. A. Hill to Gov. Scott, October 28, 1871, Scott Papers.

132. W. F. W. Williams to Gov. Scott, November 23, 1871, Scott Papers.

133. Zuczek, *State of Rebellion,* 104.

134. Warren D. Wilkes to Gov. Scott, March 20, 1872, Scott Papers.

135. David Johnson to Gov. Scott, May 4, 5, 1872, Scott Papers.

### *4. The Perils of Faction*

1. This document, usually referred to as the Fraud Report, has been used extensively by historians. It was published in S.C. General Assembly, *Reports and Resolutions of the*

*General Assembly of South Carolina, at the Regular Session, 1877–78* (Columbia, S.C.: Calvo and Patton, 1878) (hereafter cited as Fraud Report).

2. Williamson, *After Slavery,* 397. In addition, much of the new information provided by the Fraud Report was unreliable and politically motivated. Only three trials resulted from the report, and in at least one of these cases, that of Francis L. Cardozo, the report almost certainly impugns an innocent man. For a thorough discussion of the case and a compelling argument for Cardozo's innocence, see W. Lewis Burke, "Post-Reconstruction Justice: The Prosecution and Trial of Francis Lewis Cardozo," *South Carolina Law Review* 53, no. 2 (Winter 2002): 361–413.

3. Other common accusations were that one's rival was incompetent or secretly a Democrat.

4. *Charleston Courier,* August 17, 1868.

5. S.C. General Assembly, *Journal of the House of Representatives of the State of South Carolina, Being the Special Session of 1868,* (Columbia, S.C.: John W. Denny, 1868), September 15, 1868. The white Republicans who supported the civil rights bill were South Carolinians William S. Collins, George F. McIntyre, and Franklin J. Moses; North Carolinian John L. Neagle; and Massachusetts native J. H. Jenks. Neagle, who had owned slaves before the war and served in the Confederate Army during it, is not counted as a scalawag because he was a postwar migrant to South Carolina.

6. The other three meet the definition of a scalawag used in this study because they had moved to South Carolina before the war. These were Robert J. Donaldson, originally from England; James M. Allen, originally form New York; and Thomas J. Coghlan, originally from Ireland. See *Senate Journal,* Special Session, 1868, September 8, 1868.

7. *Charleston Courier,* August 31, 1868.

8. Holt, *Black over White,* 95–121.

9. Williamson, *After Slavery,* 360.

10. T. N. Tolbert to Gov. Scott, January 12, 1871, Scott Papers.

11. *Columbia Daily Union-Herald,* July 26, 1874. The *Union-Herald* got its wish, as the ticket was revised to include white Democrat John T. Sloan Jr. in a general consent ticket.

12. J. F. G. Mittag to Gov. Chamberlain, December 10, 1874, Chamberlain Papers.

13. For Klan threats to Wooley, see testimony of John H. McDevitt in *Third District Evidence,* 681.

14. *Columbia Daily Union,* May 8, 1872.

15. Ibid., August 28, 1872.

16. Quoted in Reynolds, *Reconstruction,* 304.

17. De Large was not the first to run afoul of Bowen. Scalawag Albert Gallatin Mackey was removed as collector of customs at the port of Charleston, probably because of the influence of Congressman Bowen and Senator Frederick A. Sawyer. See Mackey, *Political Treason.* Another of Bowen's rivals was carpetbagger J. H. Jenks. See John M. Morris to Sir (perhaps William Claflin, William E. Chandler, or T. L. Tullock), October 3, 1868, Chandler Papers.

18. In addition to Holt, *Black over White,* 116–20, see Walter J. Fraser Jr., *Charleston! Charleston! The History of a Southern City* (Columbia: University of South Carolina Press, 1989), 297–98.

19. Petitions and statements are found in Box 13, Folder 26, Scott Papers.

20. J. H. Hendrix, "Another Hayes Dodge!" broadsheet, n.d., Lexington County Collection, SCL.

21. The exceptions to this statement are certain wartime debts that were not related to the war and thus were honored.

22. Simkins and Woody, *South Carolina during Reconstruction,* 149–50; Reynolds, *Reconstruction,* 115–16.

23. *Charleston Daily News,* July 17, 1868.

24. Scott made this remark at least twice, once in his special message to the legislature in 1872 and again to the 1874 investigating committee (hereafter cited as the Dunn committee, after chairman Thomas C. Dunn). See S.C. General Assembly, *Journal of the House of Representatives of South Carolina,* Regular Session, 1871–72 (Columbia, S.C.: Republican Printing, 1872), January 9, 1872 (hereafter cited as *House Journal*); and testimony of Robert K. Scott, "Report of the Special Joint Committee to Ascertain what Bonds of the State Were Pledged by the Financial Agent of the State as Collateral Security for State Loans, &c.," in *Reports and Resolutions, 1874–75,* 731–32.

25. Testimony of Niles G. Parker, "Report of the Commission to Investigate the Indebtedness of the State," in *Reports and Resolutions, 1877–78,* 920. This report, compiled after Redemption had occurred, was the last of several legislative investigations made into the debt of the state; all the others took place during Reconstruction and were conducted by Republicans.

26. See, for example, Simkins and Woody, *South Carolina during Reconstruction,* 152. This first loan was negotiated at 18 or 20 percent interest, according to Governor Scott's later recollection, while the state bonds paid 6, 7, or 8 percent depending on the issue. See testimony of Robert K. Scott, Dunn committee, in *Reports and Resolutions, 1874–75,* 731.

27. *Charleston Daily News,* November 26, 1868.

28. See Williamson, *After Slavery,* 383. I have found no evidence to support the assertion. The traditional sources—Reynolds, *Reconstruction;* Simkins and Woody, *South Carolina during Reconstruction;* and the Democratic investigation of 1877—all point out the recklessness and dishonesty of the Financial Board's moves but do not suggest that they personally profited from them. Williamson's sources are Reynolds, *Reconstruction,* and a passage of the Fraud Report of 1877 that refers to a railroad scheme unrelated to the bonds here discussed.

29. See S.C. General Assembly, *Statutes at Large of South Carolina,* 14:18 and testimony of Niles G. Parker, "Report of the Commission to Investigate the Indebtedness," 920.

30. Testimony of Daniel H. Chamberlain, Dunn committee, in *Reports and Resolutions, 1874–75,* 748.

31. Testimony before Dunn committee, in *Reports and Resolutions, 1874–75,* 732, 743, 749, 750, 759, 766.

32. If detailed reports had been kept and published, the buyers of bonds, knowing which bonds they had bought at what price, would surely have detected the fraud sooner.

33. Testimony of Niles G. Parker, Fraud Report, 1581.

34. Fraud Report, 1019–20.

35. Williamson, *After Slavery,* 415.

36. Simkins and Woody, *South Carolina during Reconstruction,* 134.

37. Fraud Report, 1678.

38. Historians have generally been equivocal on whether bribes were offered prior to the phosphate bill. See Holt, *Black over White,* 140.

39. Fraud Report, 1020–22.

40. Woody, "Election of 1870," 168–73.

41. Chamberlain, *Facts and the Figures,* October 4, 1870, 2–5; Reuben Tomlinson, "Report of the State Auditor, 1869," in *Reports and Resolutions, 1869–70,* 193–207.

42. Chamberlain, *Facts and the Figures,* 5. At least one investment firm agreed: Samuel Barlow, of Barlow, Larocque, and McFarland in New York, wrote that South Carolina bonds were selling poorly because other states had repudiated, because there were fears of more bond issues, and because "it is supposed by some that when you are really reconstructed, the State authorities may be unwilling to recognise a large part of its debt created under Black rule." Samuel L. M. Barlow to James L. Orr, February 9, 1871, Orr-Patterson Papers, Southern Historical Collection, University of North Carolina, Chapel Hill.

43. F. J. Moses to Gov. Scott, August 14, 1868, and John Wooley and John McDevitt to Gov. Scott, October 27, 1868, Scott Papers.

44. Chamberlain, *Facts and the Figures,* 5.

45. Scott said this in his annual message to the legislature on December 2, 1872. See *House Journal,* Regular Session, 1872–73, 27.

46. Thornton, "Fiscal Policy." It is also possible that taxes were more onerous than the tax rate would imply because property values were assessed too high. At least, such was the claim of the Reformers' candidate for governor. See *Late Insurrectionary States* 3:241.

47. Trelease, *White Terror,* 350–51.

48. Testimony of R. B. Carpenter in *Late Insurrectionary States* 3:250.

49. See testimony of M. C. Butler in *Late Insurrectionary States* 3:240–41, 4:1187. While statewide Democratic candidates ran on the Reform ticket, Democratic candidates in white-majority districts often continued to call themselves Democrats.

50. *Late Insurrectionary States* 3:228, 240.

51. Leland, *Voice from South Carolina,* 65–69; *Late Insurrectionary States* 3:241. Carpenter told the congressional committee, "I am as certain that I received a thousand majority in that county as I am of my existence." The count returned by Crews was a thousand majority in favor of Scott.

52. *Late Insurrectionary States* 3:228.

53. Ibid.

54. Fraud Report, 1225–1385.

55. The existence of a dedicated sinking fund also promoted investor confidence, since bonds would never become worthless for lack of buyers. If the price got low enough, the state would buy back its bond.

56. Fraud Report, 1575–88; Reynolds, *Reconstruction,* 465–66. Reynolds reproduces in its entirety a letter from Chamberlain to Kimpton outlining the swindle. Chamberlain was later at pains to deny that the letter mentioned anything illegal.

57. R. J. Donaldson to Gov. Scott, September 11, 1869, Scott Papers.

58. The Land Commission scandal occurred just as black Republicans became more insistent on receiving what they considered a fair share of representation in government. Holt presents the replacement of Leslie with De Large as crucial to that movement. See Holt, *Black over White,* 108.

59. This account is based mainly on Carol R. Bleser's monograph on the Land Commission, *The Promised Land: The History of the South Carolina Land Commission, 1869–1890* (Columbia: University of South Carolina Press, 1969), especially chapter 4.

60. *Charleston Daily News,* March 31, 1871.

61. Tax-Payers' Convention of South Carolina (1871), *Proceedings of the Tax-Payers' Convention of South Carolina, Held at Columbia, Beginning May 9th, and Ending May 12th, 1871* (Charleston, S.C.: Edward Perry, 1871); Zuczek, *State of Rebellion,* 93–108, especially 104–5. Zuczek's judgment is based on Klan outrages reported to the United States Joint Select Committee in 1872 and supported by correspondence received by the governor and chief constable.

62. Thornton, "Fiscal Policy."

63. Testimony of R. B. Carpenter in *Late Insurrectionary States* 3:241–43. Carpenter's figures place South Carolina within the range of tax rates in the South cited in Thornton, "Fiscal Policy," 351. Governor Scott vigorously challenged these figures in his 1872 annual message, claiming that the millage rate was about seven, and that property was assessed "at less than one-third of its market value." See *House Journal,* Regular Session, 1872–73, 26–27.

64. The evidence that taxes were onerous comes from the amount of property sold at sheriff's sales, as advertised in the *Columbia Daily Union* and other papers, and from the governor's assertion that as much as a third of the taxes had not been paid. See *House Journal,* Regular Session, 1872–73, 26–27. For the 1871 double tax, see testimony of R. B. Carpenter in *Late Insurrectionary States* 3:241–43. Carpenter predicted that if the tax were collected, a third of the land in the state would be forfeited for taxes (242).

65. See testimony of Gabriel Cannon in *Late Insurrectionary States* 4:771–72.

66. *1868 Convention,* 457; *Late Insurrectionary States* 3:241–43.

67. *Charleston Daily News,* August 24, 1872. The speaker was Samuel Johnson, a black delegate from Anderson County. Eric Foner identifies him as a free-born literate property owner. See Foner, *Freedom's Lawmakers,* 119.

68. Capt. Felix H. Torbell to Maj. W. P. Carlin, commander U.S. troops in South Carolina, December 3, 1870, Scott Papers.

69. Simkins and Woody, *South Carolina during Reconstruction,* 156; Jerry William Norton, "South Carolina Taxpayers' Convention of 1871" (master's thesis, University of South Carolina, 1970), 36.

70. Norton, "Taxpayers' Convention," 35; Simkins and Woody, *South Carolina during Reconstruction,* 155–56.

71. Simkins and Woody stress the "casual and hasty" character of the examination and determine that the investigators were duped. Norton finds the ease with which the Democrats were misled "inexplicable." Williamson charges that the investigators were themselves invested in state bonds and so declared the debt valid out of selfish motives. See Simkins and Woody, *South Carolina during Reconstruction,* 156–59; Norton, "Taxpayers' Convention," 67; and Williamson, *After Slavery,* 384.

72. The proceedings of the 1871 Tax-Payers' Convention are reprinted in *Late Insurrectionary States* 3:472–520; quotations on 489–90.

73. Simkins and Woody, *South Carolina during Reconstruction,* 118–19; *Charleston Mercury,* February 24, 1868; *New York Times,* July 29, 1867, January 23, 1868; Bowen to Charles Sumner, May 22, 1867, Charles Sumner Papers, Houghton Library, Harvard University.

74. *Charleston Mercury,* February 24, 1868.

75. H. G. Worthington, Collector, to B. H. Bristow, Secretary of the Treasury, February 24, 1875, Records Relating to Customhouse Nominations, 1849–1910, RG 56, Box 430, National Archives II, College Park, Md. (Unfortunately, the contents of these boxes are not in chronological order.)

76. Reuben Tomlinson, State Auditor, to Gov. Scott, Dec 1, 1870, Scott Papers.

77. Holt discusses the importance of the Custom House in *Black over White,* 116–18.

78. Bleser, *Promised Land,* 75; Peggy Lamson, *The Glorious Failure: Black Congressman Robert Brown Elliott and the Reconstruction in South Carolina* (New York: W. W. Norton, 1973), 95; Fraud Report, 730; Williamson, *After Slavery,* 146.

79. Zuczek, *State of Rebellion,* 82.

80. Holt, *Black over White,* 119. Democrat Isaac McKissick, who had lost a bid for A. S. Wallace's seat in Congress, was challenging the election results as well. In April 1872 he dined at Bowen's house, where the two plotted legal strategy. McKissick wrote to his wife that Bowen's case "is to come off before mine and will benefit mine, for if the republicans would steal from and defraud a brother republican what would they do to a democrat." Isaac G. McKissick to "Sallie," April 2, 1872, James Rion McKissick Collection, SCL. McKissick was less successful; Wallace retained his seat.

81. R. W. Newhall to Gov. Scott, October 4, 1871; D. B. Broome to Gov. Scott, October 7, 1871; Samuel Edmonds to Gov. Scott, November 15, 1871; all in Scott Papers.

82. S. W. Knight to Gov. Scott, n.d., Box 18, Folder 29, Scott Papers.

83. William Emory to Gov. Scott, September 26, 1871, and David C. Tyler to Gov. Scott, October 25, 1871, Scott Papers.

84. *Reports and Resolutions, 1871–72,* 867; Simkins and Woody, *South Carolina during Reconstruction,* 159; *Commercial and Financial Chronicle,* November 11, 1871.

85. *Reports and Resolutions, 1871–72,* appendix, 13, 14, 50; 903.

86. Fraud Report, 1595–1619. The testimony of F. J. Moses appears in Fraud Report, 1607–8.

87. Ibid., 1603.

88. The impeachment fraud is detailed on pages 1597–1619 of the Fraud Report.

89. Bleser, *Promised Land,* 82–84.

90. S.C. General Assembly, *Statutes at Large of South Carolina,* 15:170–71. Scott called for this reform in his annual message of 1871. See *House Journal, 1871–72,* 43.

91. S.C. General Assembly, *Statutes at Large of South Carolina,* 15:1–3; Reynolds, *Reconstruction,* 173.

92. F. A. Sawyer, *Speech of Hon. F. A. Sawyer, of South Carolina, in the Senate of the United States, April 13, 1871.* Pamphlet in SCL.

93. *Charleston Daily News,* August 19, 20, 21, 1872.

94. Ibid., August 23, 1872.

95. Ibid., August 22, 1872. The speaker is identified as W. C. Jones, apparently a clerk for Secretary of State Cardozo.

96. Ibid., August 9, 1872.

97. Ibid., August 19, 20, 1872.

98. Ibid., August 23, 1872.

99. Ibid., August 27, 1872. His admission referred, perhaps, to his dealings with the Land Commission. In her study of that agency, Carol Bleser has concluded that Cochran

helped Governor Scott defraud the state by selling Scott's land for him. See Bleser, *Promised Land,* 54–56.

100. *Charleston Daily News,* August 27, 1872.

101. Ibid., August 29, 1872.

102. Ibid., August 24, 1872.

103. Ibid., August 23, 27, 1872.

104. Ibid. It is unclear to whom Cochran was referring. Pay certificates were signed by the Speaker of the House (Moses from 1868 to 1872) or the president of the Senate. Between 1868 and 1872, the presidents of the Senate were Lieutenant Governors Lemuel Boozer and A. J. Ransier. Boozer died in 1870, and Ransier did not bolt. The most likely targets of Cochran's accusation are C. W. Montgomery and David T. Corbin, presidents pro tem. Corbin was a bolter, but he was only president pro tem on two short occasions in 1868 and 1869, and there is no evidence he issued fraudulent pay certificates. Montgomery was president pro tem for most of the period, and many certificates he signed were included as evidence in the Fraud Report. I have not found evidence that he bolted, though. In my opinion the reference is to Whittemore, who *received* several pay certificates and therefore had to sign them in order to collect. In any case, whoever the target of Cochran's allegation was, it was literally incorrect: Moses signed many more pay certificates than anyone else. See Fraud Report, 1401–1531, for a full description of the pay certificate frauds.

105. *Charleston Daily News,* August 24, 1872.

106. Ibid., August 29, 1872.

107. This judgment is based on a list of all the Republicans whom evidence places in the bolters' camp. Of sixty-two bolters I have identified by name, only twenty-one were black. Of these, more than half were from the lowcountry. See appendix B.

108. *Columbia Daily Union,* October 21, 1872. While the report appeared in the paper after the election, it is safe to assume it had been put out in time to work to the regulars' advantage.

109. Election returns taken from *Reports and Resolutions,* 1872–73, 59–67, 129–32, and *Reports and Resolutions, 1874–75,* 084–089, 0126–0127.

110. Quoted in Simkins and Woody, *South Carolina during Reconstruction,* 467. Similar comments by other Democratic papers are quoted.

111. *Reports and Resolutions, 1872–73,* 59–67, 129–32, and *Reports and Resolutions, 1874–75,* 084–089, 0126–0127. In Charleston, perhaps thanks to Bowen's efforts, Grant and Republican congressional candidate Ransier drew over three thousand more votes than did Moses, with the balance going to Tomlinson.

112. *Columbia Daily Union,* September 4, 1872.

113. Ibid., December 19, 1872.

114. See William A. Scott, *The Repudiation of State Debts* (Boston: Thomas Y. Crowell, 1893), 78–93; Reginald McGrane, *Foreign Bondholders and American State Debts* (New York: Macmillan, 1935), 344–55; and B. U. Ratchford, *American State Debts* (Durham, N.C.: Duke University Press, 1941), 162–96.

115. Scott, *Repudiation of State Debts,* 87–88.

116. Reynolds, *Reconstruction,* 473–74.

117. R. H. Woody, "Franklin J. Moses, Jr., Scalawag Governor," *North Carolina Historical Review* 10 (April 1933): 123–24.

118. Woody, "Franklin J. Moses," 124–26.

119. *Columbia Daily Union,* December 10, 1872.
120. Holt, *Black over White,* 120.
121. Fraud Report, 629–94 (quoted line from 646); Reynolds, *Reconstruction,* 229.
122. Scott, *Repudiation of State Debts,* 88–89.

***5. Moderation in Pursuit of Justice***

1. Pike, *Prostrate State.*

2. See Robert S. Durden, *James Shepherd Pike: Republicanism and the American Negro, 1850–1882* (Durham, N.C.: Duke University Press, 1957).

3. See Durden, *James Shepherd Pike,* 201–2, 214n40.

4. Pike, *Prostrate State,* 36, 68, 67.

5. See Durden, *James Shepherd Pike,* 215–19.

6. *Atlantic Monthly,* February 1874, 233–34.

7. *Nation,* April 16, 1874, 247.

8. Tax-Payers' Convention of South Carolina (1874), *Proceedings of the Tax-Payers' Convention of South Carolina, Held at Columbia, Beginning February 17, and Ending February 20, 1874* (Charleston, S.C.: News and Courier Job Presses, 1874), 17.

9. Ibid., 16–17; Reynolds, *Reconstruction,* 250.

10. Zuczek, *State of Rebellion,* 137–38.

11. Reynolds, *Reconstruction,* 253. Later, committees of both houses "reported that the matters presented in the taxpayers' memorial were beyond the jurisdiction of Congress" (265).

12. Brooks D. Simpson, *The Reconstruction Presidents* (Lawrence: University Press of Kansas, 1998), 170; Reynolds, *Reconstruction,* 263–64. Reynolds says the offending speech was fabricated by the *Columbia Union-Herald.*

13. It was of course an oral interview, but both Democratic and Republican sources agree on the gist, and some of the exact words, of Grant's remarks. The quotes above come from Reynolds, *Reconstruction,* 263.

14. Ibid., 265.

15. Williamson, *After Slavery,* 400n105; Holt, *Black over White,* 177.

16. On the depression of 1873 and its powerful impact on national Reconstruction policy, see Foner, *Reconstruction,* 524.

17. Lamson, *Glorious Failure,* 184–85.

18. *Nation,* August 27, 1874; Williamson, *After Slavery,* 399–400.

19. *Daily Union-Herald,* September 9, 1874. Robert Woody confirms and extends the catalog. See Woody, "Franklin J. Moses," 111–32.

20. Lamson, *Glorious Failure,* 196–201; Woody, "Franklin J. Moses," 124–26; *New York Times,* June 21, 1874.

21. *Daily Union-Herald,* August 4, 1874.

22. Ibid.

23. Lamson, *Glorious Failure,* 198. Her description of a deal is not sourced but accords with newspaper accounts.

24. See *New York Times,* June 21, 1874.

25. Ibid.

26. Simkins and Woody, *South Carolina during Reconstruction,* 125; N. Louise Bailey, Mary L. Morgan, and Carolyn R. Taylor, *Biographical Directory of the South Carolina*

*Senate, 1776–1985,* 3 vols. (Columbia: University of South Carolina Press, 1986), 1:440; James S. Rogers III, "The History of Horry County, South Carolina: 1850–1876" (master's thesis, University of South Carolina, 1972), 54, 67; Catherine H. Lewis, *Horry County, South Carolina: 1730–1993* (Columbia: University of South Carolina Press, 1998), 42, 44.

27. Quote from Bailey, Morgan, and Taylor, *Biographical Directory,* 440. For Dunn's proposals for economic development, see Rogers, "Horry County," 67–70; Lewis, *Horry County,* 42.

28. The report was published in *Reports and Resolutions, 1874–75,* 723–75.

29. For example: "While he has not the audacity of Moses, [Chamberlain] is more capable as well as more adroit than that profligate debauchee, and is even less worthy than he is to fill the executive chair." And later: "We are exposing the character of a man who is as bad as Moses." These comments were made in letters from Dawson to his wife on August 2, 5, and 20, 1874. Quoted in E. Culpepper Clark, *Francis Warrington Dawson and the Politics of Restoration: South Carolina, 1874–1889* (University: University of Alabama Press, 1980), 37.

30. See *Charleston News and Courier,* August 4–10, 1874.

31. Zuczek says the Democrats wanted Grant to give Kershaw "a few public words of support"; Holt says Grant was to "secretly support" Kershaw. See Zuczek, *State of Rebellion,* 143; Holt, *Black over White,* 177. Another mystery is how much the Democrats hoped to accomplish. Zuczek implies that they intended to win the election by bringing "scalawag whites and some blacks into their camp." On the other hand, in his biography of Dawson, E. Culpepper Clark surmises that they were building a party organization for the future; he quotes Dawson as predicting Kershaw would "make a strong run, & be beaten, if the rads hold together. But we must keep on fighting till we win." See Zuczek, *State of Rebellion,* 143; Clark, *Francis Warrington Dawson,* 38.

32. The quoted statement is reported by Dawson to be the contents of a telegraph from General James Conner; Dawson's letter citing the telegraph is dated September 8, 1874. Holt, *Black over White,* 178.

33. Walter Allen, *Governor Chamberlain's Administration in South Carolina* (New York: G. P. Putnam's Sons, 1888), 8; Clark, *Francis Warrington Dawson,* 39; Lamson, *Glorious Failure,* 198–204; *Columbia Daily Union-Herald,* August 26, 1874.

34. Lamson, *Glorious Failure,* 198–204, lays out the theory described. Clark, *Francis Warrington Dawson,* 39, quotes Dawson's accusation of bribery. On the sincerity of Republicans' demands for reform, see Allen, *Governor Chamberlain's Administration,* 8.

35. *Columbia Daily Union-Herald,* September 13, 1874.

36. County-by-county vote totals are found in *Reports and Resolutions, 1874–75,* 0126 (Exhibit F). For details of the 1872 canvass, see chapter 4.

37. *Columbia Daily Union-Herald,* September 23, 1874.

38. Ibid., October 17, 23, 1874.

39. A very rough estimate indicates that over 70 percent of Democrats voted in the 1874 election, compared with 60 percent in 1870 and 40 percent in 1872. These numbers are based on the racial makeup of the state (110,000 black men of voting age; 74,000 white men) and disparities between gubernatorial and congressional voting. For example, I assume that in 1872 Republicans were much more likely to vote than Democrats, since the gubernatorial contest was between two Republicans. But the Republican total too was down 15,000 from Scott's 1870 tally. Based on congressional voting, I assume

that 10,000 of these 1870 Scott voters stayed home in 1872, and the other 5,000 voted for the bolters. Subtracting 5,000 from the bolters' total leaves just over 30,000 Democrats participating, presumably almost none of whom voted for Moses. Thus 30,000 out of 74,000 possible Democrats voted, or about 40 percent. (Incidentally, this is also the figure used by Reynolds, a conservative white South Carolinian writing in 1905, who if anything would have desired to minimize the number of whites participating in that election. See Reynolds, *Reconstruction,* 226.)

The other view, taken by Walter Edgar in his 1998 history of the state, holds that white Democrats hardly ever voted before 1876, and that 17,000 blacks (and practically all the whites) voted for Hampton in 1876. See Edgar, *South Carolina,* 393, 411, 412. This implies the absolute minimum Democratic participation before 1876: only 27,000 Democrats supported Carpenter, 5,000 supported Tomlinson, and 37,000 supported Green. That would make normal Republican voting strength a whopping 108,000.

The main problem with this theory is the voting for Congress: it assumes that Republicans showed up to vote for bolting Republicans but did not cast ballots for Republican congressional candidates. Such a proposition does not make sense. In fact, in most counties Republican congressional strength closely matched regular Republican strength in statewide contests. This fact strongly implies that most voters for the bolters were in fact Democrats.

40. See election returns in *Reports and Resolutions, 1874–75,* 085–089, Exhibit E, 0126, Exhibit F; *Reports and Resolutions, 1870–71,* 512–17, Exhibit C; *Reports and Resolutions, 1872–73,* 59–67, 129–32, Exhibit D.

41. *Columbia Daily Union-Herald,* November 21, 1874. Holt, *Black over White,* 178, quotes the number in the state house of representatives as fifty-four; Taylor, *Negro in South Carolina,* 215n7, gives it as fifty-two. Holt speculates that Democratic gains were at the expense of conservative, white Republicans from "up-country and midland areas most vulnerable to Democratic attack." See Holt, *Black over White,* 178–79. This generalization holds up for the period from 1868 to 1874, but insofar as it is intended to reflect the changes brought about by the 1874 elections, it is not accurate. Most defections from the regular Republican Party added bolters, not Democrats, as Holt points out. But of the ten new Democrats in the legislature, five came from Charleston and another from Colleton. The other four did come from midland counties (not upcountry), but they replaced blacks, not conservative whites. As Holt points out, there were ten fewer blacks in the new legislature; they were replaced by Democrats. The reduction in white Republicans Holt notes had already occurred by 1872. See *Columbia Daily Union-Herald,* October 25, 1872, November 21, 1874; Reynolds, *Reconstruction,* 226, 284. The upshot is this: the black majority in the South Carolina legislature was ended by alliances between bolting Republicans (most of them black) and Democrats.

42. Zuczek, *State of Rebellion,* 147; Foner, *Reconstruction,* 524.

43. Lamson, *Glorious Failure,* 154–55; Holt, *Black over White,* 194.

44. Lamson, *Glorious Failure,* 154–55; Holt, *Black over White,* 194.

45. Quoted in Foner, *Reconstruction,* 543.

46. The message is quoted in full in Allen, *Governor Chamberlain's Administration,* 12–28.

47. Quotes from Allen, *Governor Chamberlain's Administration,* 13, 16, 20, 21, 27.

48. Quoted in ibid., 10–11.

49. Quoted in ibid., 62.

50. Allen's account, published in 1888, quotes a number of favorable notices of the speech in South Carolina papers and in the national press. See ibid., 34–37. More recent writers have noted the Democrats' favorable response as well; see Lamson, *Glorious Failure,* 208, and Foner, *Reconstruction,* 543 ("By mid-1875, the governor had become the toast of upper-crust Democratic society.").

51. A. C. Hawthorn to Chamberlain, April 27, 1875; William Perry to Chamberlain, January 28, 1875; and T. H. Cooke to Chamberlain, March 12, 1875; all in Chamberlain Papers.

52. Rollin H. Kirk to Chamberlain, December 2, 5, 1874, Chamberlain Papers. Letter of December 2 includes affidavits.

53. Corley to Chamberlain, December 1, 1874, Chamberlain Papers.

54. James Sharp to Chamberlain, November 30, 1874, Chamberlain Papers.

55. E. S. J. Hayes to Chamberlain, December 9, 1874, Chamberlain Papers.

56. J. C. Hope to Chamberlain, December 17, 1874, Chamberlain Papers.

57. Taylor, *Negro in South Carolina,* 216. Foner, *Reconstruction,* 543; Williamson, *After Slavery,* 401; and Zuczek, *State of Rebellion,* 151, report that Chamberlain removed "many," "a large number," or "dozens" of Republican officials. Foner describes these officials as black; Williamson and Zuczek focus on the officials' actual or perceived inadequacy. Zuczek says simply that Chamberlain "replaced them with native whites"; Foner says these whites were "frequently" Democrats. Williamson (as well as Holt, *Black over White,* 180) more cautiously calls Chamberlain's policy bipartisan.

58. Figures based on Emily Bellinger Reynolds, typescript list of county officials, 1785–1968, unpublished c. 1960–68, call number P900175, SCDAH.

59. Based on Reynolds, typescript list of county officials. According to this admittedly incomplete compilation, Moses replaced twenty-two treasurers or auditors upon entering office, whereas Chamberlain replaced eighteen.

60. For figures see Holt, *Black over White,* 96–98.

61. Allen, *Governor Chamberlain's Administration,* 23–24; Foner, *Freedom's Lawmakers,* 240, 254–57, 276–77, 281. Williamson, *After Slavery,* 332, reports that Governor Scott "commissioned scores of Negroes" as trial justices; his citation, however, is to an article in the *New York Times,* which was not above exaggerating what it considered to be the evils of Reconstruction. The paper claims, for example, that Governor Moses "in almost every instance, appointed negroes of the lowest class to fill the offices." See *New York Times,* July 3, 1874, p. 2. The statement is absurd; the overwhelming majority of Moses's trial justices were white. Williamson does, however, mention by name two black judges not included in Foner's directory, proof that Foner's list is incomplete. (The two judges do not, however, add to the number of black judges removed by Chamberlain. One of the two seems to have been retained. The other, Samuel R. Dickinson of Charleston, was removed by Moses before Chamberlain took office.)

62. Appointments are listed in "List of Commissions and Appointments, 1819–1989: Appointments by Governor," manuscript, call number S213044, Secretary of State Recorded Instruments, SCDAH. This experiment is admittedly not conclusive, as most counties had numerous judges who are not to be found in the census and whose race therefore cannot be determined.

63. Foner, *Freedom's Lawmakers,* 76. The entry for Fludd states that he served in Florence County during Reconstruction, but that county was not created until 1888. Fludd served in Darlington, one of the counties from which Florence was formed.

64. Corley to Chamberlain, December 2, 1874, Chamberlain Papers. The job went to Leaphart, the newly Republican white man mentioned above.

65. H. C. Lancaster to Chamberlain, January 20, 1875, Chamberlain Papers.

66. S. W. Melton to Chamberlain, January 9, 1875, Chamberlain Papers.

67. E. S. J. Hayes to Chamberlain, December 9, 1874, Chamberlain Papers.

68. J. S. Mobley to Chamberlain, December 18, 1874, Chamberlain Papers.

69. A. M. Folger et al. to Chamberlain, May 8, 1875, Chamberlain Papers.

70. J. H. Derham to Chamberlain, February 17, April 8, 1875, Chamberlain Papers.

71. J. R. Cochran to Chamberlain, December 22, 1874, January 4, February 4, 1875; J. L. Orr to Chamberlain, January 29, 1875; all in Chamberlain Papers.

72. J. C. Winsmith to Chamberlain, November 23, 1874, Chamberlain Papers.

73. Winsmith nominated for county treasurer A. C. Merrick, a highly competent white man who claimed to "have done the labor of both offices for several years." Instead, Merrick got the auditor's office, and Chamberlain named Samuel T. Poinier, a carpetbagger, county treasurer. A. C. Merrick to Chamberlain, December 3, 1874, and J. C. Winsmith to Chamberlain, November 10, 1874, Chamberlain Papers.

74. *Columbia Daily Union-Herald,* August 2, 1874.

75. J. C. Winsmith to Chamberlain, November 23, 1874, Chamberlain Papers.

76. According to Zuczek, removals of black officials began under Governor Scott in 1871, as he tried to reduce Klan violence by offering concessions to Democrats. See Zuczek, *State of Rebellion,* 93. I have found no evidence, however, that Scott appointed many black officials even before then, at least outside Charleston.

77. See Williamson, *After Slavery,* 330–31.

78. Williamson, *After Slavery,* 331, defends Whipper but admits that "perhaps" the sizable sum of money he accumulated during Reconstruction was not all "honestly earned." Foner agrees that Whipper "did seem to have sticky fingers." Chamberlain intimated that Whipper was dishonest and, when pressed, pointed to the latter's involvement with the Sinking Fund Commission. See Eric Foner, "South Carolina's Black Elected Officials," in *At Freedom's Door: African-American Founding Fathers and Lawyers in Reconstruction South Carolina,* ed. James Lowell Underwood and W. Lewis Burke (Columbia: University of South Carolina Press, 2000), 175; and Allen, *Governor Chamberlain's Administration,* 40.

79. *Charleston News and Courier,* quoted in Allen, *Governor Chamberlain's Administration,* 39–40; *Columbia Daily Union-Herald,* December 12, 1874. Maxwell quoted in *Union-Herald.*

80. *Charleston News and Courier,* quoted in Allen, *Governor Chamberlain's Administration,* 39–40; *Columbia Daily Union-Herald,* December 12, 1874.

81. This was actually the "second Ned Tennant riot," the first having occurred in August 1874. At that time, white rifle clubs in Edgefield responded to the re-formation of the state militia by firing into the house of Tennant, captain of a local company of militia. Tennant called out the militia, white captains reciprocated, and the threat of violence was substantial. The situation was defused by the federal troops of Lt. Matthew

Leahy, who on his own initiative interposed his troops between the several dozen black militiamen and the several hundred white vigilantes. No bloodshed occurred, and both sides demobilized, "rather reluctantly on the part of the whites," as Leahy put it. For a fuller account, see Zuczek, *State of Rebellion,* 141–42.

82. Kantrowitz, *Ben Tillman,* 61–62.

83. Col. Theodore W. Parmele to Chamberlain, February 23, 1875, Chamberlain Papers.

84. Allen, *Governor Chamberlain's Administration,* 68–70. It is not true, however, that Chamberlain vetoed a bill to protect laborers discharged for their political beliefs, as Kantrowitz states. Kantrowitz, following Burton, confuses two very different bills that had in common the raising of a tax in Edgefield. The one to protect laborers was tabled in the state house of representatives and never passed; the one Chamberlain vetoed would have raised a tax to cover the arrears of the county treasurer. As T. J. Mackey pointed out, Edgefield's first three Republican treasurers all defaulted. See Kantrowitz, *Ben Tillman,* 63–64; Burton, "Ungrateful Servants?" 110–11; Reynolds, *Reconstruction,* 304–5; Allen, *Governor Chamberlain's Administration,* 74–76; *House Journal, 1874–75,* 273.

85. From Chamberlain's Special Message on January 12, 1875, quoted in Allen, *Governor Chamberlain's Administration,* 62.

86. Lamson, *Glorious Failure,* 210–11, 213, 215–19; Reynolds, *Reconstruction,* 296–98. I have followed Lamson in judging Elliott to be responsible for the effort to unseat Cardozo. Lamson, however, portrays the mechanism as that of impeachment; I believe this misses the point of Elliott's ploy. Impeachment would require nothing of Chamberlain, whereas the maneuver actually employed seems to have been intended to hurt Chamberlain in Democratic public opinion, thereby driving him back into the arms of the Republican majority.

87. *Charleston News and Courier* quoted in Allen, *Governor Chamberlain's Administration,* 84–86.

88. Allen, *Governor Chamberlain's Administration,* 80–87; Lamson, *Glorious Failure,* 217–18.

89. Lamson, *Glorious Failure,* 214–16; Clark, *Francis Warrington Dawson,* 40–48.

90. Aldrich quoted in Clark, *Francis Warrington Dawson,* 48.

91. Chamberlain to Dawson, June 24, 1875, quoted in Lamson, *Glorious Failure,* 216.

92. The story of the libel trial is presented in quite entertaining form in Clark, *Francis Warrington Dawson,* 41–45.

93. These are quoted in full in Allen, *Governor Chamberlain's Administration,* 115–39.

94. Chamberlain quoted in ibid., 23–24, 51–53, 60–61.

95. *House Journal, 1874–75,* 326, 546, 624–25; *House Journal, 1875–76,* 167, 194–95, 210, 278, 294, 303, 512–14. I have used the same votes as Thomas Holt uses to determine whether black legislators were conservative or radical and applied them to white Republicans. See Holt, *Black over White,* 190–91.

96. Lamson, *Glorious Failure,* 220–23.

97. *House Journal, 1875–76,* 194–95. In the S.C. House, fourteen white Republicans voted for Whipper, three for other candidates, and three abstained. In the state senate, four voted for Whipper, three for other candidates, and one abstained.

98. Lamson, *Glorious Failure,* 223; Allen, *Governor Chamberlain's Administration,* 195.

99. Lamson, *Glorious Failure,* 220.

100. Allen, *Governor Chamberlain's Administration,* 200–201.

101. Ibid., 196–201.

102. Edwin Parker McCravy, *Memories* (Greenville, S.C.: Observer Printing, 1941), 14. Reynolds, *Reconstruction,* 311, denies that politics was a factor, but that view conflicts with the belief of both Democratic and Republican contemporaries; it also strains common sense.

103. Reynolds, *Reconstruction,* 311–12.

104. Ibid., 284.

105. *Columbia Daily Union-Herald,* July 26, 1874.

106. Ibid., November 21, 1874.

107. Quoted in Allen, *Governor Chamberlain's Administration,* 195–96.

108. Ibid., 59.

109. Vandiver, *Traditions and History of Anderson County,* 240. Cochran was technically an independent, but he usually voted with the Republicans—for Whipper, for example.

110. J. C. Hope to C. E. Leaphart, March 7, 1876, John Christian Hope Papers, SCL (hereafter cited as Hope Papers). Hope held to his plan at least until October 13, 1876, long after most dissent had been expunged from the Democratic Party. See Hope to Leaphart, October 13, 1876, Hope Papers. Of course personal rivalries among Democrats were not new in 1876. See J. H. Derham to Chamberlain, April 8, 1875, Chamberlain Papers.

111. In February 1876, for example, a Democratic meeting found most members in favor of a straight Democratic ticket precisely for that reason. See the *Charleston News and Courier,* February 4, 1876.

112. Simkins and Woody, *South Carolina during Reconstruction,* 486–88. Facing page 486 is a political cartoon from *Harper's Weekly* that illustrates the victims of the following massacre with the caption "Impudent Niggers Daring to Celebrate the 4th."

113. Tillman quoted in Kantrowitz, *Ben Tillman,* 66–67.

114. This account of the massacre is based on Kantrowitz, *Ben Tillman,* 68–69; Zuczek, *State of Rebellion,* 163–64; and Lamson, *Glorious Failure,* 236.

115. *Charleston News and Courier,* July 20, 1876.

116. Chamberlain quoted in Allen, *Governor Chamberlain's Administration,* 324; Zuczek, *State of Rebellion,* 164–65.

117. "Plan of the Campaign," reprinted in Simkins and Woody, *South Carolina during Reconstruction,* 564–69; Kantrowitz, *Ben Tillman,* 73.

118. Testimony of T. N. Tolbert in U.S. Congress, *South Carolina in 1876: Testimony as to the Denial of the Elective Franchise in South Carolina at the Elections of 1875 and 1876, Taken under the Resolution of the Senate of December 5, 1876,* 3 vols. (Washington, D.C.: Government Printing Office, 1877) (hereafter cited as *South Carolina in 1876*), 2:91.

119. Testimony of Daniel H. Chamberlain in *South Carolina in 1876,* 1:4.

120. S. J. Patterson and others to Chamberlain, August 22, 1876, *South Carolina in 1876,* 3:548–49.

121. John Gardner to Chamberlain, August 25, 1876; P. Jenkins to Chamberlain, September 30, 1876; R. A. Cummings and others to Chamberlain, October 20, 1876; all in *South Carolina in 1876,* 3:548–49, 550, 552.

122. Kantrowitz, *Ben Tillman,* 74; Zuczek, *State of Rebellion,* 176.

123. The only officeholders on the list were Judges T. H. Cooke, C. P. Townsend, and T. J. Mackey, and state senators J. M. Smith and T. C. Andrews. Two blacks were included: Samuel Johnson of Anderson and Martin R. Delany of Charleston. M. I. Browning and D. D. McCall had themselves taken off the list, on the grounds that they had always been Democrats. See the *Charleston News and Courier,* September 23, 26, 28, October 2, 1876.

124. Ibid., October 3, 9, 16, 24, November 3, 1876.

125. Ibid., October 5, November 4, 1876.

126. Ibid., October 12, 1876; Mittag to Chamberlain, December 10, 1874, Chamberlain Papers.

127. Ibid., October 9, 1876.

128. Ibid., October 12, 1876.

129. Ibid., October 9, 13, 1876.

130. Simkins and Woody, *South Carolina during Reconstruction,* 515; Zuczek, *State of Rebellion,* 190–91.

131. Melinda Meek Hennessey, "Racial Violence during Reconstruction: The 1876 Riots in Charleston and Cainhoy," *South Carolina Historical Magazine* 86 (April 1985), 110–11; Zuczek, *State of Rebellion,* 190–92. Zuczek incorrectly states that the riot occurred on election day. It happened on November 8, as he says, but the election was held on November 7. See *South Carolina in 1876,* 3:38, 557; Lamson, *Glorious Failure,* 250. As Zuczek and Hennessey note, the riot began while Republicans and Democrats were waiting outside the offices of the *Charleston News and Courier* for news about the presidential election; that would not have begun coming in until the day following the election.

132. *South Carolina in 1876,* 2:393, 3:578.

133. This figure was arrived at by a committee of the U.S. Senate; see *South Carolina in 1876,* 3:580. The committee typically credited Hampton with every white vote in a given county, but they specifically excluded Charleston "because there is something of a white Republican element there" (579). On racial violence in Charleston, including the riot the day after election day, see Hennessey, "Racial Violence during Reconstruction," 100–112.

134. In Edgefield, 7,122 males over the age of twenty-one appear on the 1875 census, but 9,374 votes were recorded in the 1876 election.

135. *South Carolina in 1876,* 3:37–54, especially 38.

136. This anomaly is explained by repeat voting and by the Democratic tactic of casting "gossamer ballots"; ballots were printed on paper thin enough to fold over and hide inside another ballot, and when the vote was cast the ballots inside were shaken loose. See Zuczek, *State of Rebellion,* 191. Several writers have assumed a similar situation existed in Laurens. In fact, Laurens recorded almost four hundred *fewer* votes than it had eligible voters, according to the U.S. Senate's figures. See *South Carolina in 1876,* 3:578.

137. Other historians have not speculated on the board's rationale in including Laurens, since they have assumed the same problem occurred there as in Edgefield: more votes than voters. See Foner, *Reconstruction,* 575; Lamson, *Glorious Failure,* 254; Zuczek, *State of Rebellion,* 193. In fact, as discussed above, Laurens had four hundred fewer votes than eligible voters.

138. For figures, see *South Carolina in 1876,* 3:578.

139. See Simkins and Woody, *South Carolina during Reconstruction,* 523, and Zuczek, *State of Rebellion,* 193–94.

140. See Simkins and Woody, *South Carolina during Reconstruction,* 525–27, and Zuczek, *State of Rebellion,* 195–96.

141. See Simkins and Woody, *South Carolina during Reconstruction,* 528–36, and Zuczek, *State of Rebellion,* 197–99.

142. Quoted in Allen, *Governor Chamberlain's Administration,* 481.

### *Epilogue*

1. The work to begin with on the Republican Party in South Carolina after Reconstruction, despite its dated perspective, is Patton, "Republican Party in South Carolina," 91–111. Others include Cooper, *Conservative Regime;* Tindall, *South Carolina Negroes;* and Williamson, *After Slavery.* An interesting local case study is Arthur Lewis Gelston, "Radical versus Straight-out in Post-Reconstruction Beaufort County," *South Carolina Historical Magazine* 75, no. 4 (1974): 225–37. Biographies of Republican leaders Robert Smalls and Robert Brown Elliott offer their perspectives on these events. See Edward A. Miller Jr., *Gullah Statesman: Robert Smalls from Slavery to Congress, 1839–1915* (Columbia: University of South Carolina Press, 1995), and Lamson, *Glorious Failure.*

2. Williamson, *After Slavery,* 413.

3. Bleser, *Promised Land,* 121. Bleser points out that the Land Commission is never mentioned in the Fraud Report—possibly the work of Cochran, who had had shady dealings with the commission.

4. Bailey, Morgan, and Taylor, *Biographical Directory,* 314–15; Dickson, *Journeys into the Past,* 179–81.

5. David Duncan Wallace, *History of South Carolina* (New York: American Historical Society, 1934), 4:79–80.

6. Wallace, *History of South Carolina* 4:79–80; Dickson, *Journeys into the Past,* 48–49.

7. Bailey, Morgan, and Taylor, *Biographical Directory,* 315–16.

8. "James Earl Hagood," in *Cyclopaedia of Eminent and Representative Men of the Carolinas of the Nineteenth Century,* vol. 1, *South Carolina,* ed. Samuel A. Ashe and Edward McCrady Jr., 536–37 (Madison, Wis.: Brant and Fuller, 1892).

9. Ibid., 387–88.

10. Tindall, *South Carolina Negroes,* 61–65; George C. Rogers, *The History of Georgetown County, South Carolina* (Columbia: University of South Carolina Press, 1970), 475.

11. J. R. Cochran to William Henry Trescot, January 28, 1881, Trescot Papers; Robert M. Goldman, *"A Free Ballot and a Fair Count": The Department of Justice and the Enforcement of Voting Rights in the South, 1877–1893* (New York: Fordham University Press, 2001), 65–73, 92–100.

12. "James Earl Hagood," *Cyclopedia,* 1:539–40.

13. Williamson, *After Slavery,* 413.

14. For Mackey, see A. L. Gaston, *Remarks and Reminiscences,* pamphlet in author's possession, originally published in serial form by the *Chester Reporter* in July 1948. For Robertson, see his obituary in the *Columbia State,* October 14, 1897.

15. Bailey, Morgan, and Taylor, *Biographical Directory,* 401–2.

16. Ibid., 698.

17. Ibid., 1496.

18. McCravy, *Memories,* 83–85. McCravy spells the name "Stallbrand."

19. Ware, *Old Abbeville,* 139–41.

20. *Columbia Register,* September 3, 5, 6, 1880.

21. Ibid., September 3, 1880. This letter to the editor is signed "Saxe-Gotha." I have attributed authorship to Corley because it contains three traits frequently appearing in Corley's writings: unwarranted optimism about Republican prospects, wry humor ("our candidates were there in full force, making themselves agreeable to the voters and for the most part to each other"), and, most important, fulsome praise of Corley ("a citizen of great moral worth and standing . . . he is decidedly as strong a man as there is of that party in the State").

22. *State,* November 22, 1902.

23. McCravy, *Memories,* 267; Miller, *Gullah Statesman,* 229; Willard B. Gatewood, "Theodore Roosevelt and Southern Republicans: The Case of South Carolina, 1901–1904," *South Carolina Historical Magazine* 70, no. 4 (October 1969), 252–53.

24. McCravy, *Memories,* 267–68.

25. Wallace, *History of South Carolina* 4:154.

26. *State,* August 1, 1891.

27. An exception may be Lawson D. Melton, called "a leading 'lily-white'" by one historian. See Gatewood, "Theodore Roosevelt and Southern Republicans," 251–66. Lawson D. Melton was the son of Samuel W. Melton, a native white Republican during and after Reconstruction.

28. *Columbia Daily Record,* September 28, 30, 1912. For other lily-white movements, see Tindall, *South Carolina Negroes,* 49ff.

29. *Columbia Register,* September 5, 1880.

30. Bailey, Morgan, and Taylor, *Biographical Directory,* 1220–21.

31. For the extraordinary life of Franklin J. Moses Jr., see Woody, "Franklin J. Moses," 111–32.

32. Joel Williamson's statement that "a large proportion of the carpetbaggers remained and continued to work as they had before" (*After Slavery,* 413) applies much better to black carpetbaggers than to white ones.

33. See Mrs. Robert M. Wallace Diary, SCL.

34. See Bailey, Morgan, and Taylor, *Biographical Directory,* 332–33.

35. See his retrospective, "Reconstruction in South Carolina," *Atlantic Monthly* 87 (April 1901): 473–76, as well as Wilton B. Fowler, "A Carpetbagger's Conversion to White Supremacy," *North Carolina Historical Review* 43, no. 3 (1966): 286–304.

36. J. R. Cochran to William Henry Trescot, January 28, 1881, Trescot Papers. Nominally a Democrat, Trescot was something of a South Carolinian Talleyrand, preserving his influence through a remarkable series of changes of national administration. Cochran appealed to Trescot, a fellow native of Anderson County, to intercede with President Garfield to get Cochran a job. He never got one. See also Bailey, Morgan, and Taylor, *Biographical Directory,* 314–15.

37. Federal efforts to protect Republicans in their voting rights did not come to an abrupt end in 1876, as demonstrated by Goldman in his study *"Free Ballot and a Fair Count."* But even when federal prosecutors made determined efforts to prosecute election crimes, and even when the evidence of fraud was overwhelming, Democratic juries refused to convict. For South Carolina, see Goldman, *"Free Ballot and a Fair Count,"* 65–73, 92–100.

38. E. W. M. Mackey to the editor of the *Philadelphia American,* February 14, 1881, quoted in Tindall, *South Carolina Negroes,* 47.

# BIBLIOGRAPHY


*Archives*

*Houghton Library, Harvard University, Cambridge, Mass.*
Charles Sumner Papers

*Library of Congress, Washington, D.C.*
William E. Chandler Papers
Benjamin F. Butler Papers
Thaddeus K. Stevens Papers

*National Archives, East Point, Ga.*
Minute Books. U.S. Circuit Court, District of South Carolina.

*National Archives, Washington, D.C.*
Records of the Assistant Commissioner for the State of South Carolina. Bureau of Refugees, Freedmen, and Abandoned Lands. RG 105.
Records of the Commissioners of Claims (Southern Claims Commission), 1871–1881. RG 56.

*National Archives II, College Park, Md.*
Records Relating to Customhouse Nominations, 1849–1910. RG 56.

*South Carolina Department of Archives and History, Columbia*
Legislative Papers
Governors' Papers
  Daniel H. Chamberlain
  Wade Hampton III
  Franklin J. Moses Jr.
  James L. Orr
  Benjamin F. Perry
  Robert K. Scott
Reynolds, Emily Bellinger. Typescript list of county officials, 1785–1968.
Secretary of State Recorded Instruments.

*South Caroliniana Library, Columbia*
Aiken Family Papers
David Wyatt Aiken Papers
Virginia Carolina Smith Aiken Diary

Allston Family Papers
Christopher Columbus Bowen Papers
Manuel Simeon Corley Papers
John McPherson DeSaussure Papers
Martin W. Gary Papers
John Berkeley Grimball Papers
Edward Barnwell Heyward Papers
Heyward Family Papers
John Christian Hope Papers
J. A. Keller Papers
Kincaid-Anderson Papers
Lexington County Collection
Albert Gallatin Mackey Papers
E. W. M. Mackey Papers
James Rion McKissick Collection
Roderick S. McLucas Papers
Samuel W. Melton Papers
Gerhard Muller Papers
Joseph Jephtha Norton Papers
B. F. Perry Papers
Thomas Steven Powell Diary
James N. Rutland Papers
William McCreight Shannon Papers
James F. Sloan Papers
Yates Snowden Collection
William Henry Trescot Papers
Alexander Stuart Wallace Papers
Mrs. Robert M. Wallace Diary
Williams-Chesnut-Manning Papers
John Winsmith Papers

*Southern Historical Collection, University of North Carolina, Chapel Hill*
Orr-Patterson Papers
Springs Family Papers
William H. Trescot Papers

### *Published Papers and Memoirs*

Abbott, Martin, ed. "James L. Orr on Congressional Reconstruction." *South Carolina Historical Magazine* 54, no. 3 (July 1953): 141–42.

Andrews, Sidney. *The South since the War.* Boston: Ticknor and Fields, 1866; Boston: Houghton Mifflin, 1971.

*An Appeal to the Honorable the Senate of the United States, in Behalf of the Conservative People of South Carolina, against the Adoption, by Congress, of the New Constitution Proposed for South Carolina.* Columbia, S.C.: Phoenix Book and Job Power Press, 1868.

Armstrong, William J. *Speech of William J. Armstrong, delivered at Columbia, July 25, 1867.* N.p., n.d.

Chamberlain, Daniel H. *The Facts and the Figures: The Practical and Trutful* [sic] *Record of the Republican Party of South Carolina.* Columbia, S.C.: J. W. Denny, 1870.

———. "Reconstruction in South Carolina." *Atlantic Monthly* 87 (April 1901): 473–76.

*Conservative Address to the Voters of Marlborough, September,* A.D. *1874.* Charleston, S.C.: News and Courier Job Presses, 1874.

De Forest, John William. *A Union Officer in the Reconstruction.* New Haven, Conn.: Yale University Press, 1948; Baton Rouge: Louisiana State University Press, 1997.

Dennett, John Richard. *The South As It Is: 1865–1866.* New York: Viking Press, 1965.

Gaston, A. L. *Remarks and Reminiscences.* Pamphlet in author's possession. Originally published in serial form by the *Chester Reporter* in July 1948.

Leland, John A. *A Voice from South Carolina.* Charleston, S.C.: Walker, Evans & Cogswell, 1879.

McCravy, Edwin Parker. *Memories.* Greenville, S.C.: Observer Printing, 1941.

Moore, John Hammond, ed. *The Juhl Letters to the Charleston Courier: A View of the South, 1865–1871.* Athens: University of Georgia Press, 1974.

Orr, James L. *Southern Politics: Ex-Governor Orr's Reasons for Joining the Republican Party in South Carolina.* Columbia, S.C., 1870. Pamphlet in South Caroliniana Library.

Pike, James Shepherd. *The Prostrate State: South Carolina under Negro Government.* New York: D. Appleton, 1874.

*Recollections and Reminiscences, 1861–1865 through World War I.* Vol. 1. N.p.: South Carolina Division, United Daughters of the Confederacy, 1990.

Sawyer, F. A. *Speech of Hon. F. A. Sawyer, of South Carolina, in the Senate of the United States, April 13, 1871.* Pamphlet in South Caroliniana Library.

Scott, Edwin J. *Random Recollections of a Long Life, 1806–1876.* Columbia, S.C.: Charles A. Calvo Jr., 1884.

Simon, John Y., ed. *The Papers of Ulysses S. Grant.* Carbondale: Southern Illinois University Press, 1995.

*A Statement of Dr. Bratton's Case, Being Explanatory of the Ku-Klux Prosecutions in the Southern States.* London, Ont.: Free Press Steam Book and Job Printing, 1872.

Trescot, William Henry. "Letter of William Henry Trescot on Reconstruction in South Carolina, 1867." *American Historical Review* 15, no. 3 (April 1910): 574–82.

### *Published Federal and State Records*

Confederate States of America. Congress. *Journal of the Congress of the Confederate States of America, 1861–1865.* 7 vols. Washington, D.C.: Government Printing Office, 1904–5.

———. "Proceedings of the Confederate Congress." *Southern Historical Society Papers* 45:250–53; 48:187–90.

South Carolina. Constitutional Convention (1865). *Journal of the Convention of the People of South Carolina, Held in Columbia, S.C., September, 1865.* Columbia, S.C.: J. A. Selby, 1865.

South Carolina. Constitutional Convention (1868). *Proceedings of the Constitutional Convention of South Carolina, Held at Charleston, S.C., Beginning January 14th and Ending March 17th, 1868.* Charleston, S.C.: Denny and Perry, 1868.

South Carolina. Convention (1852). *Journal of the State Convention of South Carolina; Together with the Resolution and Ordinance.* Columbia, S.C.: Johnson & Cavis, 1852.

South Carolina. General Assembly. *Evidence Taken by the Committee of Investigation of the Third Congressional District, under Authority of the General Assembly of the State of South Carolina, Regular Session, 1868–1869.* Columbia, S.C.: John W. Denny, 1870.

———. *Journal of the House of Representatives of the State of South Carolina, 1868–78.*

———. *Journal of the Senate of the State of South Carolina, 1868–78.*

———. *Proceedings in the General Assembly and Supreme Court of South Carolina, on the Death of Hon. Lemuel Boozer, Judge of the Fifth Judicial Circuit.* Columbia, S.C.: J. W. Denny, 1870.

———. *Report of the Joint Investigating Committee on Public Frauds and the Election of Hon. John J. Patterson to the United States Senate Made to the General Assembly of South Carolina at the Regular Session of 1877–78.* Columbia, S.C.: Calvo and Patton, 1878.

———. *Reports and Resolutions of the General Assembly of South Carolina, at the Regular Session, 1877–78.* Columbia, S.C.: Calvo and Patton, 1878.

———. *Reports and Resolutions of the General Assembly of the State of South Carolina.* 1869–78. Columbia, S.C.: Republican Printing Company, 1870–78.

———. *Statutes at Large of South Carolina.* Vols. 13–16. Columbia, S.C.: Republican Printing, 1872–76.

Tax-Payers' Convention of South Carolina (1871). *Proceedings of the Tax-Payers' Convention of South Carolina, Held at Columbia, Beginning May 9th, and Ending May 12th, 1871.* Charleston, S.C.: Edward Perry, 1871.

Tax-Payers' Convention of South Carolina (1874). *Proceedings of the Tax-Payers' Convention of South Carolina, Held at Columbia, Beginning February 17, and Ending February 20, 1874.* Charleston, S.C.: News and Courier Job Presses, 1874.

U.S. Bureau of the Census. Censuses for 1860, 1870, and 1880. Washington, D.C., 1860, 1870, 1880.

U.S. Circuit Court (4th Circuit). *Proceedings in the Ku Klux Trials at Columbia, S.C.* Columbia, S.C.: State Printers, 1871.

United States. Congress. *Congressional Globe.* 46 vols. Washington, D.C., 1843–73.

———. *Congressional Record.* Washington, D.C., 1874–77.

———. *Papers in the Case of S. L. Hoge vs. J. P. Reed, Third Congressional District, South Carolina.* 41st Cong., 1st sess., H. Rept. 3 (Serial 1403).

———. *Papers in the Case of A. S. Wallace vs. W. D. Simpson, Fourth Congressional District, South Carolina.* 41st Cong., 1st sess., H. Rept. 5 (Serial 1403).

———. *Report of the Joint Select Committee to Inquire into the Condition of Affairs in the Late Insurrectionary States.* 13 vols. Washington, D.C.: Government Printing Office, 1872. Volumes 3–5 deal with South Carolina.

———. *South Carolina in 1876: Testimony as to the Denial of the Elective Franchise in South Carolina at the Elections of 1875 and 1876, Taken under the Resolution of the Senate of December 5, 1876.* 3 vols. Washington, D.C.: Government Printing Office, 1877.

### Newspapers

*Aiken Tribune,* 1871–76

*Anderson Intelligencer,* 1865–78

*Carolina Spartan,* 1866–76

*Charleston Daily Courier,* 1865–73

*Charleston Daily News,* 1865–73

*Charleston Daily Republican,* 1872
*Charleston Mercury,* 1865–68
*Charleston News and Courier,* 1873–78
*Chester Reporter,* 1869–78
*Columbia Daily Record,* 1912
*Columbia Daily Union,* 1872–73
*Columbia Daily Union-Herald,* 1873–75
*Columbia Register,* 1880
*Columbia State,* 1891–present
*Edgefield Advertiser,* 1865–78
*Greenville Enterprise,* 1870–73
*Greenville Republican,* 1873
*Greenville Southern Enterprise,* 1865–70
*Keowee Courier,* 1865–72
*Lexington Dispatch,* 1872–78
*New York Commercial and Financial Chronicle,* 1871–72
*New York Herald,* 1867
*New York Times,* 1865–78
*Spartanburg Herald,* 1875–78
*Sumter Watchman,* 1865–78
*Yorkville Enquirer,* 1865–78

### Secondary Works

Abbott, Martin. "County Officers in South Carolina in 1868." *South Carolina Historical Magazine* 40, no. 1 (January 1959): 30–40.

———. *The Freedmen's Bureau in South Carolina, 1865–1872.* Chapel Hill: University of North Carolina Press, 1967.

Abbott, Richard H. *For Free Press and Equal Rights: Republican Newspapers in the Reconstruction South.* Athens: University of Georgia Press, 2004.

———. *The Republican Party and the South, 1855–1877: The First Southern Strategy.* Chapel Hill: University of North Carolina Press, 1986.

Alexander, Thomas B. "Persistent Whiggery in the Confederate South, 1860–1877." *Journal of Southern History* 27 (August 1961): 305–29.

Allen, Walter. *Governor Chamberlain's Administration in South Carolina: A Chapter of Reconstruction in the Southern States.* New York: G. P. Putnam's Sons, 1888.

Anderson, Eric, and Alfred A. Moss Jr., eds. *The Facts of Reconstruction: Essays in Honor of John Hope Franklin.* Baton Rouge: Louisiana State University Press, 1991.

Anderson, George L. "The South and Problems of Post-Civil War Finance." *Journal of Southern History* 9 (May 1943): 205–16.

Ashe, Samuel A., and Edward McCrady Jr., eds. *Cyclopedia of Eminent and Representative Men of the Carolinas of the Nineteenth Century.* Vol. 1, *South Carolina.* Madison, Wis.: Brant and Fuller, 1892.

Baggett, James Alex. "Origins of Upper South Scalawag Leadership." *Civil War History* 29, no. 1 (1983): 53–73.

———. *The Scalawags: Southern Dissenters in the Civil War and Reconstruction.* Baton Rouge: Louisiana State University Press, 2003.

Bailey, N. Louise, Mary L. Morgan, and Carolyn R. Taylor. *Biographical Directory of the South Carolina Senate, 1776–1985.* 3 vols. Columbia: University of South Carolina Press, 1986.

Ball, William Watts. *The State That Forgot: South Carolina's Surrender to Democracy.* Indianapolis: Bobbs-Merrill, 1932.

Ballard, Allen B. *One More Day's Journey: The Story of a Family and a People.* New York: McGraw-Hill, 1984.

Bell, John L., Jr. "Andrew Johnson, National Politics, and Presidential Reconstruction in South Carolina." *South Carolina Historical Magazine* 82, no. 4 (1981): 354–66.

Benedict, Michael Les. "Preserving the Constitution: The Conservative Basis of Radical Reconstruction." *Journal of American History* 61 (June 1974): 65–90.

Bleser, Carol R. *The Promised Land: The History of the South Carolina Land Commission, 1869–1890.* Columbia: University of South Carolina Press, 1969.

Boddie, William Willis. *History of Williamsburg.* Spartanburg, S.C.: Reprint Company, 1980.

Boles, John B., and Evelyn Thomas Nolen. *Interpreting Southern History: Historiographical Essays in Honor of Sanford W. Higginbotham.* Baton Rouge: Louisiana State University Press, 1987.

Bolick, Julian Stevenson. *A Laurens County Sketchbook.* N.p., n.p., 1973.

Brock, Euline W. "Thomas W. Cardozo: Fallible Black Reconstruction Leader." *Journal of Southern History* 47 (May 1981): 183–206.

Burke, W. Lewis. "Post-Reconstruction Justice: The Prosecution and Trial of Francis Lewis Cardozo." *South Carolina Law Review* 53, no. 2 (Winter 2002): 361–413.

Burton, Vernon. "Edgefield Reconstruction Political Black Leaders." *Proceedings of the South Carolina Historical Association,* 1988, 27–38.

———. "Race and Reconstruction: Edgefield County, South Carolina." *Journal of Social History* 12 (Fall 1978): 31–56.

Byars, Merlene Hutto. *South Carolina Scrapbook: Learn about Your Heritage with the Saxe Gothans.* Cayce, S.C.: Saxe Gotha Historical Society, 1994.

Carter, Dan T. *When the War Was Over: The Failure of Self-Reconstruction in the South, 1865–1867.* Baton Rouge: Louisiana State University Press, 1985.

Cauthen, Charles Edward. *South Carolina Goes to War, 1860–1865.* Chapel Hill: University of North Carolina Press, 1950.

*Central Midlands Historic Preservation Survey.* Lexington, S.C.: Central Midlands Regional Planning Council, 1974.

Channing, Steven A. *Crisis of Fear: Secession in South Carolina.* New York: W. W. Norton, 1974.

Charles, Allan D. *The Narrative History of Union County South Carolina.* Spartanburg, S.C.: Reprint Company, 1987.

Clark, E. Culpepper. *Francis Warrington Dawson and the Politics of Restoration: South Carolina, 1874–1889.* University: University of Alabama Press, 1980.

———. "Sarah Morgan and Francis Dawson: Raising the Woman Question in Reconstruction South Carolina." *South Carolina Historical Magazine* 81, no. 1 (1980): 8–23.

Clark, Thomas D. *The Southern Country Editor.* Indianapolis: Bobbs-Merrill, 1948.

Cooper, William J., Jr. *The Conservative Regime: South Carolina, 1877–1890.* 1968. Reprint, Columbia: University of South Carolina Press, 2005.

Coulter, E. Merton. *The South during Reconstruction 1865–1877.* Baton Rouge: Louisiana State University Press, 1947.

Crow, Jeffrey J. "Thomas Settle, Jr., Reconstruction, and the Memory of the Civil War." *Journal of Southern History* 62, no. 4 (November 1996): 689–726.

Crow, Jeffrey J., Paul D. Escott, and Charles L. Flynn Jr., eds. *Race, Class, and Politics in Southern History: Essays in Honor of Robert F. Durden.* Baton Rouge: Louisiana State University Press, 1989.

Cummings, Charles M. "The Scott Papers: An Inside View of Reconstruction." *Ohio History* 79, no. 2 (1970): 112–18.

Current, Richard N. *Lincoln's Loyalists: Union Soldiers from the Confederacy.* Boston: Northeastern University Press, 1992.

———. *Those Terrible Carpetbaggers: A Reinterpretation.* New York: Oxford University Press, 1988.

Davidson, James. "The Post-Bellum Poor-White as Seen by J. W. De Forest." *Southern Folklore Quarterly* 24, no. 2 (1960): 101–8.

Degler, Carl N. *The Other South: Southern Dissenters in the Nineteenth Century.* Boston: Northeastern University Press, 1982.

Dickson, Frank A. *Journeys into the Past: The Anderson Region's Heritage.* Published by the Author, 1975.

Donald, David. "The Scalawag in Mississippi Reconstruction." *Journal of Southern History* 10 (November 1944): 447–60.

Doster, James. "Vicissitudes of the South Carolina Railroad, 1865–1878: A Case Study in Reconstruction and Regional Traffic Development." *Business History Review* 30, no. 2 (1956): 175–95.

Drago, Edmund Lee. *Hurrah for Hampton! Black Red Shirts in South Carolina during Reconstruction.* Fayetteville: University of Arkansas Press, 1998.

Du Bois, W. E. B. *Black Reconstruction.* New York: Harcourt, Brace, 1935.

Durden, Robert F. *James Shepherd Pike: Republicanism and the American Negro, 1850–1882.* Durham, N.C.: Duke University Press, 1957.

Eaton, Clement. *The Freedom-of-Thought Struggle in the Old South.* New York: Harper and Row, 1964.

Edgar, Walter. *South Carolina: A History.* Columbia: University of South Carolina Press, 1998.

Ellem, Warren A. "Who Were the Mississippi Scalawags?" *Journal of Southern History* 38, no. 2 (1972): 217–40.

Fitzgerald, Michael W. "Radical Republicanism and the White Yeomanry during Alabama Reconstruction, 1865–1868." *Journal of Southern History* 54 (November 1988): 565–96.

———. *The Union League Movement in the Deep South: Politics and Agricultural Change during Reconstruction.* Baton Rouge: Louisiana State University Press, 1989.

Foner, Eric. *Freedom's Lawmakers: A Directory of Black Officeholders during Reconstruction.* 2nd ed. Baton Rouge: Louisiana State University Press, 1996.

———. *Nothing But Freedom: Emancipation and Its Legacy.* Baton Rouge: Louisiana State University Press, 1983.

———. *Reconstruction: America's Unfinished Revolution, 1863–1877.* New York: Harper and Row, 1988.

Ford, Lacy K. *Origins of Southern Radicalism: The South Carolina Upcountry, 1800–1860.* New York: Oxford University Press, 1988.

———. "Rednecks and Merchants: Economic Development and Social Tensions in the South Carolina Upcountry, 1865–1900." *Journal of American History* 71 (September 1984): 294–318.

Fowler, Wilton B. "A Carpetbagger's Conversion to White Supremacy." *North Carolina Historical Review* 43, no. 3 (1966): 286–304.

Fraser, Walter J., Jr. *Charleston! Charleston! The History of a Southern City.* Columbia: University of South Carolina Press, 1989.

Fredrickson, George M. *The Black Image in the White Mind: The Debate on Afro-American Character and Destiny, 1817–1914.* New York: Harper and Row, 1971.

Frey, Sylvia. "Republicanism: Sources, Meanings, and Uses in American History." *Historical Journal* 35, no. 2 (1992): 471–85.

Gatewood, Willard B., Jr. "'The Remarkable Misses Rollin': Black Women in Reconstruction South Carolina." *South Carolina Historical Magazine* 92, no. 3 (1991): 172–88.

———. "Theodore Roosevelt and Southern Republicans: The Case of South Carolina, 1901–1904." *South Carolina Historical Magazine* 70, no. 4 (October 1969): 251–66.

Gelston, Arthur Lewis. "Radical versus Straight-out in Post-Reconstruction Beaufort County." *South Carolina Historical Magazine* 75, no. 4 (1974): 225–37.

Genovese, Eugene D. "Yeomen Farmers in a Slaveholders' Democracy." *Agricultural History* 44 (April 1975): 331–42.

Gergel, Belinda, and Richard Gergel. *In Pursuit of the Tree of Life: A History of the Early Jews of Columbia, South Carolina, and the Tree of Life Congregation.* Columbia, S.C.: Tree of Life Congregation, 1996.

Gillette, William. *Retreat from Reconstruction, 1869–1879.* Baton Rouge: Louisiana State University Press, 1979.

Goldman, Robert M. *"A Free Ballot and a Fair Count": The Department of Justice and the Enforcement of Voting Rights in the South, 1877–1893.* New York: Fordham University Press, 2001.

Goodrich, Carter. "Public Aid to Railroads in the Reconstruction South." *Political Science Quarterly* 71 (September 1956): 407–42.

Graydon, Nell S. *Tales of Columbia.* Columbia, S.C.: R. L. Bryan, 1964.

Green, Fletcher Melvin, ed. *Essays in Southern History: Presented to Joseph Gregoire de Roulhac Hamilton, Ph.D., LL.D., by His Former Students at the University of North Carolina.* Chapel Hill: University of North Carolina Press, 1949.

Gregorie, Anne King. *History of Sumter County.* Sumter, S.C.: Library Board of Sumter County, 1954.

Hahn, Steven. *The Roots of Southern Populism: Yeoman Farmers and the Transformation of the Georgia Upcountry, 1850–1890.* New York: Oxford University Press, 1983.

Hamer, Philip M. *The Secession Movement in South Carolina, 1847–1852.* Allentown, Pa.: H. Ray Haas, 1918.

Harding, Vincent. *There Is a River: The Black Struggle for Freedom in America.* New York: Harcourt Brace Jovanovich, 1981.

Harris, William C. *The Day of the Carpetbagger: Republican Reconstruction in Mississippi.* Baton Rouge: Louisiana State University Press, 1979.

Hennessey, Melinda M. "Racial Violence during Reconstruction: The 1876 Riots in Charleston and Cainhoy." *South Carolina Historical Magazine* 86 (April 1985): 100–112.

Hesseltine, William B. "Economic Factors in the Abandonment of Reconstruction." *Mississippi Valley Historical Review* 22 (September 1935): 191–210.

Hewett, Janet B., and Joyce Lawrence. *South Carolina Confederate Soldiers, 1861–1865.* Vol. 1, *Name Roster.* Wilmington, N.C.: Broadfoot, 1998.

Hine, William C. "The 1867 Charleston Streetcar Sit-ins, A Case of Successful Black Protest." *South Carolina Historical Magazine* 77, no. 2 (1976): 110–14.

———. "Black Politicians in Reconstruction Charleston, South Carolina: A Collective Study." *Journal of Southern History* 49, no. 4 (1983): 555–84.

Hollis, Daniel Walker. *The University of South Carolina.* Columbia: University of South Carolina Press, 1956.

Hollis, John P. *The Early Period of Reconstruction in South Carolina.* Baltimore: Johns Hopkins Press, 1905.

Holt, Michael F. *The Rise and Fall of the Whig Party: Jacksonian Politics and the Onset of the Civil War.* New York: Oxford University Press, 1999.

Holt, Thomas. *Black over White: Negro Political Leadership in South Carolina during Reconstruction.* Urbana: University of Illinois Press, 1977.

Howe, Daniel Walker. *The Political Culture of the American Whigs.* Chicago: University of Chicago Press, 1979.

Hudson, Janet. "From Constitution to Constitution, 1868–1895: South Carolina's Unique Stance on Divorce." *South Carolina Historical Magazine* 98, no. 1 (1997): 75–96.

Hyman, Harold M., ed. *New Frontiers of the American Reconstruction.* Urbana: University of Illinois Press, 1966.

Hyman, Michael R. *The Anti-Redeemers: Hill-Country Political Dissenters in the Lower South from Redemption to Populism.* Baton Rouge: Louisiana State University Press, 1990.

———. "Taxation, Public Policy, and Political Dissent: Yeoman Disaffection in the Post-Reconstruction Lower South." *Journal of Southern History* 55 (February 1989): 49–76.

Jarrell, Hampton M. *Wade Hampton and the Negro: The Road Not Taken.* Columbia: University of South Carolina Press, 1950.

Jordan, Laylon Wayne. "'The New Regime': Race, Politics, and Police in Reconstruction Charleston, 1865–1875." *Proceedings of the South Carolina Historical Association,* 1994, 45–53.

Kantrowitz, Stephen. *Ben Tillman and the Reconstruction of White Supremacy.* Chapel Hill: University of North Carolina Press, 2000.

Kibler, Lillian A. *Benjamin F. Perry: South Carolina Unionist.* Durham, N.C.: Duke University Press, 1946.

———. "Unionist Sentiment in South Carolina in 1860." *Journal of Southern History* 4 (August 1938): 346–66.

Kirkland, Thomas J., and Robert M. Kennedy. *Historic Camden: Part Two, Nineteenth Century.* Columbia, S.C.: State, 1926.

Klein, Rachel N. *Unification of a Slave State: The Rise of the Planter Class in the South Carolina Backcountry, 1760–1808.* Chapel Hill: University of North Carolina Press, 1990.

Kloppenberg, James T. "Republicanism in American History and Historiography." *Toqueville Review* 13, no. 1 (1992): 119–36.

Klosky, Beth Ann. *The Pendleton Legacy.* Columbia, S.C.: Sandlapper Press, 1971.

Kolchin, Peter. "The Business Press and Reconstruction." *Journal of Southern History* 33 (May 1967): 183–96.

———. "Scalawags, Carpetbaggers, and Reconstruction: A Quantitative Look at Southern Congressional Politics, 1868–1872." *Journal of Southern History* 45, no. 1 (February 1979): 63–76.

Lamson, Peggy. *The Glorious Failure: Black Congressman Robert Brown Elliott and the Reconstruction in South Carolina.* New York: W. W. Norton, 1973.

Leemhuis, Roger P. *James L. Orr and the Sectional Conflict.* Washington, D.C.: University Press of America, 1979.

Lesesne, J. Mauldin. *The Bank of the State of South Carolina: A General and Political History.* Columbia: University of South Carolina Press, 1970.

Lewis, Catherine H. *Horry County, South Carolina: 1730–1993.* Columbia: University of South Carolina Press, 1998.

Logue, Cal M. "Racist Reporting during Reconstruction." *Journal of Black Studies* 9, no. 3 (1979): 335–49.

Lonn, Ella. *Desertion during the Civil War.* New York: Century, 1928.

McCully, Robert S. "Letter from a Reconstruction Renegade." *South Carolina Historical Magazine* 77, no. 1 (1976): 34–40.

McGrane, Reginald. *Foreign Bondholders and American State Debts.* New York: Macmillan, 1935.

McKitrick, Eric L. *Andrew Johnson and Reconstruction.* Chicago: University of Chicago Press, 1960.

McKivigan, John R. "James Redpath in South Carolina: An Abolitionist's Odyssey in the Reconstruction Era South." In *The Moment of Decision: Biographical Essays on American Character and Regional Identity,* edited by Randall M. Miller and John R. McKivigan, 188–210. Westport, Conn.: Greenwood Press, 1994.

McPherson, James M., and William J. Cooper Jr., eds. *Writing the Civil War: The Quest to Understand.* Columbia: University of South Carolina Press, 1998.

Mering, John V. "Persistent Whiggery in the Confederate South: A Reconsideration." *South Atlantic Quarterly* 69 (Winter 1970): 124–43.

Miller, Edward A., Jr. *Gullah Statesman: Robert Smalls from Slavery to Congress, 1839–1915.* Columbia: University of South Carolina Press, 1995.

Miller, Wilbur R. *Revenuers and Moonshiners: Enforcing Federal Liquor Law in the Mountain South, 1865–1900.* Chapel Hill: University of North Carolina Press, 1991.

Moneyhon, Carl H. *The Impact of the Civil War and Reconstruction on Arkansas: Persistence in the Midst of Ruin.* Baton Rouge: Louisiana State University Press, 1994.

Moore, John Hammond. *Columbia & Richland County: A South Carolina Community, 1740–1990.* Columbia: University of South Carolina Press, 1993.

———. "Getting Uncle Sam's Dollars: South Carolinians and the Southern Claims Commission, 1871–1880." *South Carolina Historical Magazine* 82 (1981): 248–62.

———. "South Carolina's Reaction to the Photoplay, *The Birth of a Nation.*" *Proceedings of the South Carolina Historical Association, 1963* (1964): 30–40.

———. *Southern Homefront: 1861–1865.* Columbia, S.C.: Summerhouse Press, 1998.

Moore, Robert J. "Governor Chamberlain and the End of Reconstruction." *Proceedings of the South Carolina Historical Association,* 1977, 17–27.

Norton, Jerry William. "South Carolina Taxpayers' Convention of 1871." Master's thesis, University of South Carolina, 1970.

O'Brien, Michael, and David Moltke-Hansen, eds. *Intellectual Life in Antebellum Charleston.* Knoxville: University of Tennessee Press, 1986.

Otten, James T. "Disloyalty in the Upper Districts of South Carolina during the Civil War." *South Carolina Historical Magazine* 75 (1974): 95–110.

Pease, William H., and Jane H. Pease. *James Louis Petigru: Southern Conservative, Southern Dissenter.* Athens: University of Georgia Press, 1995.

Perman, Michael. *Reunion without Compromise: The South and Reconstruction, 1865–1868.* New York: Cambridge University Press, 1973.

———. *The Road to Redemption: Southern Politics, 1869–1879.* Chapel Hill: University of North Carolina Press, 1984.

Pope, Thomas H. *The History of Newberry County, South Carolina.* Vol. 2, *1860–1990.* Columbia: University of South Carolina Press, 1992.

Powers, Bernard E., Jr. "Community Evolution and Race Relations in Reconstruction Charleston, South Carolina." *South Carolina Historical Magazine* 95, no. 1 (1994): 27–46.

Rable, George C. *But There Was No Peace: The Role of Violence in the Politics of Reconstruction.* Athens: University of Georgia Press, 1984.

———. "Southern Interests and the Election of 1876: A Reappraisal." *Civil War History* 26 (December 1980): 347–61.

Ratchford, B. U. *American State Debts.* Durham, N.C.: Duke University Press, 1941.

Reid, Bill G. "Confederate Opponents of Arming the Slaves." *Journal of Mississippi History* 22 (1960): 249–70.

Reynolds, John Schreiner. *Reconstruction in South Carolina, 1865–1877.* Columbia, S.C.: State, 1905.

Roark, James L. *Masters without Slaves: Southern Planters in the Civil War and Reconstruction.* New York: Norton, 1977.

Robinson, Armstead L. "Beyond the Realm of Social Consensus: New Meanings of Reconstruction for American History." *Journal of American History* 68 (September 1981): 276–97.

———. "Explaining the Failure of Democratic Reform in Reconstruction South Carolina." *Reviews in American History* 8 (December 1980): 521–30.

Rodgers, Daniel T. "Republicanism: The Career of a Concept." *Journal of American History* 79, no. 1 (1992): 11–38.

Rogers, George C. *The History of Georgetown County, South Carolina.* Columbia: University of South Carolina Press, 1970.

Roper, John Herbert. "A Reconsideration: The University of South Carolina during Reconstruction." *Proceedings of the South Carolina Historical Association,* 1974, 46–57.

Rose, Willie Lee. *Rehearsal for Reconstruction: The Port Royal Experiment.* Indianapolis: Bobbs-Merrill, 1964.

Saville, Julie. *The Work of Reconstruction: From Slave to Wage Laborer in South Carolina, 1860–1870.* New York: Cambridge University Press, 1994.

Schaper, William A. "Sectionalism and Representation in South Carolina." *Annual Report of the American Historical Association for the Year 1900,* 2 vols. Washington, D.C.: Government Printing Office, 1901.

Schwalm, Leslie A. *A Hard Fight for We: Women's Transition from Slavery to Freedom in South Carolina.* Urbana: University of Illinois Press, 1997.

Scott, William A. *The Repudiation of State Debts.* Boston: Thomas Y. Crowell, 1893.

Scroggs, Jack B. "Carpetbagger Constitutional Reform in the South Atlantic States, 1867–1868." *Journal of Southern History* 27 (November 1961): 475–93.

Seip, Terry L. *The South Returns to Congress: Men, Economic Measures, and Intersectional Relationships, 1868–1879.* Baton Rouge: Louisiana State University Press, 1983.

Sellers, W. W. *A History of Marion County, South Carolina, from Its Earliest Times to the Present, 1901.* Columbia, S.C.: R. L. Bryan, 1902.

Shalhope, Robert E. "Toward a Republican Synthesis: The Emergence of Understanding of Republicanism in American Historiography." *William and Mary Quarterly,* 3rd ser., 29 (January 1972): 49–80.

Shapiro, Herbert. "The Ku Klux Klan during Reconstruction: The South Carolina Episode." *Journal of Negro History* 49, no. 1 (1964): 34–55.

Sharkey, Robert P. *Money, Class, and Party: An Economic Study of Civil War and Reconstruction.* Baltimore: Johns Hopkins University Press, 1967.

Sheppard, William Arthur. *Red Shirts Remembered: Southern Brigadiers of the Reconstruction Period.* Atlanta: Ruralist Press, 1940.

Simkins, Francis B. "The Election of 1876 in South Carolina." *South Atlantic Quarterly* 21 (July–October 1922): 225–40; 335–51.

———. "The Ku-Klux Klan in South Carolina, 1868–1871." *Journal of Negro History* 12 (October 1927): 606–47.

———. "New Viewpoints of Southern Reconstruction." *Journal of Southern History* 5 (February 1939): 49–61.

———. "The Problems of South Carolina Agriculture after the Civil War." *North Carolina Historical Review* 7 (January 1930): 46–78.

———. "The Solution of Post-Bellum Agriculture Problems in South Carolina." *North Carolina Historical Review* 7 (April 1930): 192–219.

Simkins, Francis B., and Robert S. Woody. *South Carolina during Reconstruction.* Chapel Hill: University of North Carolina Press, 1932.

Simpson, Brooks D. *The Reconstruction Presidents.* Lawrence: University Press of Kansas, 1998.

Singletary, Otis A. *Negro Militia and Reconstruction.* Austin: University of Texas Press, 1957.

Spartanburg Unit of the Work Projects Administration in the State of South Carolina. *A History of Spartanburg County.* Spartanburg, S.C.: Band and White, 1940.

Stagg, J. C. A. "The Problem of Klan Violence: The South Carolina Up-Country, 1868–1871." *Journal of American Studies* 8 (December 1974): 303–18.

Stampp, Kenneth M. *The Era of Reconstruction, 1865–1877.* New York: Alfred A. Knopf, 1969.

St. Clair, Kenneth E. "Debtor Relief in North Carolina during Reconstruction." *North Carolina Historical Review* 18 (July 1941): 215–35.

Summers, Mark W. *Railroads, Reconstruction, and the Gospel of Prosperity: Aid under the Radical Republicans, 1865–1877.* Princeton, N.J.: Princeton University Press, 1984.

Sweat, Edward F. "The Union Leagues and the South Carolina Election of 1870." *Journal of Negro History* 61, no. 2 (1976): 200–214.

Taylor, Alrutheus Ambush. *The Negro in South Carolina during the Reconstruction.* Washington, D.C.: Association for the Study of Negro Life and History, 1924.

Taylor, Joe Gray. "The White South from Secession to Redemption." In *Interpreting Southern History: Historiographical Essays in Honor of Sanford W. Higginbotham,* edited by John B. Boles and Evelyn Thomas Nolen, 162–98. Baton Rouge: Louisiana State University Press, 1987.

Thompson, Henry T. *Ousting the Carpetbagger from South Carolina.* Columbia, S.C.: R. L. Bryan, 1926.

Thornton, J. Mills, III. "Fiscal Policy and the Failure of Radical Reconstruction in the Lower South." In *Region, Race, and Reconstruction: Essays in Honor of C. Vann Woodward,* edited by J. Morgan Kousser and James M. McPherson, 349–94. New York: Oxford University Press, 1982.

———. *Politics and Power in a Slave Society: Alabama: 1800–1860.* Baton Rouge: Louisiana State University Press, 1978.

Tindall, George Brown. *South Carolina Negroes, 1877–1900.* Columbia: University of South Carolina Press, 1952.

Todd, Richard Cecil. *Confederate Finance.* Athens: University of Georgia Press, 1954.

Trelease, Allen W. *White Terror: The Ku Klux Klan Conspiracy and Southern Reconstruction.* New York: Harper and Row, 1971; Baton Rouge: Louisiana State University Press, 1995.

———. "Who Were the Scalawags?" *Journal of Southern History* 29 (November 1963): 445–68.

Tunnell, Ted. *Crucible of Reconstruction: War, Radicalism, and Race in Louisiana, 1862–1877.* Baton Rouge: Louisiana State University Press, 1984.

Underwood, James Lowell, and W. Lewis Burke. *At Freedom's Door: African-American Founding Fathers and Lawyers in Reconstruction South Carolina.* Columbia: University of South Carolina Press, 2000.

Uya, Okon Edet. *From Slavery to Public Service: Robert Smalls, 1839–1915.* New York: Oxford University Press, 1971.

Vandiver, Louise Ayer. *Traditions and History of Anderson County.* Atlanta: Ruralist Press, 1928.

Wallace, David Duncan. *History of South Carolina.* 4 vols. New York: American Historical Society, 1934.

Wallenstein, Peter. *From Slave South to New South: Public Policy in Nineteenth-Century Georgia.* Chapel Hill: University of North Carolina Press, 1987.

Ware, Lowry. *Old Abbeville: Scenes of the Past of a Town Where Old Time Things Are Not Forgotten.* Columbia: SCMAR, 1992.

Wells, Edward Laight. *Hampton and Reconstruction.* Columbia, S.C.: State, 1907.

Wiggins, Sarah Woolfolk. *The Scalawag in Alabama Politics, 1865–1881.* University: University of Alabama Press, 1977.

Williams, Alfred Brockenbrough. *Hampton and His Red Shirts: South Carolina's Deliverance in 1876.* Charleston, S.C.: Walker, Evans & Cogswell, 1935.

Williams, Lou Falkner. *The Great South Carolina Ku Klux Klan Trials, 1971–1872.* Athens: University of Georgia Press, 1996.

Williamson, Joel. *After Slavery: The Negro in South Carolina during Reconstruction, 1861–1877.* Chapel Hill: University of North Carolina Press, 1965.

Wingard, Nancy F., and Clayton B. Kleckley. *Brief History of Lexington County and Schedule for Lexington County Tricentennial Activities.* Lexington, S.C.: Lexington County Historical Society, 1970.

Woody, R. H. "Behind the Scenes in the Reconstruction Legislature of South Carolina: Diary of Josephus Woodruff." *Journal of Southern History* 2 (February 1936): 78–102; 3 (May 1936): 233–59.

———. "Franklin J. Moses, Jr., Scalawag Governor of South Carolina, 1872–74." *North Carolina Historical Review* 10 (April 1933): 111–32.

———. *Republican Newspapers of South Carolina.* Charlottesville, Va.: Historical Publishing, 1936.

———. "Some Aspects of the Economic Condition of South Carolina after the Civil War." *North Carolina Historical Review* 7 (July 1930): 346–64.

———. "The South Carolina Election of 1870." *North Carolina Historical Review* 8 (April 1931): 168–86.

Zuczek, Richard. *State of Rebellion: Reconstruction in South Carolina.* Columbia: University of South Carolina Press, 1996.

### *Theses and Dissertations*

Bradley, John Calvin, Jr. "The Political Reconstruction of Spartanburg County, 1865–1868." Honors thesis, South Carolina College, 1983.

Breibart, Solomon. "The Constitutional Convention of 1868." Master's thesis, University of North Carolina, 1938.

Briggs, Michael. "South Carolina Reapportionment, 1776–1978." Master's thesis, University of South Carolina, 1978.

Burton, Orville Vernon. "Ungrateful Servants? Edgefield's Black Reconstruction: Part 1 of the Total History of Edgefield County, South Carolina." Ph.D. diss., Princeton University, 1975.

Ford, Lacy K., Jr. "One Southern Profile: Modernization and the Development of White Terror in York County, 1856–1876." Master's thesis, University of South Carolina, 1976.

Hume, Richard L. "The 'Black and Tan' Constitutional Conventions of 1867–1869 in Ten Former Confederate States: A Study of Their Membership." Ph.D. diss., University of Washington, 1969.

Lancaster, James L. "The Scalawags of North Carolina, 1850–1868." Ph.D. diss., Princeton University, 1974.

Mims, Julian Landrum. "Radical Reconstruction in Edgefield County, 1865–1877." Master's thesis, University of South Carolina, 1969.

Norton, Jerry William. "South Carolina Taxpayers' Convention of 1871." Master's thesis, University of South Carolina, 1970.

Oliver, Robert T. "A Faithful Heart: The Journals of Emmala Thompson Butler Reed 1866–67." Master's thesis, Clemson University, 1997. Unbound typed manuscript at South Caroliniana Library.

Olsberg, Robert Nicholas. "A Government of Class and Race: William Henry Trescot and the South Carolina Chivalry, 1860–1865." Ph.D. diss., University of South Carolina, 1972.

Pritchard, Claudius Hornsby, Jr. "Colonel D. Wyatt Aiken, 1828–1887: South Carolina's Militant Agrarian." Master's thesis, Longwood College, 1965.

Rogers, James S., III. "The History of Horry County, South Carolina: 1850–1876." Master's thesis, University of South Carolina, 1972.

Storey, Margaret deMontcourt. "Southern Ishmaelites: Wartime Unionism and Its Consequences in Alabama, 1860–1874." Ph.D. diss., Emory University, 1999.

Thompson, Michael. "Blacks, Carpetbaggers, and Scalawags: A Study of the Membership of the South Carolina Legislature, 1868–1870." Ph.D. diss., Washington State University, 1975.

# INDEX